Did He
or Didn't He?

Also by Mart Martin

The Voyeur's Guide to Men and Women in the Movies
 (Contemporary Books)
*Did She or Didn't She? Behind the Bedroom Doors of 201 Famous
 Women* (Citadel Press)

Did He
or Didn't He?

*The Intimate Sex Lives
of 201 Famous Men*

MART MARTIN

CITADEL PRESS
Kensington Publishing Corp.
www.kensingtonbooks.com

Dedicated to

Perry J. Schwartz
known for his devotion to
Faith, Family, Friends, and Fun.
Thank you for your all-inclusive attitude to life.

CITADEL PRESS books are published by

Kensington Publishing Corp.
850 Third Avenue
New York, NY 10022

All Kensington titles, imprints, and distributed lines are available at special quantity discounts for bulk purchases for sales promotions, premiums, fund raising, educational, or institutional use. Special book excerpts or customized printings can also be created to fit specific needs. For details, write or phone the office of the Kensington special sales manager: Kensington Publishing Corp., 850 Third Avenue, New York, NY 10022, attn: Special Sales Department, phone 1-800-221-2647.

Kensington and the K logo Reg. U.S. Pat. & TM Office
Citadel Press is a trademark of Kensington Publishing Corp.

First printing October 2000

10 9 8 7 6 5 4 3 2 1

Printed in the United States of America

Library of Congress Cataloging-in-Publication Data
Martin, Mart.
      Did he or didn't he? : the intimate sex lives of 201 famous men /
Mart Martin.
          p.   cm.
      "A Citadel Press book."
      Includes bibliographical references.
      ISBN 0-8065-2130-9 (pbk.)
      1. Men—United States—Sexual behavior.   2. Celebrities—United
States—Sexual behavior.   3. Entertainers—United States—Sexual
behavior.   I. Title.
HQ28.M39   1997
306.7'081—dc21   97-29955
                                                                                CIP

Contents

"Everyone poked everyone in Hollywood. I think actors will put it anywhere it will go." —Sheilah Graham

Preface

....

*D*id he or didn't he? Frankly, I don't know for certain—and it seems highly unlikely that anyone will ever know for certain what's fact and what's fantasy about these men. What we do have to assist in our assessment is what they have told on themselves, along with what others have gossiped about them in various autobiographies, biographies, and reams of reminiscences.

Did he or didn't he . . . have a string of lovers and multiple marriages? A swashbuckling screen idol summed up the frustration that many men in the public eye must feel sometimes when he snapped, "I'm just a goddamned phallic symbol to the world." It might have been a curse, but it was a curse these men certainly enjoyed. For as one of them put it, "I was in Hollywood a week before I got laid. I don't know, that may just be a record."

Did he or didn't he . . . have a reputation among those who knew him that was vastly different from the public's perception of him? Many of these men did. For example, even though one man, characterized as having a carefree and breezy personality, raised photogenic children from two well-publicized "happy" marriages, in reality he was a child-thrashing, borderline alcoholic about whom a friend said, "You could make one wrong move and he'd never speak to you again." It's no wonder that he even said about himself, "If they ever find me out, I'm a goner."

Did he or didn't he . . . spread his charms around while he ascended to fame? Admittedly, some of these men tossed their charms quite broadly. One screen legend who did, said, "You know, I've had my cock sucked by some of the big names in Hollywood." A longtime reigning sex king was just as blunt about the female costars at his studio after he became famous. According to him, "They're all beautiful and I've had every one of them." Another screen idol made no excuses for himself when he said, "Why frustrate people? If I'm feeling horny at the time and I like them, I'll oblige them." The star's spouse was more succinct. His problem, according to her, was that he "could never say no to anyone."

Did he or didn't he . . . always tell the truth about his love life? Maybe so and maybe not. Probably so in some cases and just as probably not in others. Maybe director Alfred Hitchcock was being more honest than we realize when he told us, "All love scenes started on the set are continued in the dressing room after the day's shooting is done."

My original intention when I began peeking into bedrooms was to concentrate solely on men from the cinema. Then, various other men began appearing with more and more frequency among the original cast of characters. It seemed as if they were almost demanding to be included. Especially since some of them had given so much—to so many—in order to reach their high station in life. All these men are public figures and most are performers, which has caused me to reach a conclusion about them: their ultimate sexual consummation seems to be not between the sheets of a bed, but on the sheets of the newsprint they've generated. Author Richard Porier stated it most aptly, in *The Performing Self:* "For artists, sometimes performing their art isn't enough, so they turn their lives into an artistic performance."

Did he or didn't he? We can only rely on the quoted remarks, facts, and information on these pages to help us try to decide. They came from a vast number of books and journals—especially biographical and autobiographical works—anecdotal volumes dealing with specific individuals and with films in general; and articles, reviews, and interviews published in newspapers and magazines. The bibliography lists all this material for those interested in delving further into the lives of specific individuals.

Now, before turning this page to peek behind some interesting bedroom doors and wonder who we might find there, it would be wise to remember screenwriter Wilson Mizner's words about romantic involvements: "Some of the greatest love affairs I've known involved one actor or actress, unassisted."

Did He
or Didn't He?

Brian Aherne 1902–1986

✦ He Said

Accept hospitality only from the rich, who don't expect you to ask them back.

I have always referred to the great women stars as the Monsters, and monsters indeed most of them are.

One sometimes wonders how a Spaniard or a Frenchman can ever be contented with the American woman, who, for all her lively charm and beauty, is so often spoiled and unhappy.

✦ They Said

Brian feels about homosexuals the way most people feel about ghosts; he just can't believe they exist. —John Van Druten, author

✦ First Sexual Experience

Unknown.

✦ Wives

Joan Fontaine, actress
Eleanor de Liagre Labrot

✦ Did You Know?

As a proper young man in England, Aherne said that he used to feel "faint" at the sight of a lovely young lady. His fainting spells apparently lasted for a number of years, because, according to him, he was well into his twenties before he became serious (i.e., had sexual relations) with a woman.

Lovers, Flings, or Just Friends?

Wendy Barrie, actress

Ruth Chatterton, actress

Marlene Dietrich, singer-actress (costar in *Song of Songs,* '33)

Doris Duke, tobacco heiress

Clare Eames, actress

Ann Harding, actress (costar in *The Fountain,* '34)

Merle Oberon, actress

Woody Allen 1935–

✦ He Said

Bathing is snobbism. Bathing isn't good for you. It washes off the natural juices that keep you young. . . . I douse myself with talcum and liberal helpings of spice. I break down about every third day and have a shower.

Everything I learned about comedy writing, I learned from Danny Simon. —Referring to Neil's brother

✦ They Said

A face that convinces you that God is a cartoonist. —Jack Kroll, film critic

I find him neurotic. —George C. Scott, actor

Woody is a genius. —Mel Brooks, actor and fellow director

I have a four-year-old and I wouldn't want Woody around her. —Tisa Farrow, sister of ex-lover Mia, taking her big sister's side in the Allen-Farrow child molestation Korean poontang imbroglio

✦ First Sexual Experience

Probably lost his virginity to first wife, Harlene, since his friend Eliott Mills has said that before the marriage he walked around with Woody "explaining what a clitoris is. I drew a picture in the dirt, the blind leading the blind."

✦ Wives

Harlene Rossen, student
Louise Lasser, comedienne-actress

✦ Did You Know?

As a young teenager, Woody saw his first Ingmar Bergman film—*Summer With Monika* ('53)—because he and his friends had heard it had a nude woman in it.

Did Woody receive the virginity of Soon-Yi, Korean adopted daughter of Mia Farrow, for his fifty-seventh birthday on December 1, 1992? Only Woody and Soon-Yi know for certain.

Desi Arnaz 1917–1986

✦ He Said

Your wife is your wife . . . your fooling around can in no way affect your love for her. Your relationship is sacred and a few peccadilloes mean nothing.

I don't take out other broads—I take out hookers.

The world was my oyster. What I wanted I needed only to ask for.

✦ They Said

Desi didn't know the difference between sex and love. To put it bluntly, love was a good fuck. Desi could get that anywhere. —Anonymous musician friend

Desi loved sex. He couldn't get enough. —Cesar Romero, actor

What a lech! Anything female from thirteen to thirty, he'd go after. —Roger C. Carmel, actor

I don't believe he ever intended to settle down and become a good, steady, faithful husband. —Lucille Ball, angry at her ex-hubby later in life

Congratulations, Desi, you are the only person in the world to screw Harry Cohn, Columbia Pictures, Paramount, Cecil B. De Mille, and your wife, all at the same time. —Cecil B. De Mille, director, on learning that Lucy was pregnant by Desi and would have to forgo a role in his latest epic

✦ First Sexual Experience

Desi almost lost his virginity at age twelve, when he tried to seduce the daughter of his family's cook in Cuba, but he got caught before he could accomplish anything. At age fifteen, his father took him to Casa Marino, the best brothel in Santiago, Cuba, and he finally lost his virginity.

✦ Wives

Lucille Ball, actress (costar in *The Long, Long Trailer*, '54)

Edith McSkiming Hirsch, widow of the Kal Kan dog food manufacturer

✦ Did You Know?

While he was in high school in Miami, Florida, Desi's best friend was Al "Sonny" Capone Jr., son of the famed mobster. He later sued Arnaz, unsuccessfully, for $1 million over the TV series *The Untouchables.*

Lovers, Flings, or Just Friends?

Pat Dane, actress

Renée DeMarco, dancer

Brenda Frazier, socialite deb

Betty Grable, actress

Lorenz Hart, homosexual lyricist

Sonja Henie, ice skater–actress

Richard Kollmar, husband of columnist Dorothy Kilgallen

Barbara Nichols, actress

Liz Renay, starlet-model

Cesar Romero, actor

Lana Turner, actress

plus a redheaded whore managed by New York's infamous madam, Polly Adler, *and,* on one eventful evening, *all* the girls managed by Adler, along with many other nurses, starlets, and local pickups, preferably well built and blond

Fred Astaire 1899–1987

✦ He Said

I make love with my feet.

✦ They Said

They seem a very decent sort of American. —King George V of Great Britain, referring to the appearance of Fred and dancing partner–sister Adele on the London stage

Can't act. Can't sing. Balding. Can dance a little. —Assessment after a Paramount Studios screen test

. . . the nimble tread of the feet of Fred Astaire . . . —"You're the Top," by Cole Porter

✦ First Sexual Experience

Unknown, but probably some female he met during one of his many early stage appearances.

✦ Wives

Phyllis Baker Potter, socialite-divorcée

Robyn Smith, jockey

✦ Did You Know?

Astaire made his film debut in 1914, when he appeared in a silent two-reeler called *Fanchon the Cricket* starring Mary Pickford.

Astaire even danced with Joan "Mommie Dearest" Crawford. Catch the duo high-stepping in *Dancing Lady* ('33) to see how Fred puts Joan through her dancing paces.

The British Royals loved Fred. He taught the Prince of Wales how to tap dance, and during a London sojourn in the twenties, the then–Duchess of York, now the Queen Mum, sent a personal note inviting him to drop by and "see the baby," her new first-born, now known as Queen Elizabeth II.

Lovers, Flings, or Just Friends?

Lillian Bostwick

Barrie Chase, dancer

Audrey James, British socialite companion of the Prince of Wales

Carol Lynley, actress

Marilyn Miller, actress

Jesse Reed, dancer-divorcée

Ginger Rogers, actress-dancer (costar in *Flying Down to Rio*, '33)

Tina Sinatra, daughter of singer-actor Frank

Jean-Pierre Aumont 1909–

✦ He Said

An actor exists only in front of his audience. He's a little like a man who can make love only in front of voyeurs.

I've always had more faith in pure chance than in elaborate schemes.

✦ They Said

Your accent is your main asset. I'd rather see you come back without a leg than without your accent. —Louis B. Mayer, head of MGM, sending Aumont off to fight in World War II

Nothing to write home about. —Guthrie McClintic, producer, on first seeing Aumont in person

✦ First Sexual Experience

Unknown.

✦ Wives

Blanche Montel, actress
Maria Montez, actress (costar in *Siren of Atlantis*, '48)
Marisa Pavan, actress (and twin sister of actress Pier Angeli)

✦ Did You Know?

As a child Aumont attended a boarding school where he and the other boys were whipped each morning by a one-armed professor. The man's rationale: the boys had been up all night every evening indulging in masturbation. They hadn't, but Aumont says the group soon decided to investigate the pleasure for which they were being wrongly punished each morning.

Lovers, Flings, or Just Friends?

Annie Berrier, chanteuse (who also had a fling with King Farouk of Egypt)
Joan Crawford, actress
Grace Kelly, actress
Hedy Lamarr, actress
Vivien Leigh, actress
Barbara Stanwyck, actress

Alec Baldwin 1958–

Lovers, Flings, or Just Friends?

Holly Gagnier, actress
Jill Goodacre, model
Janine Turner, actress

✦ He Said
You meet beautiful women, you've got a lot of time on your hands, people pay attention to you a lot more than you deserve—I acted on that as much as most young guys do who come to that place. —Remarking on his days as a self-described "womanizing jerk"

Women come up to me at parties and tell me they like my butt.

People ask me where I get all my energy. I don't do drugs or drink at all. I'm just always wired in the morning.

I have no desire to know most actors.

✦ They Said
Alec Baldwin is too mean looking to be a sex symbol. . . . He looks like he would beat you up if you said one word wrong. —Ursula Andress, actress

He has a potbelly, but I could get over that. —Rosie Perez, actress

He has eyes like a weasel. He makes Clint Eastwood look like a flirt. —Sandy Dennis, actress

✦ First Sexual Experience
Unknown.

✦ Wives
Kim Basinger, actress (costar in *The Marrying Man,* '91)

✦ Did You Know?
While he was a student at George Washington University, Baldwin ran for president of the student body. He lost by two votes.

According to a celebrity gossip appearing on Joan Rivers's television show, Baldwin has someone visit him twice a month for a hot wax treatment—to remove the hair from his back.

Antonio Banderas 1960–

✦ He Said

It was fun. I had success with the girls. —Remembering his early years as an actor

Every morning when I wake up, I look in front of the mirror and it says "sex symbol." Once I see that, I go back to bed.

I am not a homosexual. I like to be a devil sometimes.

I don't want anything I don't deserve, [but] if they offer me more money, I'm not a-stupid.

✦ They Said

He probably has a small penis or something. My God! There has to be something wrong with him because nobody can be that perfect. —Madonna, singer-actress

Antonio has a little cock, but that is not a problem—at least for us. We can manage in Europe. Even if it's a little dick, he knows what to do. It's not the meat, it's the motion. In any case, he's a great actor. —Victoria Abril, Spanish actress, who's costarred in several of Banderas's films where he had nude scenes

He's the only guy I know who's better than Don in bed. —Melanie Griffith, comparing him to her ex-husband, actor Don Johnson

Men and women like him equally because he doesn't have that macho baggage. —David Frankel, director

Because I get to play a man who lives with Antonio Banderas, I am the envy of, I'm not sure of the numbers, but I think it's 95 percent of the women in the world and 22 percent of the men. —Tom Hanks, on being able to play Banderas's gay lover in a film

✦ First Sexual Experience
Unknown.

✦ Wives
Ana Leza, Spanish actress
Melanie Griffith, actress

✦ Did You Know?

Banderas's lustful fans of all sexes thought they were getting a real eyeful of him in mid-1997 when *Playgirl* ran an enticing, full-frontal nude that resembled the actor. Were they ever fooled! It turned out the guy in the photo—who looked remarkably like the actor—was a male "model" from one of the homosexually oriented photography studios who had posed for the shot back in the early eighties.

Lovers, Flings, or Just Friends?

Banderas fooled around prior to his first marriage and he appears to have been quite the charming ladies' man, but most of them were not well-known personalities. After his first marriage, if he managed to continue spreading his charm around he also avoided any publicity about doing so, despite being singled out by Madonna, who proclaimed her desire to sample his wares.

John Barrymore Sr. 1882–1942

✦ He Said

Don't trust any of them as far as you can throw Fort Knox. They're all twittering vaginas. —Advice given to actor Anthony Quinn

Do you think if I screwed you, you'd leave me alone? —Snapping at Tallulah Bankhead, who'd been pestering him for a long time to have sex with her

✦ They Said

There are few men about whom there has been more vicious gossip. He is reputed to have witnessed and indulged in every known vice. —Douglas Fairbanks Jr.

His jealousy was dreadful to behold. —Dolores Costello, actress and spouse

It takes an earthquake to get Jack out of bed, a flood to make him wash, and the United States army to put him to work. —Lionel Barrymore, brother

✦ First Sexual Experience

Lost his virginity to his stepmother, Mamie Floyd. She seduced him when he was fifteen years old. One doctor, who treated him later in life for his alcoholism, said that it seemed to date from about this same period.

✦ Wives

Katherine Harris, socialite
Blanche Oelrichs Thomas, socialite (whose convent education ended after she was caught eating foie gras sandwiches in bed)
Dolores Costello, actress (costar in *The Sea Beast*, '26)
Elaine Jacobs (Barrie), student

✦ Did You Know?

Barrymore's wild behavior was often accompanied by memorable quips. When a Hollywood producer's wife discovered him urinating into the corner of a ladies' rest room, she chastised him, saying, "Mr. Barrymore, this is for ladies!" The actor whirled around, waggled his penis at her, and announced, "So, madam, is this!"

One rumor says Barrymore's first introduction to Katharine Hepburn was on their film *A Bill of Divorcement* ('32). She was making her film debut and came to his dressing room to rehearse. It's said that Barrymore told her, "Perhaps you'd like to take off your clothes and lie on the couch." When Hepburn declined indignantly, Barrymore—not the least bit ashamed—said, "I see, then let's just go over the lines."

Lovers, Flings, or Just Friends?

Hazel Allen, actress

Sally Allen, starlet

Mary Astor, actress (costar in *Beau Brummel*, '24)

Tallulah Bankhead, actress

Vivian Blackburn, actress

Lotta Faust, actress

Irene Fenwick, actress (who later married his brother Lionel)

Irene Frizzelle, actress

Elsie Janis, actress

Carole Lombard, actress (costar in *Twentieth Century*, '34)

Bonnie Maginn, actress

Evelyn Nesbit, the Girl in the Red Velvet Swing and mistress of architect Stanford White

Nita Naldi, actress

Grace Palatta, actress

and a month he spent frolicking in a Calcutta whorehouse

Cecil Beaton 1904–1980

✦ He Said

My attitude to women is this—I adore to dance with them and take them to theaters and private views and talk about dresses and plays and women, but I'm really much more fond of men.

Perhaps the world's second worst crime is boredom. The first is being a bore.

✦ They Said

He was a very passionate, very ardent man and quite unlike the way people normally think of him. —Coral Browne, actress

Some people, when you were very young and effeminate, may have found you most obnoxious to begin with, but you worked and proved yourself useful. —Greta Garbo, actress, speaking to Beaton

Your sleeves are too tight, your voice is too high and precise. —Noël Coward, playwright-entertainer

Now, Cecil may have been from the middle classes but he didn't have a middle-class bone in his body. —Diana Vreeland, doyenne of *Vogue*

✦ First Sexual Experience

Possibly with Gordon Fell-Clark, a fellow student at Harrow, on, as Beaton put it, "a stupid field day years ago." Fred Astaire's sister and dancing partner, Adele, and model Marjorie Oelrichs gave him his first heterosexual experiences.

✦ Wives

Beaton remained a bachelor his entire life.

✦ Did You Know?

As a young man, Beaton often let his fingernails grow to exaggerated lengths—at one time his left thumbnail was almost two inches long—and painted them. Once, while walking on London's Bond Street, Beaton's nails were spotted by a male stranger, who glared at him and said, "Ought not to be allowed on the streets."

At their first meeting, Garbo pulled a single yellow rose from a vase and gave it to Beaton. He saved the flower and pressed it in a book, then framed it and hung it above his bed where it remained until his death. It was auctioned off after his death to a New Zealand photographer for more than $1,000.

Lovers, Flings, or Just Friends?

Tris Bennett, Harrow schoolmate

Coral Browne, actress

Doris Castlerose, spouse of a gossip columnist (Winston Churchill said, "She'd make a corpse come")

Lord Charles Cavendish, British nobleman

Gary Cooper, actor

Marlene Dietrich, singeractress

Sir Michael Duff, British socialite

Gordon Fell-Clark, Harrow schoolmate

Greta Garbo, actress

Edward Gathome-Hardy, British socialite

Jimmy, a black boxer

Kin, a male art historian

Tilly Losch, dancer

Rudolph Nureyev, ballet dancer

Marjorie Oelrichs, model

June Osborn, widow

Adela Rogers St. Johns, writer

Stephen Tennant, British socialite

Benjamin Thomas, Cambridge schoolmate

Victor William "Peter" Watson, wealthy British playboy

and two American sailors in Honolulu, who, after he'd fellated them, were going to steal his cameras, until Truman Capote scared them off

Warren Beatty 1937–

✦ He Said

I'm a very normal guy. But I've made one rule for myself. Never tell lies to women. And I've always told my girlfriends the truth, however painful it might be to both of us.

I'm not going to appear bare-assed. It's a hangup I have. —To director Roman Polanski, while reviewing the script of *Papillon* ('73)

✦ They Said

Every time I go on a talk show, I am invariably asked about Warren Beatty's sex life. I have a stock answer: He should be in a jar at the Harvard Medical School. —Rex Reed, critic

Warren is a pussy. . . . He's a wimp. —Madonna

He is like a masculine dumb blonde. —Anouk Aimée, actress

Sex is his hobby, you could say. —Shirley MacLaine, older sister

Warren would proposition a chair if it looked at him sideways. —Jackie Collins

Three, four, five times a day every day was not unusual for him. And he was able to accept phone calls at the same time. —Joan Collins

God! I must be the only woman in L.A. or New York that Warren hasn't tried to shtup. —Sue Mengers, Hollywood agent

✦ First Sexual Experience

Unknown.

✦ Wives

Annette Bening, actress (costar in *Bugsy,* '91)

✦ Did You Know?

No beefcake photos, please! Beatty, since his early films like *Splendor in the Grass* ('61) and *Bonnie and Clyde* ('67), and despite his reputation as a ladykiller, reportedly doesn't sign contracts that require him to be filmed minus his shirt.

Madonna has said that what Mr. B. packs in his pants is "a perfectly wonderful size," but another admitted Warren admirer—actress Jennifer Lee—has said that he is not "that well endowed."

Tennessee Williams has told a tale of how eager Warren was to be cast in his film of *The Roman Spring of Mrs. Stone.* First, Warren "read" for the part of Paolo, a gigolo, and Williams told him he could play the part. Later that same evening, Warren supposedly showed up at Williams's hotel room wearing a bathrobe. Tennessee said, "Go to bed, Warren. I said you had the part."

Lovers, Flings, or Just Friends?

Candace Bergen, actress

Judy Carne, actress

Leslie Caron, actress (costar in *Promise Her Anything,* '66)

Cher, singer-actress

Julie Christie, actress (costar in *McCabe and Mrs. Miller,* '71)

Joan Collins, actress

Britt Ekland, actress

Jane Fonda, actress

Germaine Greer, feminist

Barbara Hershey, actress

Anjelica Huston, actress

Bianca Jagger, wife of rock singer Mick

Diane Keaton, actress

Madonna, singer-actress

Joni Mitchell, singer

Mary Tyler Moore, actress

Christina Onassis, shipping heiress

Jacqueline Kennedy Onassis, wealthy widow

Michelle Phillips, singer

Lee Radziwill, socialite sister of Jackie Onassis

Vanessa Redgrave, actress

Diana Ross, singer-actress

Jessica Savitch, telejournalist

Jean Seberg, actress

Carly Simon, singer

Barbra Streisand, actress-singer

Elizabeth Taylor, actress

Liv Ullman, actress

Mamie Van Doren, actress

Natalie Wood, actress

Jean-Paul Belmondo 1933–

✦ He Said

One thing they can never say about Belmondo is that he was just another pretty face.

They compare me to Humphrey Bogart and John Garfield. Nonsense. I am me!

✦ They Said

You can live without Hollywood. Look at Belmondo. He's never been there. He doesn't speak a word of English. But that has not stopped him from becoming an international success. —Jean Moreau, actress

One of the three best actors in the world. —Henry Fonda, actor

✦ First Sexual Experience

Unknown.

✦ Wives

Elodie, ballerina

✦ Did You Know?

To what does Belmondo—self-admittedly not the most handsome of men—attribute his success with women? As he put it, "Hell, everybody knows that an ugly guy with a good line gets the chicks."

Lovers, Flings, or Just Friends?

Ursula Andress, actress

Laura Antonelli, actress (costar in *Docteur Popoul*, '72)

Brigitte Bardot, actress

Geraldine Chaplin, actress

Anna Karina, actress

Christina Onassis, shipping heiress

Jean Seberg, actress (costar in *Breathless*, '59)

Ingmar Bergman 1918–

✦ He Said

Jesus punished me with a gigantic infected pimple right in the middle of my pallid forehead. —Remembering what happened to him when he first started masturbating

Film work is a powerfully erotic business. . . . The intimacy, devotion, dependency, love, confidence, and credibility in front of the camera's magic eye become a warm, possibly illusory security . . . the atmosphere is irresistibly charged with sexuality.

When you are born and brought up in a vicarage, you are bound at an early age to peep behind the scenes of life and death.

A film is a tapeworm, a tapeworm twenty-five hundred meters long that sucks the life and spirit out of me.

✦ They Said

You don't necessarily need to like genius, but you can stand aside and admire it. —Mai Zetterling, Swedish actress and director

✦ First Sexual Experience

Lost his virginity to Anna Lindberg, a schoolmate, when he was about fourteen or fifteen years old.

✦ Wives

Else Fisher, dancer-choreographer
Ellen Lundström, choreographer
Gun Hagberg, writer
Käbi Laterei, pianist
Ingrid von Rosen

✦ Did You Know?

Bergman's brother was one of the founders of Sweden's largest fascist group—the Swedish National Socialist Party.

Milton Berle 1908–

✦ He said

For me, drag is another way to get laughs. My drag is too gay to be gay. —Discussing his propensity to appear in his television skits while in drag

✦ They Said

They say the two best-hung men in Hollywood are Forrest Tucker and Milton Berle. What a shame. It's never the handsome ones. The bigger they are, the homelier. —Betty Grable, actress

Go ahead, Milton, just take out enough to win. —Unnamed friend encouraging Berle to win a bet about whether he was exceptionally endowed

✦ First Sexual Experience

Lost his virginity at age twelve to a dancer in the Broadway show *Florodora,* in which he was appearing.

✦ Wives

Joyce Mathews, showgirl
Joyce Mathews, showgirl
Ruth Cosgrove, publicity agent

✦ Did You Know?

Can you imagine Milton with long yellow curls? Well, he had them way back when he was a child performing in vaudeville and early silents.

Berle made one of his earliest screen appearances when he was six years old, with comedian Charlie Chaplin in *Tillie's Punctured Romance* ('14). Chaplin saw Berle's photo in an ad for Buster Brown shoes and brought him to Hollywood to be in the film.

Famed in the early fifties as Mr. Television and Uncle Miltie, Berle made his first television appearance in 1929, performing on a closed-circuit experimental broadcast.

Actor Stephen Boyd, the evil Messala in *Ben-Hur* ('59), dropped dead in Berle's arms during a chat outside the Beverly Hills Hotel.

Lovers, Flings, or Just Friends?

Lucille Ball, actress
Theda Bara, actress
Wendy Barrie, actress
Lita Grey Chaplin, ex-wife of actor Charlie
Louise Cook, belly-dancer
Evelyn Cromwell, an Earl Carroll's Vanities girl
Linda Darnell, actress
Frances Heenan, actress
Mary Beth Hughes, actress
Betty Hutton, actress
Fran Kegan, actress
Dorothy Kilgallen, columnist
Veronica Lake, actress
Judy Malcolm, dancer
Audrey Meadows, actress
Aimee Semple McPherson, evangelist
Marilyn Monroe, actress
Ann Sheridan, actress
and some of the girls from Polly Adler's New York whorehouse

Leonard Bernstein 1918–1990

✦ He Said

Maybe people do think of me as just another pinko faggot, a do-gooder, but that's what I am.

I look like a well-built dope fiend.

✦ They Said

He would verge on a relationship with a woman, but he was unsuccessful with them. —Edys Merrill, a female roommate and close friend

Lennie is a short-timer regarding sexual relationships. —David Diamond, friend, who also complained that Bernstein attempted affairs "with all my boyfriends"

What an egotist! When not getting all the attention, he sits in a chair with closed eyes, pretending to be asleep. —Tennessee Williams, recounting a sojourn in Mexico City with friends when Bernstein was also a guest

I like Lenny Bernstein, but not as much as he does. —Oscar Levant, pianist-composer

Being kissed by him was like an assault by a sort of combination of sandpaper and sea anemones! —Jonathan Miller, theatrical director

✦ First Sexual Experience

Lost his virginity to Renée Longy Miquelle, one of his music teachers, or so he once confided to a friend.

✦ Wives

Felicia Montealegre Cohn, Chilean music student and actress

✦ Did You Know?

Bernstein would have willingly left music altogether to pursue a career in film if things had worked out correctly, but they didn't. It was announced on three separate occasions that he had been signed to appear as the star of a film, but none of the projects ever came to fruition.

Composer Aaron Copland used to refer to Bernstein as a PH, for phony homosexual. He apparently wasn't all that phony, as Bernstein participated in a homosexual orgy organized by author Gore Vidal in Rome in 1970.

During the New York Philharmonic's 1958 tour of South America, Bernstein's wife left the tour early and flew home because he had flirted outrageously with men in Chile, her native country, which humiliated her.

Lovers, Flings, or Just Friends?

Ellen Adler, daughter of acting teacher Stella Adler

Tallulah Bankhead, actress

Marc Blitzstein, playwright

Marlon Brando, actor

Aaron Copland, composer

Farley Granger, actor

Robert Lee Kirkland III, journalist

Tommy Kothran, radio station musical director

John Kriza, dancer

Harold Lang, dancer

John Mehegan, jazz pianist

Renée Longy Miquelle, music teacher

Dmitri Mitropoulos, Greek conductor

Rudolph Nureyev, ballet dancer

David Oppenheim, musician

David Prall, philosophy professor

Jerome Robbins, choreographer

Ned Rorem, composer

Charles Roth, conducting student

Anna Sokolow, dancer

Aaron Stern, music conservatory dean

Mark Adams Taylor, speechwriter

Jennie Tourel, British singer

Lana Turner, actress

Arthur Weinstein, interior decorator

Humphrey Bogart 1899–1957

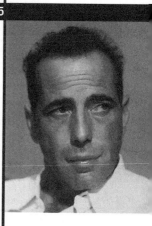

✦ He Said

I had had enough women by the time I was twenty-seven to know what I was looking for in a wife.

I don't go for those top-heavy dames at all. That isn't sexy to me, but then, I'm not a bosom man.

Anybody who would stick a cock in one of those girls would throw a rock through a Rembrandt. —Referring to a group of eight young, beautiful girls who were attending a stag party

To have a love affair breaks a bond between husband and wife— and even if your partner doesn't know about it, the relationship must be less open, so something very important will never be the same.

Okay, but don't put it in your mouth. —His answer to Truman Capote's request to have sex with him

Women are funny. Just because of that little triangle they have, they think they can get by with anything.

✦ They Said

When a woman appealed to him, he waited for her the way a flame waits for the moth. —Louise Brooks, actress

Bogie is no ladies' man. Maybe it is deep-down decency. He has very set ideas about behavior and morals in that respect. —Peter Lorre, actor

✦ First Sexual Experience
Unknown.

✦ Wives
Helen Menken, actress
Mary Philips, actress
Mayo Methot, actress
Lauren Bacall, actress (costar in *To Have and Have Not,* '44)

✦ Did You Know?

Bogart was a nervous nose picker; the more nervous he got, the faster he picked.

One tale says that Bogart caused Bette Davis to see her first set of male genitals. It happened during the filming of *Bad Sister* ('31). Davis was supposed to diaper a baby and had made the rash assumption that the infant would be female. It wasn't, and the view gave the still-virginal and highly embarrassed Bette her first view of male sexual equipment.

Lovers, Flings, or Just Friends?

Louise Brooks, actress

Truman Capote, author and bon vivant

Ginette Richer, friend and companion of French chanteuse Edith Piaf

Margaret Sullavan, actress

Verita Thompson, personal secretary

Lovers, Flings, or Just Friends?

Marie Bell, French actress

Constance Dowling, actress

Alice Field, actress

Katharine Hepburn, actress (costar in *Break of Hearts*, '35)

Gaby Morlay, French actress

Natalie Paley, French actress (costar in *L'Epervier*, '33)

Sandra Ravel, actress

Charles Boyer 1899–1978

✦ He Said

I believed I was past the age of falling in love. It was something that happened to younger men, and as a younger man I made every effort not to do it. I could not afford love and I was selfish enough to avoid it. —Remarking on how he felt about falling in love, finally, at age thirty-four

✦ They Said

Terribly serious about his looks . . . a wig, a corset, lifts in his shoes and so on. When he took all that off, he must have looked like the Pillsbury Doughboy. —Bette Davis, actress, his costar in *All This and Heaven Too* ('40)

Sex on a movie set is almost taken for granted, and any actress has to keep her legs crossed unless she just doesn't care. Maybe not every man is after it, but it's pretty much of a custom, and easy as pie for a male star. Charles is one of the exceptions, though. —Actress in a Boyer film

We've got a French actor here on a six-month option, but I'm letting him go home because nobody can understand the guy's accent. —Irving Thalberg, producer

✦ First Sexual Experience

Unknown.

✦ Wives

Pat Paterson, British actress

✦ Did You Know?

Boyer—in the mid-1940s—smoked up to six packs of cigarettes a day.

Boyer committed suicide two days after his wife's funeral. They had been married more than forty-five years, and their only child, a son, had committed suicide several years earlier.

Marlon Brando 1924–

✦ He Said

Should sex and desire die in me, it would be the end. It doesn't matter if I have almost never been happy with a woman.

I've never been circumcised, and my noble tool has performed its duties through thick and thin without fail.

It makes me look as if I'm about to suck every cock in Holly-wood. —Showing his contempt for a bust of him, modeled after his role of Marc Antony in *Julius Caesar* ('54), by Hollywood sculptor Constantine

✦ They Said

Physically Marlon is not well appointed. He screens that deficiency by undue devotion to his sex organ. —Anna Kashfi, ex-wife

He was just about the best looking man I had ever seen, with one or two exceptions. And I have never played around with actors. It is a point of morality with me. And anyhow, Brando was not the type to get a part that way. —Tennessee Williams, playwright, on first seeing Brando, then telling why he didn't try to sample his charms

As far as I am concerned, he can drop dead. He has the manners of a chimpanzee, the gall of a Kinsey researcher, and a swelled head the size of a navy blimp. —Louella Parsons, whom Brando called "the fat one," expressing her dislike of Mr. Mumbles

✦ First Sexual Experience

Lost his virginity at age nineteen in New York City to Estrelita Rosa Maria Consuelo Cruz, a married Colombian woman.

✦ Wives

Movita Castenada, Mexican actress
Anna Kashfi, actress

✦ Did You Know?

Brando got especially annoyed with James Dean, who after seeing him in *The Wild One* ('54), fell in love with him, then constantly telephoned him. But Brando did try and help Dean by getting him to see a psychiatrist.

Hollywood trashy behavior chronicler and voyeur extraordinaire Kenneth (*Hollywood Babylon*) Anger was asked by the Australian publication *Campaign* if it is true that he has a photo of Marlon Brando giving head. He replied: "I do. It was taken in 1952. He is going down on his roommate Wally Cox, a television actor. I've tried to publish it a couple of times, but publishers have always refused."

Lovers, Flings, or Just Friends?

Stella Adler, acting teacher
Ursula Andress, actress
Pier Angeli, actress
James Baldwin, author
Tallulah Bankhead, actress
Jossanne Mariani Berenger, French governess
Leonard Bernstein, composer-conductor
Joan Collins, actress
Wally Cox, actor
Yvonne De Carlo, actress
Doris Duke, heiress
Faye Dunaway, actress
Bob Dylan, singer-actor
Anne Ford, fashion designer
Juliette Greco, actress-singer
Bianca Jagger, wife of Mick
Katy Jurado, actress
Barbara Luna, actress
Christian Marquand, French actor
Marilyn Monroe, actress
Rita Moreno, actress
France Nuyen, actress
Pina Pellicer, actress
Liz Renay, model
Maria Schneider, actress
Tarita Teriipaia, Tahitian actress and longtime companion
Gore Vidal, author
Shelley Winters, actress
and, based on a friend's statement, almost every Japanese woman associated with *Sayonara* ('57)

George Brent 1904–1979

✦ He Said

I'd rather have a screwball around my house than a solid something from Pasadena. —Describing the personality he sought in a wife

I saved my money. You can't play Shirley Temple all your life. —Explaining how he eased himself out of films and acting

✦ They Said

Brent bent. —Ann Sheridan, actress and spouse, describing Brent's sexual equipment; her comment, unprintable at the time, was made to a Hollywood gossip columnist who asked why their marriage broke up so quickly

One of the most attractive men this town had. —Bette Davis, actress

Very hard to get to know, very removed and withdrawn. —Geraldine Fitzgerald, actress

Where has he been all my life? —Ruth Chatterton, actress, on seeing a screen test of Brent; she married him shortly thereafter

✦ First Sexual Experience

Unknown.

✦ Wives

Helen Campbell
Ruth Chatterton, actress (costar in *The Rich Are Always With Us,* '32)
Constance Worth, actress
Ann Sheridan, actress (costar in *Honeymoon for Three,* '41)
Janet Michael, dress designer

✦ Did You Know?

Brent, an Irishman, fought against the British in the Irish struggle for independence, fleeing his home country to Canada after he became a "wanted" man.

Brent and Garbo used to put on boxing gloves and spar with each other in his backyard.

Lovers, Flings, or Just Friends?

Diana Barrymore, actress

Bette Davis, actress (costar in *Housewife,* '34)

Olivia de Havilland, actress

Kay Francis, actress (costar in *Living on Velvet,* '35)

Greta Garbo, actress (costar in *The Painted Veil,* '34)

Ilona Massey, actress (costar in *International Lady,* '41)

Merle Oberon, actress (costar in *'Til We Meet Again,* '40)

Minna Wallis, agent and sister of producer Hal Wallis

Loretta Young, actress (costar in *They Call It Sin,* '32)

Yul Brynner 1915–1985

✦ He Said

Girls have an unfair advantage over men. If they can't get what they want by being smart, they can get it by being dumb.

It's far, far better to be a lover off the stage than on it. You need time to get inside a woman's skin to really understand her.

People don't know my real life and they're not about to find out.

✦ They Said

He is very, very handsome and very, very sensual. —Deborah Kerr, actress

Goody, goody, he has cancer! Serves him right! —Marlene Dietrich, scribbling on a newspaper photo of Brynner, which she sent to her daughter. After a long, torrid affair, Yul had dumped Marlene rather abruptly, something that rarely happened to her.

One of the biggest shits I've ever come across in show business. He was just a pig. —William Holden

✦ First Sexual Experience

Unknown for certain, possibly lost his virginity to a woman ten years older, named Eva, who trained him as a high-wire acrobatic flier in Paris.

✦ Wives

Virginia Gilmore, actress
Doris Kleiner, fashion house executive
Jacqueline de Thion de la Chaume de Croisset, French *Vogue* editor
Kathy Lee, dancer

✦ Did You Know?

Brynner was once addicted to smoking opium. In fact, he met and became close friends with Jean Cocteau through their smoking opium together.

Lovers, Flings, or Just Friends?

Tallulah Bankhead, actress

Anne Baxter, actress (costar in *The Ten Commandments*, '56)

Ingrid Bergman, actress (costar in *Anastasia*, '56)

Claire Bloom, actress

Joan Crawford, actress

Yvonne De Carlo, actress

Marlene Dietrich, singer-actress

Frankie, Austrian singer

Judy Garland, actress

Serge Lifar, dancer

Gina Lollobrigida, actress (costar in *Solomon and Sheba*, '59)

Marilyn Monroe, actress

Andrée Peyraud, French artist

Nancy Davis (Reagan), actress and, later, political wife

Maria Schell, actress (costar in *The Brothers Karamazov*, '58)

plus many other costars, young ladies, and members of his casts and audiences

Raymond Burr 1917–1993

✦ He Said

My attitude is: the public understands perfectly everything I choose to show them in roles as an actor. Everything else is none of their business.

This is the kind of guts that you have before you're twenty. Somebody asks you to play Macbeth, you say, "I'll be ready tomorrow." Now I'd say, "Yes, but I need a year to work on it."
—Describing how he accepted an offer to join a repertory company in England when he was quite young

✦ They Said

Even to those of us who knew him well, he was a very private person. —Charles Macaulay, close friend

Although not a lawyer, Mr. Burr strove for such authenticity . . . that we regard his passing as though we lost one of our own.
—R. William Ide III, president of the American Bar Association, commenting on the death of TV's Perry Mason portrayer

✦ First Sexual Experience
Unknown.

✦ Wives
Annette Sutherland, actress
Isabella Ward
Laura Andrina Morgan

✦ Did You Know?
To mask his homosexuality Burr claimed to have been married three times. Was he? Doubts exist that he was even married once.

Burr played in more than fifty films, yet he'll always be remembered as television's favorite attorney—Perry Mason. Probably his most notable film role was as the killer in *Rear Window* ('54), where he almost got his hands on Grace Kelly.

Richard Burton 1925–1984

✦ He Said

It is not really a triumph to be a success with these Hollywood ladies, because they have so little opportunity with men.

If there's a dame on this set I can't screw, my name's not Richard. —Boast made on the set of *Ice Palace* ('60)

Perhaps most actors are latent homosexuals and we cover it with drink. I was once a homosexual, but it didn't take.

She's going to make me a star. I'm going to use her, that no-talent Hollywood nothing. —Referring to Elizabeth Taylor, shortly before they became involved during filming *Cleopatra* ('63)

✦ They Said

I get an orgasm just listening to that voice of his. —Elizabeth Taylor, actress and two-time spouse

He's like all these drunks. Impossible when he's drunk and only half there when he's sober. —John Boorman, director

He deserves an Oscar for sheer gall. He should stick to Shakespearean roles. —Eddie Fisher, singer-actor, snapping about Burton's role in the breakup of his marriage to Elizabeth Taylor

He was a clever actor, but a shit, an absolute shit. —Stewart Granger, actor

✦ First Sexual Experience

Lost his virginity to Lil, an usherette at the theater where he first performed as an actor.

✦ Wives

Sybil Williams, actress
Elizabeth Taylor, actress
Elizabeth Taylor, actress
Suzy Hunt, model
Sally Hay, publicity assistant

✦ Did You Know?

Burton marched onto the set of *Cleopatra* ('63) one morning in March 1962 and announced, "I finally fucked E. Taylor in the back of my Cadillac."

An actor who knew him well was once asked about Burton's reputation for having seduced every actress with whom he worked. When he was challenged to name an actress Burton had not seduced, the actor replied, "Louise Dressler." The inquisitor said, "But she's dead," to which the actor responded, "I know."

Lovers, Flings, or Just Friends?

Jeanne Bell, *Playgirl* centerfold

Claire Bloom, actress (costar in *Look Back in Anger,* '59)

Florinda Bolkan, Brazilian actress

Geneviève Bujold, actress (costar in *Anne of the Thousand Days,* '69)

Nathalie Delon, French actress and wife of actor Alain

M'el Dowd, actress

Elizabeth, princess of Yugoslavia

Zsa Zsa Gabor, actress

Ava Gardner, actress (costar in *The Night of the Iguana,* '64)

Tammy Grimes, actress

Roberta Haynes, actress (costar in *Ice Palace,* '60)

Joey Heatherton, dancer-actress (costar in *Bluebeard,* '72)

Virna Lisi, actress (costar in *Bluebeard,* '72)

Sophia Loren, actress (costar in *Brief Encounter,* '74)

Diane McBain, actress

Laurence Olivier, actor

Rachel Roberts, actress

Jean Simmons, actress

Susan Strasberg, actress

Barbra Streisand, actress-singer

Lana Turner, actress

Raquel Welch, actress

and an almost toothless, middle-aged Jamaican maid

James Caan 1939–

✦ He Said

I won't mention names, but in my career, the most talented people invariably are the easiest and nicest to get along with. The ones that are difficult try to camouflage the fact that they haven't got shit to offer.

My acting technique is to look up at God just before the camera rolls and say, "Give me a break."

I'm the kind of guy, when work is done I've got to be with my friends. I've got to blow it off like going to the rodeo, drinking, or whoring.

✦ They Said

He likes to kiss and cuddle. —Leesa Roland, actress

In another age, the cheerful swaggering presence of James Caan would have made him the major star he is often said to be. —David Denby, film critic

✦ First Sexual Experience

Lost his virginity when he was thirteen years old in a Miami whorehouse, to a forty-year-old woman. During the sex act, his ass was badly bitten by mosquitoes.

✦ Wives

Dee Jay Mattis, dancer
Sheila Ryan, model
Ingrid Hajek

✦ Did You Know?

During his days of cavorting around the Playboy Mansion, Caan once invited Dorothy Stratten—director Peter Bogdanovich's lover, who was later murdered by her estranged husband—to his room. Once there, Caan began to make love to another Playmate in front of her, obviously hoping that Stratten would join them. She refused to indulge, saying later, "He was never very nice to me afterward."

When ex-spouse Sheila Ryan informed him that she might marry again, Caan lost his top. According to her, Caan "struck me repeatedly on my head and arms. I have no idea how many times he hit me, but it must have been six or seven." She started an assault action against him, but later dropped the charges.

What is Caan "crazy about" sexually? If a tattling prostitute is to be believed, then it is—according to her—"licking pussy." She says she spent hours "squatting over his face" while he worked her over.

Lovers, Flings, or Just Friends?

Heidi Fleiss, Hollywood madam (she says they had sex; he denies it)

Connie Kreski, *Playboy* centerfold

Leesa Ann Roland, actress (who sued him in July 1994 claiming he physically abused her)

and lots of *Playboy* centerfolds and models, of whom Caan says he "balled an astounding number . . . bam, bam, bam, in a row"

Nicolas Cage 1964–

✦ He Said

I think I'm average looking at best. But it's really about attitude. If you believe you're sexy, then you're sexy.

I dig affection, baby, but not while I'm driving.

The original reason was because I thought I could meet girls. —Revealing why he went into acting

One of the first signs of being depressed is that you lose interest in things. That's why I think it is important to stay passionate.

I tend to be at times more sensitive than a lot of fathers.

✦ They Said

Nic winks at his own intensity. —Shirley MacLaine, actress

To me, Nicky is a Renaissance man. —Cher, singer-actress

We were kissing and kissing and kissing. —Patricia Arquette, tattling about their first date

✦ First Sexual Experience

Unknown.

✦ Wives

Patricia Arquette, actress

✦ Did You Know?

Cage certainly has a romantic streak about him. He and wife Patricia Arquette met and dated for three weeks some nine years ago, then drifted apart. The couple didn't really see each other for almost eight years but maintained telephone contact. They finally met again and rekindled the relationship, ending up at the altar. That might have been expected, since Cage has said, "I know she has haunted me for eight years."

Lovers, Flings, or Just Friends?

Kristina Fulton, actress
Samantha Mathis, actress
Uma Thurman, actress
Jenny Wright, actress
Kristen Zang, model

Lovers, Flings, or Just Friends?

Noël Coward, playwright-entertainer

Merle Oberon, actress

James Cagney 1899–1986

✦ He Said

Show business is as unpredictable as a bicycle in heavy traffic.

I've always maintained that in this business you're only as good as the other fellows think you are.

A player should be able to demand what he is worth as long as he is worth it.

✦ They Said

The bad thing about Cagney was that he was short, not good-looking, and had to prove himself as an actor. —Charles Einfeld, director

No thanks. He's nothing but a little runt. —Howard Hughes, rejecting a fellow producer's offer to loan Cagney to him for a screen role

He just didn't seem interested in fraternizing with the studio crowd. —June Travis, actress, who costarred with Cagney in *Ceiling Zero* ('35)

He wasn't as tough as he seemed to be—only nervous and very obstinate. —Hal Wallis, producer at Warner Bros., Cagney's home studio with which he had a running feud

Jimmy's a swell hitter. —Joan Blondell, actress, on how she felt about being batted around by Cagney in his screen roles

✦ First Sexual Experience
Unknown.

✦ Wives
Frances Willard Vernon, actress-dancer

✦ Did You Know?
Cagney's first role on the stage was in drag, as a chorus girl, a far different image from that he developed later in his films.

Cagney required take after take on a scene while filming *Boy Meets Girl* ('38) because sexy, dumb-blonde Marie Wilson was required to sit in his lap and he kept getting an erection. Later Marie said, "Sitting on Jimmy's lap was like being on top of a flag-pole."

Michael Caine 1933–

✦ He Said

If you come on with no clothes on, nobody's going to be looking at your eyes. They're all going to be saying, "Oh, I thought it'd be a bit bigger than that."

A woman who tried to go out with me wearing a see-through blouse, an extremely low-cut dress, or a miniskirt where [everyone] can see her crotch and pants would be given the elbow immediately and forever.

Men and women like sex equally, right? But after the act itself is over and you're lying there in bed thinking about it, women need an excuse to justify it to themselves. So you have to give them that justification. And the greatest excuse of all is to tell them you love them. —Explaining his seduction technique to fellow actor and one-time roommate Terence Stamp

I just can't stay with the same woman for twenty-four hours a day, every day of my life. Anyway, why make one woman hate you for the rest of your life, instead of having a lot of women loving you for moments of it?

✦ They Said

He was very old-fashioned in some ways and he has a thing about not making love to virgins. —Edina Ronay, former lover

Caine was unkind, superficial, and kept me like I was his geisha. —Bianca Jagger, reflecting on her affair with Caine

He is an overfat, flatulent, sixty-two-year-old windbag, a master of inconsequence now masquerading as a guru. —Richard Harris, actor, who was annoyed at having been labeled—along with Richard Burton and Peter O'Toole—as a drunk by Caine in an interview

✦ First Sexual Experience
Unknown.

✦ Wives
Patricia Haines, British actress
Shakira Baksh, Miss Guyana 1967 and a starlet

✦ Did You Know?
Caine was stationed in Korea with the British army, where he fought in the Korean War. While there Marilyn Monroe visited to entertain the Allied troops. Caine remembered, "I reckon we all dreamed about her for weeks afterward."

Lovers, Flings, or Just Friends?

Alexandra Bastedo, British starlet

Marie Devereaux, British actress

Faye Dunaway, actress (costar in *Hurry, Sundown*, '67)

Elizabeth Ercy, French model-actress

Minda Feliciano, Philippine Airlines stewardess

Anna Karina, French actress (costar in *The Magus*, '68)

Bianca Perez Morena de Macais (Jagger), model-actress

Luciana Paluzzi, Italian actress

Edina Ronay, British starlet

Camilla Sparv, Swedish starlet

plus lots of young ladies, models, and starlets who lived with him for short periods before he became a star

Truman Capote 1924–1984

✦ He Said

I didn't feel as if I were imprisoned in the wrong body. I wasn't a transsexual. I just felt things would be easier for me if I were a girl. —Reflecting on his childhood, when he was regarded as a sissy

I always had a marked homosexual preference, and I never had any guilt about it.

It's too bad I don't like going to bed with women. I could have had any woman in the world, from Garbo to Dietrich. . . . I can't understand why anyone would want to go to bed with a woman. It's boring, boring, boring.

I am an alcoholic. I am a drug addict. I am a homosexual. I am a genius.

✦ They Said

His voice today is identical to what it was in the fourth grade. I hear him on television or the radio and I recall him as a young boy. —One of his Alabama schoolteachers

He is tart as a grand aunt, but in his way he is a ballsy little guy. —Norman Mailer, author

The pimple on the face of American literature. —Katherine Anne Porter, author

He's got the warmth of an alligator. —Estelle Winwood, actress

Capote despises the people he talks about. Using, using all the time. He builds up his friends privately and knocks them down publicly. —Marella Agnelli, Italian socialite

✦ First Sexual Experience

Occurred at about age twelve when he was enrolled at St. John's Military Academy in Ossining, New York. When the lights went out at night in his dormitory, Capote was usually forced into the bed of a bigger, stronger boy. As he said, "They took sex very seriously."

✦ Wives

Capote never married, although he had several long-running relationships with males.

✦ Did You Know?

Although he had sex with handsome film actors like Errol Flynn and John Garfield, who was the one actor that Tru, as he put it, always had "a yen for"? Lloyd Nolan, not your standard matinee idol.

Lovers, Flings, or Just Friends?

Newton Arvin, literature professor and literary critic

Humphrey Bogart, actor

Rick Brown, bartender

Howard Doughty, author

Jack Dunphy, author

Errol Flynn, actor

Denham Fouts, renowned male whore

John Garfield, actor

Boze Hadleigh, author

John Huston, director

Jack O'Shea, bank employee–personal manager

Lee Radziwill, socialite sister of Jackie Onassis

Gore Vidal, author

and an air-conditioning repairman from Palm Springs, California, among others

Johnny Carson 1925–

✦ He Said

If I had given as much to marriage as I gave to the Tonight Show, *I'd probably have a hell of a marriage.*

It is impossible for a comedian to be all things to all people.

I just found out that I do not drink well.

✦ They Said

Johnny was very oversexed. He was a man who liked to keep his body in the best shape. —Mamie Van Doren, actress

When I knew him, he really had no friends. The only time he came alive was on camera. —Truman Capote, author and social gadfly

He's not a sophisticated man. I wouldn't want to wake up and sit across the breakfast table with him. —Alicia Bond, Israeli actress

He's an anaesthetist. Prince Valium. —Mort Sahl, comedian

✦ First Sexual Experience

Lost his virginity to "Francine," a girl of "easy virtue," in the backseat of his family's 1939 green Chrysler Royal when he was seventeen years old in the town of Norfolk, Nebraska. Carson has said it was "a disaster."

✦ Wives

Joan "Jody" Morrill Wolcott, college student
Joanne Copeland, stewardess
Joanna Holland, fashion model
Alexis Maas, stockbroker's secretary

✦ Did You Know?

Carson sued a firm that was marketing portable toilets with the punchline, "Here's Johnny!" He won the suit.

October 1, 1962, was Johnny's first night as permanent host of the *Tonight Show*. His guests? Joan Crawford and Rudy Vallee.

Lovers, Flings, or Just Friends?

Alicia Bond, Israeli actress
Jill Corey, singer
Angie Dickinson, actress
Morgan Fairchild, actress
Sally Field, actress
Phyllis McGuire, singer and "close" friend of mobster Sam Giancana
Mary Kane "Emm-Jay" Tokel, production assistant
Mamie Van Doren, actress

Lovers, Flings, or Just Friends?

Joan Barry, starlet

Louise Brooks, actress

May Collins, actress

Dorothy Comingore (Linda Winters), actress

Marion Davies, actress

Florence Deshon, actress

Dagmar Godowsky, actress

Signe Holmquist, actress

Peggy Hopkins Joyce, Ziegfeld girl

Hetty Kelly, dancer

Hedy Lamarr, actress

Carole Landis, actress

Neysa McMein, artist

Aimee Semple McPherson, evangelist

Pola Negri, silent film actress

Mabel Normand, silent film actress

Edna Purviance, silent film actress

May Reeves, socialite

Clare Sheridan, sculptress-writer

Moussia Sodskay, French cabaret singer

Geraldine Spreckels, sugar heiress

Estelle Taylor, actress (and later Mrs. Jack Dempsey)

Lupe Velez, actress

Claire Windsor, actress

and lots of bimbos and girls in the brothels he liked to frequent

Charlie Chaplin 1899–1977

✦ He Said

The most beautiful form of life is the very young girl just starting to bloom.

Like everyone else's, my sex life went in cycles. Sometimes I was potent, other times disappointing.

Acting is 99 percent sweat and 1 percent talent. But that talent better be good.

✦ They Said

Now, Chaplin was short and his nose was average, but his pecker was really big-time. —Mae West, actress

There were nights after our marriage when Charlie was good for as many as six "bouts," as he called them, in succession—with scarcely five minutes' rest in between. —Lita Grey, second wife (when she complained to Charlie, he said, *I'm a stallion, Lita, and you better resign yourself to it*)

If people don't sit at Chaplin's feet, he goes and stands where they're sitting. —Herman J. Manckiewicz, screenwriter

He was a mean man. Sadistic. I saw him torture his son, humiliating him, insulting him. —Marlon Brando, referring to how son Sydney Chaplin was treated while making *A Countess From Hong Kong* ('67)

Chaplin is the one man in the world I want to meet. —V. I. Lenin, leader of the Russian Revolution

✦ First Sexual Experience

Not known for certain, but given the era, probably with a prostitute, most likely in London.

✦ Wives

Mildred Harris, actress (who was sixteen, and claimed to be pregnant)

Lita Grey, actress (and costar in *The Gold Rush*, '25)

Paulette Goddard, actress

Oona O'Neill, eighteen-year-old daughter of playwright Eugene O'Neill

✦ Did You Know?

After sharing a shower with him, Orson Welles described Chaplin's genitals as being like "a little peanut," but Chaplin himself claimed he possessed a twelve-inch penis, which he referred to as "the eighth wonder of the world."

Maurice Chevalier 1888–1972

✦ He Said

I do not look on myself as a great lover. I just want to make people happy.

I don't think the French make the best lovers. It's just that they like to talk about it more.

I had the most beautiful women in the world in Hollywood, but, in fact, the only thing that mattered to me was the public.

When a man falls in love with a woman, it is so easy to be a prisoner of the flesh. It is that which ruins most entertainers, especially singers.

✦ They Said

You're the greatest thing to come from France since Lafayette. —Al Jolson

The biggest bottom-pincher I ever came across. —Jeanette MacDonald, singer-actress and frequent costar

A trivial song with him can become a gem. —Charles Boyer, actor, close friend, and fellow Frenchman

✦ First Sexual Experience

Lost his virginity at about fourteen years old to a blond girl named Marguerite who appeared on the bill with him at La Parisiana, a fashionable Paris music hall. He described her as a "robust, chesty girl singer."

✦ Wives

Yvonne Vallée, French entertainer (costar in the French version of *The Playboy of Paris*)

✦ Did You Know?

As a child Chevalier used to earn money standing outside houses where neighbors were conducting extramarital affairs. If he saw an unsuspecting spouse approaching, he'd whistle loudly to alert the lovers inside.

Chevalier's first song in English on a professional stage was "How You Gonna Keep 'Em Down on the Farm After They've Seen Paree?"

Lovers, Flings, or Just Friends?

Josephine Baker, entertainer

Evelyn Brent, actress

Claudette Colbert, actress (costar in *The Big Pond*, '30)

Lily Damita, actress

Anna de Noailles, poetess-socialite

Marlene Dietrich, singer-actress

Muriel Ferguson, actress-dancer

Jacqueline Francelle, actress

Kay Francis, actress

Fréhel, French cabaret star

Miriam Hopkins, actress

Elsie Janis, music-hall entertainer

Anita Loos, playwright-author-screenwriter

Jeanette MacDonald, singer-actress (costar in *The Love Parade*, '29)

Janie Michels, artist

Marilyn Miller, actress

Mistinguette, French entertainer

Jacqueline Noël, dancer

Merle Oberon, actress

Nita Raya, actress

Toby Wing, starlet

plus many prostitutes from the Montmartre district of Paris and lots of music-hall entertainers, singers, and dancers

Lovers, Flings, or Just Friends?

Ben Bagley, record producer

Judy Balaban, teenager

Donna Carnegie, actress

Arline Cunningham, secretary

Dino, Italian airline pilot

Lehman Engel, musical conductor

Irmegaard Hassler, socialite

Libby Holman, singer

"Josh," actor

Jack Larson, actor (who played Jimmy Olson, cub photographer, in the 1950s TV series *Superman*)

Ann Lincoln, actress

Myrna Loy, actress (costar in *Lonelyhearts,* '59)

Claude Perrin, erstwhile dress designer

Mira Rostova, actress–drama coach

Maria Schell, actress

Dr. William Silverberg, psychiatrist

Elizabeth Taylor, actress (costar in *A Place in the Sun,* '51)

Phyllis Thaxter, actress

Manfred von Linde, plastic surgeon

Thornton Wilder, playwright

plus a variety of partners (male and female) from all occupations

Montgomery Clift 1920–1966

✦ He Said

I don't understand it, I love men in bed, but I really love women.

I don't feel particularly sexual and besides, what does sexuality have to do with my work?

If you're good at what you do, nobody can get at you.

✦ They Said

I think it was the secret tragedy of his life. —Ben Bagley, on Clift's embarrassment over his small penis (in the first, unexpurgated editions of *Hollywood Babylon,* Clift was referred to as Princess Tiny Meat, until his attorney had the references removed)

The guy acts like he has a Mix Master up his ass and doesn't want anyone to know it. —Marlon Brando, taking a swipe at a fellow actor (had Marlon been there, and was he speaking from a personal point of view?)

He wanted to love women, but he was attracted to men, and he crucified himself for it. —Deborah Kerr, costar in *From Here to Eternity,* '53

He'd say "Oh, Jesus! Look at that disgusting fag." When I saw him at a cast party making love to that same fag actor, I left the room. —Edward Dmytryk, who directed Clift in *The Young Lions,* '58

✦ First Sexual Experience

He was taught how to masturbate when he was thirteen years old by his older brother in an attic. He probably lost his virginity to Lehman Engel, a musical conductor.

✦ Wives

Clift never married.

✦ Did You Know?

While visiting director John Huston, Clift seduced an English journalist, who'd come to interview Huston, and spent the night with him. Huston was outraged, saying, "The incident seemed trashy—I felt Monty had insulted me. It was messy. I wish he'd consulted me and my family and how I felt about it."

Clift refused *Sunset Blvd.* ('50) because of its young man and older woman love theme, saying, "I don't think I could be convincing making love to a woman twice my age." His statement was laughable, because he was involved in just such a romance with singer Libby Holman at the time.

Harry Cohn 1891–1958

✦ He Said

Lemme tell ya what this business is about. It's cunt and horses!

I kiss the feet of talent.

Fuck the critics. They're like eunuchs. They can tell you how to do it, but they can't do it themselves.

Great pictures make great stars. . . . Send me your mother or your aunt and we will do the same for them.

✦ They Said

He reels off smut like a berserk, unexpurgated Chaucer. —Henry Mollison, actor

The man you stood in line to hate. —Hedda Hopper, gossip columnist

Harry Cohn was mean and nasty, but if he told you something, you could count on it. —Blake Edwards, director-screenwriter

He liked to be the biggest bug in the manure pile. —Elia Kazan, director

He was the meanest man I ever knew—an unreconstructed dinosaur. —Budd Schulberg, producer

It proves what they always say: Give the public what they want and they'll come out to see it. —Red Skelton, comedian, commenting on the crowd at Cohn's funeral

✦ First Sexual Experience

Unknown.

✦ Wives

Rose Barker Cromwell, divorcée

Joan Perry, starlet (who later became the second Mrs. Laurence Harvey)

✦ Did You Know?

Cohn maintained a secret passageway that led directly from his office into a dressing room that was assigned to lots of actresses during his tenure at Columbia Pictures; it facilitated his sexual access to the ladies.

Cohn wore his monogrammed silk shirts only once before disposing of them. He usually gave them to the nanny of his children, who sent them on to her father in Scotland.

Lovers, Flings, or Just Friends?

Lucille Ball, actress

Marlene Dietrich, singer-actress

Marilyn Monroe, actress

Grace Moore, opera singer and actress

plus lots of actresses, starlets, and extras, because Cohn thought, as head of a studio, that he was entitled to a share of their "favors" for employing them

Ronald Colman 1891–1958

Lovers, Flings, or Just Friends?

Mary Astor, actress

Vilma Banky, actress (costar in *The Dark Angel*, '25)

Majorie Daw, actress

Marlene Dietrich, singer-actress (costar in *Kismet*, '44)

Bessie Love, actress

Merle Oberon, actress

Lois Wilson, actress

Shelley Winters, actress (costar in *A Double Life*, '47)

✦ He Said

Hollywood is the most physical city in the world. I don't mean sex alone. Take athletics. They all go in for them.

✦ They Said

He was never promiscuous; it was not in his nature, only when something tickled his fancy. —Al Weigand, close friend

Insofar as women were concerned . . . he was scared of them. When friends started to matchmake during the course of a conversation, he would just clam up. —Percy Marmont, actor

I had some lines to say, and when I turned to him, he was so beautiful that I forgot every word I was supposed to say, didn't remember a darned thing—just sat there and looked at him. —Irene Rich, one of Colman's early costars, describing the effect he had on her

He had no personality of his own, only an appearance, and for that reason he was an almost perfect actor for the fictional screen. —Graham Greene, author

Ronald Colman was a gentle, dear man, not at all actorish. —Lois Moran, silent screen star

✦ First Sexual Experience

Unknown.

✦ Wives

Thelma Raye, British actress

Benita Hume, British actress (and the third Mrs. George Sanders)

✦ Did You Know?

During his tenth year in Hollywood, a poll was taken of actresses to determine who they thought was the handsomest man in films. Colman won the poll, taking twenty-two votes to Gable's eight and Fredric March's seven.

Sean Connery 1930–

✦ He Said

There was never any trouble getting girls, but it's big trouble getting rid of them.

The girls always want to sketch me up close. It's embarrassing.
—Comment made when he was posing in a G-string for art classes

Stars get so submerged by success they can't lift a tissue to wipe their nose without someone there to help.

Good God, no. Why should I? I've made more pictures than you.
—Replying to a female actress (probably Streisand) who had asked if he would be directed by her if she had a part for him in her next film

✦ They Said

The young Sean was magnificent in the nude and certainly lacked nothing "down there." In fact, he was the biggest I've ever seen. It made me drop my charcoal pencil! —Anonymous student in one of the classes in which Connery posed nude for art studies

Sean has a voice that makes you melt. —Kim Basinger, actress

Much more attractive without his wig on. —Barbara Carrera, actress

✦ First Sexual Experience

Lost his virginity at age fourteen to an attractive older woman in a military uniform who accosted him while he was walking down a street.

✦ Wives

Diane Cilento, actress
Micheline Roquebrune, French divorcée

✦ Did You Know?

Given the amount of "artistic" posing that Connery indulged in as a young man, and his youthful sexuality, it is reasonable to assume that some interesting nudes, photographs and drawings, do exist of him. While none have yet surfaced, there have been photographs published of him in a G-string.

Sean Connery a singing star? Yes. In *Darby O'Gill and the Little People* ('59) he warbles "Pretty Irish Girl" to his love interest. In fact, his version of the song was even released as a single.

Lovers, Flings, or Just Friends?

Ursula Andress, actress (costar in *Dr. No*, '62)

Claudine Auger, actress (costar in *Thunderball*, '65)

Brigitte Bardot, actress (costar in *Shalako*, '68)

Kim Basinger, actress (costar in *Never Say Never Again*, '83)

Lyndsey de Paul, singer

Zsa Zsa Gabor, actress

Julie Hamilton, British photographer

Magda Knopka, Polish model-actress

Sue Lloyd, British actress

Carol Sopel, British actress

Jill St. John, actress (costar in *Diamonds Are Forever*, '71)

Lana Turner, actress (costar in *Another Time, Another Place*, '58)

Shelley Winters, actress

Lana Wood, actress and sister of actress Natalie (costar in *Diamonds Are Forever*, '71)

Lovers, Flings, or Just Friends?

Tallulah Bankhead, actress (costar in *Devil and the Deep,* '32)

Cecil Beaton, photographer and costume designer

Ingrid Bergman, actress (costar in *Saratoga Trunk,* '45)

Clara Bow, actress (costar in *It,* '27)

Claudette Colbert, actress (costar in *His Woman,* '31)

Marlene Dietrich, singer-actress (costar in *Morocco,* '30)

Dorothy, Countess di Frasso, socialite with an Italian title

Edmund Goulding, director (directed him in *Paramount on Parade,* '30)

Sheilah Graham, gossip columnist

Cary Grant, actor

William Haines, actor

Rod La Rocque, actor

Anderson Lawler, wealthy homosexual tobacco heir

David Lewis, producer

Carole Lombard, actress

Patricia Neal, actress

Merle Oberon, actress

Randolph Scott, actor

Barbara Stanwyck, actress (costar in *Meet John Doe,* '41)

Anna Sten, actress (costar in *The Wedding Night,* '35)

Lupe Velez, actress (costar in *Wolf Song,* '29)

Mae West, actress

Gary Cooper 1901–1961

✦ He Said

It happens that I've made friendships with women who have aided me in my work.

We'll go look at the tits of the pretty girls on Fifth Avenue. —Answering a press agent's query on how they'd spend their time after finding that a press conference had been canceled

Hollywood personalities are really partly applesauce. We deceive the public, and get paid for it. I get paid pretty well, so I deceive the public good.

✦ They Said

Coop's hung like a horse and can go all night. —Clara Bow, actress

Cooper found out pretty quick that he could do two things well . . . ride a horse and fuck. —An anonymous friend, describing Cooper's talents

I think the men were more interested in him than the women, because he was such a role model. —Loretta Young, actress

I don't doubt that he had a man occasionally. They wouldn't leave him alone, you know. —One of Cooper's many female conquests

Dahling, they offered me all that money. So I decided I'd go to Hollywood and fuck that divine Gary Cooper. —Tallulah Bankhead, telling why she decided to leave the stage for films

✦ First Sexual Experience

Unknown.

✦ Wives

Veronica "Rocky" Balfe, socialite-actress

✦ Did You Know?

Cooper's mother dressed him as a girl, and he wore skirts until he went to school, because she had wanted a girl when he was born.

Cecil Beaton said that bisexual director Edmund Goulding "worshiped Cooper twice a day."

Cooper ate a big can of sauerkraut each morning, because he thought it kept him "regular."

While they were going together Cooper drew a face—using her nipple as its nose—on one of Lupe Velez's breasts with lipstick. She was so proud of his artistic endeavor, she kept pulling her breast out to show her lover's handiwork to everyone on the film she was making at the time.

Jackie Cooper 1922–

✦ He Said

Joan Crawford wasn't the only older woman I had an affair with. There were half a dozen friends of my mother, bored with their husbands.

I grew up with pressure and responsibility. Most children don't experience them until they are teenagers, if then. I had it from the time I was seven or eight.

✦ They Said

Cooper as a kid was a smart little son of a bitch. I'll tell you something else about him. He could always get the broads. —Bill Smith, who caught Cooper in bed with an older vaudeville actress

He needed a lot of reassurance, and he has not always picked the ladies who could give it to him. —Dr. Arnold Hutschnecker, who treated Cooper for a while

✦ First Sexual Experience

Lost his virginity at age thirteen to a twenty-year-old girl who lived across the street from him in Ocean Beach.

✦ Wives

June Horne, film extra
Hildy Parks, actress
Barbara Kraus

✦ Did You Know?

Thought of as the WASPy, all-American boy, some have speculated that Cooper was the illegitimate son of a Jewish father and an Italian mother. Others have said that he was actually the son of his supposed "uncle," director Norman Taurog.

Lovers, Flings, or Just Friends?

Joan Crawford, actress (she seduced him when he was seventeen)

Judy Garland, singer-actress

Bonita Granville, actress

June, a Beverly Hills High coed

Kathryn, a chorus girl (he was thirteen, she was twenty)

Mrs. Martin, a divorced friend of his mother's

Janis Paige, actress

Pat Stewart, student

and a hooker disguised as a nurse whom Broderick Crawford sent over

Lovers, Flings, or Just Friends?

Halle Berry, actress

Angie Everhart, actress

Joan Lunden, actress

Sheri Stewart, nightclub hostess

Marla Maples Trump, model-socialite

Kevin Costner 1955–

✦ He Said

I never really dated in high school . . . I think I had just one date, at the senior prom. That was it, period!

I'd like to put on buckskins and a ponytail and go underwater with a reed, hiding from the Indians . . . to me, that's sexy.

I'm more comfortable with a horse than a woman. —Talking about the closeness required with his costars

What bothers me more than anything is now everyone knows how I kiss. —Remarking on the sex scenes in his films

People say all these women want to have sex with me, but that's bullshit.

What turns me on is not graphic sex, but the potential for romance.

My affairs were very short-lived. You couldn't even call them affairs. They were like collisions. —Remarking on the wild days before his marriage

✦ They Said

Kevin is sexy and very mysterious. He's not girly at all, like some men who know they're attractive. —Rae Dawn Chong, actress

Costner is a guy who women find attractive and men are not put off by. He never has to resort to being weird. —Phil Alden Robinson, director

He reminds me of my friend Gary Cooper. Coop was always looking for a place to spit and Kevin has that same puckered look. —Anthony Quinn, actor

He isn't macho; he's pure male. —James Earl Jones, actor

✦ First Sexual Experience
Unknown.

✦ Wives
Cindy Silva, college student

✦ Did You Know?
No car backseats for Kevin's playroom. During the filming of *No Way Out* ('87), with its steamy limousine rear-seat love scene, Costner claimed he polled the cast and crew of the film to see how many had indulged in rear-seat romps. Most had, he's said, but claimed that he himself had never indulged.

Noël Coward 1899–1973

✦ He Said

All that open plumbing absolutely revolts me. I can only imagine that being in bed with a woman would be like feeling the skin of a snake. —Answering a query on what he specifically objected to about being in bed with a woman

God preserve me in future from female stars. I don't suppose he will.

I take ruthless stock of myself in the mirror before going out. A polo jumper or unfortunate tie exposes one to danger.

I was a talented child, God knows, and—when washed and smarmed down a bit—possibly attractive.

Talent, dear boy, sheer talent. —Explaining his success

Do what pleases you, and if that does not please the public, get out of the entertainment business.

✦ They Said

Noël was a terrible cunt in many ways. —Rex Harrison, actor

No one could prick the bloom of pomposity quite like Noël. —Lord Louis Mountbatten, British nobleman

✦ First Sexual Experience

Coward once confessed that he'd lost his virginity at age thirteen to Gertrude Lawrence, two years older, whom he met on a train.

✦ Wives

Coward remained a bachelor his entire life, although he formed several long-lasting homosexual relationships.

✦ Did You Know?

Coward, in Hollywood waiting for a boat to Asia, stayed with silent screen idol John Gilbert. One evening, after a party, when the other guests had gone home, Gilbert and his guest sat beside the fireplace enjoying a nightcap. Coward kept moving his chair closer and closer, until he was close enough to rest his hand on Gilbert's knee. Then, slowly but surely, his hand crept upward until it rested on his host's crotch. Coward said he "hoped their acquaintanceship would flower into a close friendship." Gilbert, startled by the gesture, but not wanting to insult his esteemed guest, was perplexed over how to handle the awkward situation. He finally just laughed—which sent Coward storming upstairs in a snit over his rejected overture.

Lovers, Flings, or Just Friends?

Jeffrey Amherst, friend
Bobby Andrews, actor
Michael Arlen, author
Richard Attenborough, director-actor
James Cagney, actor
Louis Hayward, actor
John Eakins, actor
Stewart Foster, Coldstream Guardsman
Cary Grant, actor
Peter Lawford, actor
Laurence Olivier, actor
Graham Payn, actor-singer
Tyrone Power, actor
Prince George, the Duke of Kent
Michael Redgrave, actor
Ned Rorem, composer
Philip Streatfield, painter
Alan Webb, actor
Michael Wilding, actor
John Chapman "Jack" Wilson, manager-producer
Keith Winter, playwright
Esmé Wynne, actress

Lovers, Flings, or Just Friends?

Joan Bennett, actress (costar in *Mississippi*, '35)

Ingrid Bergman, actress (costar in *The Bells of St. Mary's*, '45)

Peggy Bernier, actress

Joan Blondell, actress (costar in *Two for Tonight*, '35)

Joan Caufield, actress (costar in *Welcome Stranger*, '47)

Joan Corbett, starlet

Ghislain de Baysson, French friend

Frances Farmer, actress (costar in *Rhythm on the Range*, '36)

Rhonda Fleming, actress

Mona Freeman, actress

Betty Hannon, dancer

Miriam Hopkins, actress (costar in *She Loves Me*, '34)

Betty Hutton, actress (costar in *Here Come the Waves*, '44)

Grace Kelly, actress (costar in *The Country Girl*, '54)

Dorothy Lamour, actress (costar in *The Road to Zanzibar*, '41)

Mary Martin, actress (costar in *Rhythm on the River*, '40)

Jane Rankin, socialite

Inger Stevens, actress (costar in *Man on Fire*, '57)

Jane Wyman, actress (costar in *Just for You*, '52)

Bing Crosby 1904–1977

✦ He Said
If they ever find me out, I'm a goner.

✦ They Said
There was ice water in all the Crosby veins, but especially in Bing's. —Rudy Vallee, entertainer

I became sick from all the stress that man caused me. —Inger Stevens, actress, who was sleeping with Crosby when he abruptly married his second wife, Kathryn. When she heard a radio announcement that he had just gotten married, Stevens was working in a house Crosby owned, decorating it because she thought that's where they would live after their marriage.

Nobody was close to Bing. —Carroll Carroll, radio scriptwriter

You could make one wrong move and he'd never speak to you again. —Anonymous friend

✦ First Sexual Experience
Unknown.

✦ Wives
Dixie Lee, singer-starlet
Kathryn Grant, actress

✦ Did You Know?
Crosby had an ermine-covered toilet, but his was extra special: It was covered in ermine on both sides.

Crosby once had a private audience with Pope Pius XII, probably to seek a special papal annulment of his marriage to Dixie Lee. The reason for his intended annulment: Dixie was an incurable alcoholic. What Bing most likely didn't explain to the pontiff was that he was greatly responsible for her alcoholism.

Tom Cruise 1962–

✦ He Said

Women to me are not a mystery. I get along easily with them.

I like bright, sexy, sexy women.

Wherever I go people recognize me and stare. For the longest time, I kept wondering if my fly was open.

Everything I've been through helps me understand more.

I appreciate the fact that someone appreciates my work. And it's not bad to be adored by a lot of people.

Love scenes make me nervous. It's very strange to get in bed with someone you don't really know.

We're so happy together. Honestly. —Two weeks before he and wife Mimi Rogers separated and divorced

✦ They Said

A magnet for women. —Tony Scott, director

I'm waiting for the moment when I don't have to talk about that fucking name anymore. I've had it welded onto mine for years now. —Mimi Rogers, ex-spouse, complaining about always being referred to as the ex–Mrs. Tom Cruise or Tom Cruise's ex-wife

✦ First Sexual Experience

Unknown.

✦ Wives

Mimi Rogers, actress
Nicole Kidman, actress (costar in *Days of Thunder*, '90)

✦ Did You Know?

Is Tom Cruise the sexiest man around? Evidently more than twenty-seven thousand people once thought so. They voted him Sexiest Man in the World during a call-in on the television show *Entertainment Tonight* in 1987.

Was Cruise really undisturbable during the filming of *A Few Good Men* ('92)? One rumor says that no one was permitted to knock on the door of his dressing room trailer when he was needed for filming. Instead, according to the rumor, Cruise was summoned to the set by having a fax sent to his accommodations.

Lovers, Flings, or Just Friends?

Cher, singer-actress

Rebecca de Mornay, actress (costar in *Risky Business*, '83)

Heather Locklear, actress

George Cukor 1899–1983

✦ He Said

Devoted. —Cukor's response to Louis B. Mayer's asking him if he was a homosexual

It was absolutely all right to be gay in Hollywood, as long as you were not living with a man.

Personally, I adore clothes. I think they're one of the better inventions of mankind.

Never underestimate the stupidity of actors.

Don't give away the secret: It's the easiest job in the world. —Commenting on directing to someone who was approaching his first directorial job

✦ They Said

George was really queen of the roost. —Joseph L. Mankiewicz, screenwriter-director

His homosexuality bothered me. Perhaps, above all, because he was so ugly, and that made it ludicrous. —Gottfried Reinhardt, producer

George Cukor never disguised his sexuality, yet he never carried it as a pin on his lapel. —Joseph L. Mankiewicz, screenwriter-director

I won't be directed by a fairy. I have to work with a real man! —Clark Gable, actor, snarling about Cukor on the set of *Gone With the Wind* ('39), from which he had Cukor replaced as director

Basically Cukor is a theater man who neither cares about nor understands the camera. —Gene Kelly, dancer-actor

✦ First Sexual Experience
Unknown.

✦ Wives
Cukor never married, nor did he develop any long-lasting relationships with males.

✦ Did You Know?
Cukor was famed for hosting Sunday afternoon soirees at his home for members of Hollywood's gay set, as was Cole Porter. Cukor and Cole were referred to as the Rival Queens of Hollywood.

Lovers, Flings, or Just Friends?

Edward Crandall, actor

James Dean, actor

Joe Dallesandro, actor

George Hoyningen-Huene, photographer

Peter Lawford, actor

Anthony Quinn, actor

Aldo Ray, actor

Bob Seiter, actor–film editor

George Towers, companion-student-attorney

Forrest Tucker, actor

and a male telephone operator at London's tony Savoy Hotel; *plus* lots of sailors from Long Beach, California, preferably young; *and* many, many heterosexual, masculine men whom he paid for their favors

Tony Curtis 1925–

✦ He Said

I went around with a lump in my pants and chased all the girls. This is what I reflected on the screen. There wasn't anything deeper or less deep than that. —Reflecting on his early acting career

In the movie profession a lot of girls would give you anything to get an introduction to a director or a studio. It still goes on.

The secret to youth is to marry a girl younger than yourself.

You don't have to be like a cat in an alley. But you have to be courageous in the bedroom, just as you have to be courageous in life.

✦ They Said

The trouble with you, Tony, is that you're only interested in tight pants and wide billing. —Billy Wilder, director, arguing with Curtis about his billing on a film

Tony Curtis is a perfect example of what ambition and bad career choices can do to fabulous good looks over the years. —John Gielgud, actor

He's one of the few actors I have not got along with. —Joan Collins, actress

✦ First Sexual Experience

Curtis ejaculated when he was about ten or eleven years old while holding hands with a girl in a dark movie theater. He finally lost his virginity in a Panama City whorehouse when he was almost eighteen years old, while he was serving in the navy.

✦ Wives

Janet Leigh, actress
Christine Kaufmann, actress (costar in *Taras Bulba*, '62)
Leslie Allen, model
Lisa Deutsch, attorney

✦ Did You Know?

Gay costume designer Orry-Kelly, an old boyfriend of Curtis's idol Cary Grant, once told Marilyn Monroe that Curtis's ass was better-looking than hers; she wasn't amused by the comparison.

During his early, money-tight years in Hollywood, Curtis peddled photos—which he had autographed himself—of Deanna Durbin to unsuspecting tourists.

Lovers, Flings, or Just Friends?

Suzan Ball, actress
Lucille Barkley, actress
Ann Blyth, actress
Susan Cabot, actress
Danyel Cheeks, porn actress
Yvonne De Carlo, actress
Gloria DeHaven, actress (costar in *So This Is Paris*, '54)
Peggy Dow, starlet
Anita Ekberg, actress
Sue England, starlet
Mona Freeman, actress (costar in *I Was a Shoplifter*, '50)
Coleen Gray, starlet
Wanda Hendrix, starlet
Joyce Holden, starlet
Martha Hyer, actress (costar in *Mister Cory*, '57)
Soraya Khashoggi, socialite
Karen Kupcinet, starlet
Piper Laurie, actress (costar in *The Prince Who Was a Thief*, '51)
Barbara Lawrence, starlet
Kelly LeBrock, actress
Marilyn Monroe, actress (costar in *Some Like It Hot*, '59)
Andrea Savio, actress
Jaclyn Smith, actress
Mamie Van Doren, actress (costar in *The All-American*, '53)
and a girl from the Universal Studios distributing office who gave him a blowjob

Bobby Darin 1936–1973

✦ He Said

The sex element is the most important in this business. I'm very self-conscious about my physiognomy. But the fact remains, you must sell sex.

Conceit is thinking you're great; ego is knowing it.

Cocky is my favorite word.

My entire life has been a lie. —Referring to the way his family concealed his illegitimacy from him

✦ They Said

I used to laugh when people told me how Bobby was an arrogant little son of a bitch. —Dick Clark, television host

I think he was a wonderful actor. —Stanley Kramer, director, who directed him in *Pressure Point* ('62)

He could be warm, thoughtful, and enormous fun. But when he wanted to be, he could be the meanest son of a bitch alive. —A close relative

✦ First Sexual Experience

Lost his virginity as a teenager to a woman he also later caught in bed with his stepfather.

✦ Wives

Sandra Dee, actress (costar in *Come September,* '60)
Andrea Yeager, divorcée

✦ Did You Know?

When Darin began to consider running for a political office in California, his real mother, Nina, finally confessed that she wasn't the older "sister" she'd pretended to be all his life. She was afraid that his opposition would discover his illegitimacy and use it against him.

Darin's dead body was donated to UCLA medical research.

Sammy Davis Jr. 1925–1990

✦ He Said

I make no bones about the fact that when they started making explicit sex films, I became an immediate and avid collector.

Complete ugliness, utter ugliness, like mine, is most attractive. Yes, I'm convinced that a really ugly man, in the end, seems attractive.

If God ever took away my talent, I would be a nigger again.

The only person I ever hurt was myself and even that I did to the minimum.

✦ They Said

He had the sexual stamina of a bull. . . . You couldn't be alone in a room with Sammy for five minutes without giving him a blowjob. —Kathy McGee, singer

God made Sammy as ugly looking as He could, and then hit him in the face with a shovel. —Robert Sylvester, columnist

✦ First Sexual Experience

Unknown.

✦ Wives

Loray White, showgirl
May Britt, actress
Altovise Gore, dancer-actress

✦ Did You Know?

Davis married Loray White, a dancer at Las Vegas's Silver Slipper, after mobsters told him he had twenty-four hours in which to marry a black girl. Harry Cohn, head of Columbia Pictures, had become incensed that Davis was dating Kim Novak, one of his biggest stars, and wanted their relationship stopped. So, he had mobsters take Davis out into the desert and threaten him with the loss of his one remaining eye. White later told writer James Bacon that the marriage was never consummated, and that Davis gave her $25,000 after six months when the marriage ended.

Davis practiced Satanism for a while, even having one fingernail painted red, a signal used by Satanists to identify themselves to each other. He claimed he only "dabbled around the edges of it for sexual kicks."

Lovers, Flings, or Just Friends?

Claudine Auger, actress
Marilyn Chambers, porno actress
Ava Gardner, actress
Peggy Lipton, actress
Linda Lovelace, porno actress and fellatrice extraordinaire
Kathy McGee, singer
Marilyn Monroe, actress
Kim Novak, actress
Romy Schneider, actress
Jean Seberg, actress
Georgina Spelvin, porno actress
Tempest Storm, stripper

Daniel Day-Lewis 1958–

✦ He Said

At school, boys were always jumping in bed with each other. You got the feeling they were only practicing until girls came along.

Marriage has no meaning to me as an idea. It's not a concept I think about.

I'm like most human beings. I want what I don't have at the time. I want to be alone when I'm with someone and with someone when I'm alone.

In the end it's no different from doing Romeo and Juliet *with someone you don't know.* —On acting in gay roles in films

The nude scenes presented me with enormous difficulties. They were a harrowing experience, I felt so vulnerable. —On performing his first nude scene on camera

✦ They Said

Daniel Day-Lewis has what every actor in Hollywood wants. Talent. And what every British actor wants. Looks. —John Gielgud, actor

He likes his women dark and mysterious. —Unnamed friend

It was painful . . . but it was delicious. —Isabelle Adjani, on their relationship

✦ First Sexual Experience
Unknown.

✦ Wives
Rebecca Miller, actress and daughter of playwright Arthur Miller

✦ Did You Know?

Is Day-Lewis a cad? Rumors were that he broke off his mysterious relationship with French actress Isabelle Adjani when she admitted she was pregnant with his child. That didn't deter her; she had the child anyway.

James Dean 1931–1955

✦ He Said

You know, I've had my cock sucked by some of the big names in Hollywood.

I'm certainly not going through life with one hand tied behind my back.

I came to Hollywood to act, not to charm society.

To me the only success is immortality.

✦ They Said

He was small, ugly, hunchbacked with a potbelly, and bow-legged. . . . If he'd have lived he'd have a larger potbelly, wear a wig, and have died of AIDS. —Marlene Dietrich, singer-actress

I've known many actors who have been twisted up in their sex lives, but never anybody as, as, I guess, unhealthy *is the word, as sick and unhealthy as Dean was.* —Elia Kazan, director

I don't mean to speak ill of the dead, but he was a prick. —Rock Hudson, costar in *Giant* ('56)

He was intensely determined not to be loved or to love. —Nicholas Ray, director

The little son of a bitch was one of the most unspeakably detestable fellows I ever knew in my life. —Ruth Goetz, producer

We never became lovers, but we could have—like that. —Sal Mineo, costar in *Rebel Without a Cause* ('55)

✦ First Sexual Experience

Occurred with Dr. James DeWeerd, the pastor of the Wesleyan Church in Fairmount, Indiana, during Dean's senior year in high school. DeWeerd also delivered the eulogy at Dean's funeral.

✦ Wives

Dean was still single when he died at age twenty-four.

✦ Did You Know?

James Dean probably holds the dubious distinction of being the film star whose penis was seen by the largest number of people— live, in person—at one time. The incident occurred during the filming of *Giant* ('56) in Marfa, Texas. A large group of townspeople were gathered behind a rope watching a scene be set up for shooting. Dean strolled over to face the crowd, unzipped his fly, and, with penis in full view, proceeded to urinate. After he finished, he sauntered back onto the set to resume filming.

Lovers, Flings, or Just Friends?

Nick Adams, actor

Ursula Andress, actress

Lemuel Ayers, theatrical producer

Tallulah Bankhead, actress

Marshall Barer, friend

Bill Bast, actor and roommate

Rogers Brackett, advertising executive

Richard Davalos, actor (costar in *East of Eden*, '56)

Alfredo de la Vega, wealthy heir

David Diamond, composer

Jonathan Gilmore, actor

Barbara Hutton, Woolworth heiress

Eartha Kitt, singer-actress

Toni Lee, singer

Sal Mineo, actor (costar in *Rebel Without a Cause*, '55)

Betsy Palmer, actress

Nicholas Ray, director (directed in him *Rebel Without a Cause*, '55)

Elizabeth Sheridan, actress-dancer

Jack Simmons, actor

Robert Stevens, television director

Susan Strasberg, actress

Clifton Webb, actor

Alec W. Wilder, composer

Natalie Wood, actress

plus a black man he fellated in front of the other guests at a party

Alain Delon 1935–

✦ He Said

Next to being an actor, I would have enjoyed being a gangster.

I am not a star. I am an actor. I have been fighting for ten years to make people forget that I am just a pretty boy with a beautiful face. It's a hard fight, but I will win it.

✦ They Said

He's much too pretty. He's prettier than I am. —Vivien Leigh, actress, rejecting him for the role of the gigolo in her film *The Roman Spring of Mrs. Stone* ('61)

In his beauty, there is something mean and furtive. —Luchino Visconti, Italian director

He was a real sex machine. —Marisa Mell, actress

✦ First Sexual Experience

Unknown.

✦ Wives

Nathalie Delon (Francine Canovas), actress

✦ Did You Know?

In October 1968, Delon and his wife got caught up in what came to be known in France as *l'affaire de Markovic*. It began when the body of Stefan Markovic, the Delons' Yugoslavian bodyguard-chauffeur, was discovered in a garbage dump, having been beaten to death with a blunt instrument. Charges and countercharges swirled around the couple: that Markovic was her lover, his lover, arranged orgies for the couple, and other unsavory things. As the investigation continued, many prominent politicians and entertainment personalities found their names being mentioned in connection with the whole affair until finally it seemed that it was suddenly hushed up. When the case was closed, no charges were ever filed against either of the Delons or any of the other names mentioned.

Robert De Niro 1943–

✦ He Said

Some women never give me a look unless they find out who I am.

I'm not one of those actors who goes around in private giving off that macho thing.

I don't mind being a bastard, as long as I'm an interesting bastard.

There's nothing more offensive to me than watching an actor act with his ego.

✦ They Said

I had a bigger romance with Bobby than I did with any of my lovers. Better change that to read "my husbands." —Shelley Winters, actress

If he ever wants me, he can have me. No questions asked. —Oprah Winfrey, talk show host–actress

A class-A bastard. —Liza Minnelli, actress and costar in *New York, New York,* '77

Do you know you are going to be the most incredible star? —Sally Kirkland, actress, on first seeing De Niro act in a play

✦ First Sexual Experience
Unknown.

✦ Wives
Diahnne Abbott, actress
Grace Hightower

✦ Did You Know?
While researching his role of Jake LaMotta in *Raging Bull* ('80), De Niro spent time with LaMotta's ex-wife Vicki. She's said that since he had already assumed much of Jake's character in preparation for the role when he visited her, she thought it only natural for De Niro and her to make love. Robert chose to keep their relationship very businesslike, however, and declined to discover how Jake felt in Vicki's embraces. Vicki lamented about the situation, "I should have attacked him or something."

Lovers, Flings, or Just Friends?

Naomi Campbell, model

Gillian De Terville, British model

Whitney Houston, singer-actress

Ashley Judd, actress (costar in *Heat,* '95)

Sally Kirkland, actress

Jennifer Rubin, actress

Stefania Sandrelli, Italian actress

Toukie Smith, actress-model

Helena Lisandrello (a.k.a. Helena Springer), singer

Uma Thurman, actress (costar in *Mad Dog and Glory,* '93)

Shelley Winters, actress

Johnny Depp 1964–

✦ He Said

It's not, like, every week I get an envelope of pubes. —Remarking about receiving envelopes containing the pubic hair of some of his female fans

I've never been one of those guys who goes out and screws everything in front of him.

I'm an old-fashioned guy who wants marriage and kids.

Feet are fascinating, don't you think? They tell you so much about people.

If I could have another mouth grafted onto my face to smoke more, I would do it.

I don't want to be remembered in the year 2030 for being on some kid's lunchbox or thermos.

✦ They Said

Johnny changes wedding plans the way some people change socks. —Unnamed columnist commenting on Depp's wedding plans, none completed, with several different women

He always believes in this pure way about love. —Faye Dunaway, actress

He's got real sex appeal for women. —Wes Craven, director

Johnny invented grunge. I don't remember a movie star with that look before him. —John Waters, director

✦ First Sexual Experience

Lost his virginity at age thirteen, by his own account, but hasn't revealed to whom.

✦ Wives

Lori Ann Allison, sister of one of his band members

✦ Did You Know?

Depp has claimed, perhaps in jest, that he offered to do a cameo in the porno takeoff of his film *Edward Scissorhands* called *Edward Penishands.*

Lovers, Flings, or Just Friends?

Christina Applegate, actress

Tally Chanel, actress

Sherilyn Fenn, actress

Jennifer Grey, actress

Juliette Lewis, actress (costar in *What's Eating Gilbert Grape*, '93)

Kate Moss, model

Nina Patterson

Winona Ryder, actress (costar in *Edward Scissorhands*, '90)

Kirk Douglas 1916–

✦ He Said

An erection is a mysterious thing. There's always that fear, each time one goes, that you won't be seeing it again.

As a matter of fact, my father and my mother had a dimple. My six sisters have the same. Actually, it's a weakness of the muscle. It's so perfectly formed, some people think I had it put in.

People don't dislike me because I'm a perfectionist. They hate me because I'm me.

✦ They Said

Boastful, egotistical, resentful of criticism—if anyone dare give it. —Sheilah Graham, Hollywood columnist

He has always believed the back is a real turn-on. —Janet Leigh, actress

I've worked with him many times over the years. . . . He is the most difficult and exasperating man that I know—except for myself. —Burt Lancaster, longtime friend

Go ask Mr. Douglas for his autograph. He's a great actor. Of course, you probably didn't recognize him without his built-up shoes. —Burt Lancaster, replying to a fan's request for an autograph

✦ First Sexual Experience

Appears to have lost his virginity, when he was in his early teens, to Mrs. Louise Livingston, an English teacher, with whom he had a long relationship.

✦ Wives

Diana Dill, actress
Anne Buydens, film publicist

✦ Did You Know?

As a young man Douglas worked one summer as a bellboy in a small hotel owned by a vicious, anti-Semitic woman. Since she didn't know he was Jewish, she spouted her hatred of Jews all summer long. At the end of the season, she seduced Douglas. During sex, he whispered loudly into her ear, "That is a circumcised Jewish cock inside you. . . . I am a Jew. You are being fucked by a Jew."

Early in his career, Douglas was "auditioned" by Mae West for a part. Mae's auditions usually consisted of the actors being required to strip to skimpy briefs, or less, and let her "inspect" them. Douglas didn't make the grade.

Lovers, Flings, or Just Friends?

Pier Angeli, actress (costar in *The Story of Three Loves*, '53)

Lauren Bacall, actress (costar in *Young Man With a Horn*, '50)

Joan Crawford, actress

Linda Darnell, actress (costar in *The Walls of Jericho*, '48)

Marlene Dietrich, actress

Peggy Diggins, student-model

Rita Hayworth, actress

Evelyn Keyes, actress

Elsa Martinelli, actress

Patricia Neal, actress

Ann Sothern, actress (costar in *A Letter to Three Wives*, '49)

Princess Safia Tarzi of Afghanistan

Gene Tierney, actress

Lana Turner, actress (costar in *The Bad and the Beautiful*, '52)

Irene Wrightsman, socialite

Michael Douglas 1945–

✦ He Said

Women I've never laid eyes on claim they've slept with me.

Growing up with my father was like growing up with the Kennedys. We were taught that women were just there to be used.

It's hard trying to create the fuck of the century twelve hours a day for five days when you orchestrate or choreograph all the moves and try lots of different angles and just want it to be over so you can go home.

Hollywood is littered with the bodies of the sons and daughters of the famous who didn't make it.

I don't mind looking into the mirror and seeing my father.

✦ They Said

He's full of charm and humor, but don't ever cross him. —Kathleen Turner, actress and costar in *The War of the Roses* ('89)

I want my sons to surpass me, because that's a form of immortality. —Kirk Douglas, actor and father

✦ First Sexual Experience
Unknown.

✦ Wives
Diandra Lukens, Washington socialite

✦ Did You Know?

In addition to his Oscar for Best Actor for *Wall Street* ('87), Douglas once won another memorable award. While working at a gas station, he was selected as a Mobil Man of the Month.

After tabloid reports surfaced that his wife had supposedly caught Douglas in a hotel room with one of her best friends, Douglas was reputed to have sought treatment for an addiction to sex. He's also said those reports were, "Bullshit. It's bullshit."

Lovers, Flings, or Just Friends?

Sherri Lansing, production executive

Taryn Power, actress

Brenda Vaccaro, actress (costar in *Summertree*, '71)

Clint Eastwood 1933–

✦ He Said

Sex is a small part of life. It's a good thing—great—but 99 per-cent of your life is spent doing other things.

I don't think I was ever attacted to a girl who didn't like music, who didn't have some interest in it.

I've been on film sets where after lunch girls come up and asked for my dirty plates or empty beer bottles.

✦ They Said

I think you'd have to be around for a year before you saw his ugly side, assuming he has one. —Norman Mailer

I thought he hung the moon. —Sondra Locke, frequent costar with whom he conducted a long-running affair

As a director, Eastwood is not as good as he thinks he is. As an actor, he is probably better than he allows himself to be. —Richard Schickel, film critic

✦ First Sexual Experience

Lost his virginity at age fourteen. To whom is still a mystery, which he's made more intriguing by his comment, "I had nice neighbors."

✦ Wives

Maggie Johnson
Dina Ruiz, television newsanchor

✦ Did You Know?

When news of his illegitimate daughter, Kimber Tunis Eastwood, and her son, Eastwood's first grandchild, surfaced, he was reputed to have withdrawn the support for her that he had provided for years.

Sondra Locke, with whom Eastwood conducted a multiyear relationship, sued him for $70 million in a palimony action after their association ended. Eastwood said of her suit, "This is not at all classy." Among other things she alleged: she aborted two pregnancies at his direction and had her tubes tied, again at his request. Her suit was finally settled out of court at somewhere between $6 and $40 million according to press reports, with Locke supposedly being prevented from ever writing a book about their relationship.

Lovers, Flings, or Just Friends?

Frances Fisher, actress (costar in *Unforgiven*, '92)

Jo Ann Harris, actress (costar in *The Beguiled*, '70)

Dani Janssen, widow of David Janssen

Sondra Locke, actress-director (costar in *The Gauntlet*, '77)

Barbara Minty, model (and the third Mrs. Steve McQueen)

Sierra Pecheur, actress

Bernadette Peters, actress (costar in *The Pink Cadillac*, '89)

Jacelyn Reeves, flight attendant

Jean Seberg, actress (costar in *Paint Your Wagon*, '69)

Susan St. James, actress

Barbra Streisand, actress-singer

Roxanne Tunis, actress

Mamie Van Doren, actress

Nelson Eddy 1901–1967

✦ He Said

His crowd thinks I'm a fag. —Complaining about how actor Clark Gable and his circle regarded him

Most film actresses are incredibly boring.

Generally speaking, I think an actor or actress shouldn't marry another in the profession, for in time one almost always overshadows the other.

✦ They Said

Nelson Eddy was no fairy! I was deliciously devoured by a hungry man. —Lina Basquette, actress

Even without his fabulous voice he could have easily slept his way to the top. —Marie Collick, close friend

✦ First Sexual Experience

Unknown.

✦ Wives

Ann Denitz Franklin, divorced socialite

✦ Did You Know?

Eddy was a foot fetishist and loved to rub women's feet.

Whenever Eddy's mother could track him down at one of his sexual liaisons, she did so with a fury. She'd telephone demanding that he abandon the woman and come home to her. He usually did.

Country singer Dottie West has an unusual connection to Eddy. He provided financial support for her upbringing as a child after an accident killed one of her uncles, who had been a favorite of Eddy's.

Lovers, Flings, or Just Friends?

Lina Basquette, actress

Alice Brady, actress

Mamo Clark, actress

Alice Faye, actress

Helen Jepson, singer

Isabel Jewell, actress

Lila Lee, actress

Anita Louise, actress

Jeanette MacDonald, singer-actress (costar in *Naughty Marietta*, '35)

Mae Mann, newspaper writer

Frances Marion, screenwriter

Maybelle Marston

Grace Moore, singer-actress

Maryon Murphy, wife of a producer

Norma Nelson, script girl

Eleanor Powell, dancer-actress (costar in *Rosalie*, '37)

Gale Sherwood, singing partner

Eleanor Steber, opera singer

Risë Stevens, singer-actress (costar in *The Chocolate Soldier*, '41)

Sybil Thomas, widow of a banker

Edward Kennedy "Duke" Ellington 1899–1974

✦ He Said

My mother taught me to gravitate toward beauty, so I have. —His come-on line when he'd approach a woman for the first time

✦ They Said

He could no more be faithful to one woman than he could be to one piece of music. —Don George, close friend

He was a man that loved and wanted love and knew nothing but love. —Bernice Wiggins, cousin

✦ First Sexual Experience

Unknown.

✦ Wives

Edna Thompson, neighbor and schoolmate

✦ Did You Know?

Joan Crawford, attending a Pepsi awards dinner in the same Dallas, Texas, hotel where Ellington's band was playing for a charity benefit, was invited to come help dispense some of the charity's door prizes. She graciously agreed to do so, but soon after she arrived, passed out—probably from her liquor intake—and fell into the saxophone section of the band. After she had lain there for several minutes, a hotel staff member came and picked her up. When he was asked why he hadn't helped Crawford, Ellington replied, "I wouldn't lay my hand on a white woman in Texas."

Ellington created the scores for two films: *Anatomy of a Murder* ('59) and *Paris Blues* ('61). He received an Oscar nomination for his *Paris Blues* score but didn't win the award.

Lovers, Flings, or Just Friends?

Josephine Baker, entertainer

Mildred Dixon, dancer

Beatrice (Evie) Ellis, chorus girl

Oriana Fallaci, journalist

Lena Horne, singer-actress

Jeanette MacDonald, singer-actress

Countess Fernanda de Castro Monte, singer

Freddi Washington, actress-dancer

Anna Mae Wong, actress

Douglas Fairbanks Jr. 1909–2000

✦ He Said
I was not really the man to fall seriously for just any pretty young ship that passed in the night.

✦ They Said
That guy Fairbanks has so goddamn many faggot friends that I was beginning to worry about him, too. This kinda thing is a relief and it'll prove he's no fairy. —Jack Warner, expressing his delight when Fairbanks was named a party in a divorce suit

There's only one Fairbanks! —Douglas Fairbanks Sr., stating his opposition to his son's intention of pursuing a film career

✦ First Sexual Experience
Unknown.

✦ Wives
Joan Crawford, actress
Mary Lee Hartford, socialite
Vera Shelton, home shopping network merchandiser

✦ Did You Know?
Clifton Webb, Hollywood's notorious "mama's boy" and close friend of Joan Crawford, Fairbanks's wife, once put the make on the actor. Fairbanks had offered him a ride to the studio, when Webb began expressing his true feelings, then placed his hand on Fairbanks's thigh. Being undecided how to act at first—whether to express anger, contempt, or annoyance—Fairbanks finally decided to handle the situation by laughing and treating it as a joke. Webb became infuriated and insisted Fairbanks stop the car so he could get out and call a cab. Webb didn't make it to the studio that day; he called in with an "upset stomach."

At his first meeting with Bette Davis—at a party—Fairbanks, who was still married to Joan Crawford at the time, chatted politely, then quickly thrust his hand into Davis's bra. He felt up her tits, then recommended that she use ice on her nipples, like his wife did. Davis was appalled at his behavior.

Composer-playwright Noël Coward probably had quite a crush on the young, handsome Fairbanks in his heyday. It's been widely rumored that he wrote his song "Mad About the Boy" about Fairbanks.

Douglas Fairbanks Sr. 1883–1939

✦ He Said

I've done everything—twice.

You mustn't listen to talk in Hollywood. The idlers have nothing to do but spread rumors, and busy people can't afford to spend all their time denying them.

✦ They Said

He didn't drink or smoke, so he thought he had the right to some kind of vice. He chose women. He went after every girl who crossed the studio lot. And most women couldn't resist Doug's attention. —Anita Loos, writer

He's got a face like a cantaloupe and he can't act. —D. W. Griffith, director

He's not good-looking. But he has a world of personality—just worlds of it. —Gladys "Grace" George, actress

In his private life Douglas always faced a situation in the only way he knew, by running away from it. —Mary Pickford, second wife

✦ First Sexual Experience

Unknown.

✦ Wives

Anna Beth Sully, heiress
Mary Pickford, actress (costar in *The Taming of the Shrew,* '29)
Lady Sylvia Ashley, socialite (and the fourth Mrs. Clark Gable)

✦ Did You Know?

In 1917, Mount Fairbanks, a peak in an Alaskan national park, was named for the actor.

Lovers, Flings, or Just Friends?

Maria Alba, actress (costar in *Mr. Robinson Crusoe,* '32)

Majorie Daw, silent screen actress

Lila Lee, silent screen actress

Lupe Velez, actress (costar in *The Gaucho,* '27)

Peter Finch 1916–1977

✦ He Said

A high libido and a sense of life's absurdities can breed queer bedfellows, and in the good old public days, I landed up in some pretty queer situations.

✦ They Said

He was a fairly weak character—an angel, a darling man, no evil in him—but he was content to just love life and eat and drink and sleep with lovely ladies. —Maxine Audley, actress

He was a piss-pot and a hell-raiser. —Yolande Turnbull, second wife

It was very difficult to know Peter Finch the man—very easy to know Peter Finch the actor. —Jim Davidson, broadcast bandleader

The irony of Peter's career is that he achieved fame in the medium he used openly to despise and ridicule, namely cinema. —A close friend

✦ First Sexual Experience

Unknown.

✦ Wives

Tamara Tchinarova, dancer
Yolande Turnbull, South African performer
Eletha Barrett, Jamaican hairdresser

✦ Did You Know?

Finch used his half-sister Flavia to help him keep track of his women—he was often juggling multiple affairs. He'd give his ladies ("dollybirds" in his words) her telephone number and ask them to keep in touch with her while he was elsewhere making films. Finch's instructions to his sister: "Keep the dollybirds under your thumb in London. Don't let them wander off with anyone else."

Lovers, Flings, or Just Friends?

Maxine Audley, British actress

Shirley Bassey, singer

Florrie Christmas, screenwriter

Bette Dickson, Australian actress

Donald Friend, Australian painter

Margaret Hoyter, Australian socialite

Kay Kendall, actress (costar in *Simon and Laura*, '56)

Vivien Leigh, actress

Trisha Locke, model agency owner

Sheila Smart, Australian socialite

Mai Zetterling, actress

plus lots and lots of other women, including a Sabena Air Lines stewardess, a German princess, the daughter of an African chieftain, a professor of Greek, and many prostitutes, actresses, and starlets

Albert Finney 1936–

✦ He Said

I don't flaunt my infidelities.

No security; perfect training for the actor's life. —Musing on all the moves his family made during his childhood because of his father's profession—as an illegal bookie

✦ They Said

Albie's just plain wonderful. That's all there is to it. —Audrey Hepburn, actress

✦ First Sexual Experience

Unknown.

✦ Wives

Jane Wenham, actress

Anouk Aimée, actress

✦ Did You Know?

As bizarre as it seems, Finney cut a record album in 1977 on the Motown label; not being a "chart buster," it disappeared quickly.

Lovers, Flings, or Just Friends?

Elizabeth Ashley, actress

Samantha Eggar, actress

Cathryn Harrison, actress

Audrey Hepburn, actress (costar in *Two for the Road,* '67)

Diane Keaton, actress (costar in *Shoot the Moon,* '82)

Jean Marsh, actress

Diana Quick, actress

Rachel Roberts, actress (costar in *Saturday Night and Sunday Morning,* '60)

Edina Ronay, British starlet

Billie Whitelaw, actress

Shelley Winters, actress

Eddie Fisher 1928–

✦ He Said

Well, I love her and I never loved you. —Telling Debbie Reynolds why he was ditching her for Elizabeth Taylor

Elizabeth was beautiful, a famous Hollywood star, but as far as I was concerned, she could also be a pain in the ass, a spoiled brat.

✦ They Said

The reason I drink is because when I'm sober I think I'm Eddie Fisher. —Dean Martin, singer-actor

He's a needy, dependent person. I don't know what to compare him to. He's like an elevator that can't find the floor. —Debbie Reynolds, actress

Let me pat you, dear boy, let me touch it. —Noël Coward, encountering a nude Fisher in the steam room aboard the ocean liner *Queen Elizabeth* and asking permission to touch Fisher's rear; he was denied his request

✦ First Sexual Experience

Lost his virginity, when he was about fourteen years old, to a neighborhood girl named Tootsie Stern.

✦ Wives

Debbie Reynolds, actress
Elizabeth Taylor, actress
Connie Stevens, actress-singer
Terry Richards, beauty queen
Betty Young Lin, businesswoman

✦ Did You Know?

Fisher has admitted that during one period of two or three months he spent about $200,000 on cocaine.

One of Fisher's idols when he was young was actor John Garfield. After seeing the actor at Grossinger's resort in the Catskills of New York, he followed Garfield around. He watched as the actor pinched women on the ass, and even heard him say to one waitress, "Hey, sweetheart, you want to fuck?" Fisher finally was introduced to Garfield, but didn't tell him what all he had been observed doing.

During a trip to Japan while in the armed services, Fisher was billeted at an exclusive geisha resort, usually reserved for top brass. Condoms were provided in the bedrooms, and he said Susan Hayward's picture appeared on the wrapper.

Lovers, Flings, or Just Friends?

Edie Adams, singer-actress

Pier Angeli, actress

Ann-Margret, singer-actress

Renata Boeck, German model

Judith Campbell, lady friend of President Kennedy and mobster Sam Giancana

Lyn Davis, teacher

Nathalie Delon, actress (and wife of actor Alain)

Marlene Dietrich, singer-actress

Mia Farrow, actress

Judy Garland, singer-actress

Hope Lange, actress

Jane Morgan, singer

Merle Oberon, actress

Stephanie Powers, actress

Juliet Prowse, dancer

Maria Schell, actress

Pat Shean, Las Vegas showgirl

Pamela Turnure, press secretary to Jacqueline Kennedy

Mamie Van Doren, actress

Virginia Warren, daughter of Chief Justice Earl Warren

Joan Wynne, showgirl

plus lots and lots of hookers (a different girl each night) from a Los Angeles madam who made "serving the stars" her specialty

F. Scott Fitzgerald 1896–1940

✦ He Said

The little hard face of a successful streetwalker on a jumping jack. —Describing the face of teenage singing actress Deanna Durbin

I am half feminine—that is, my mind is.

Isn't Hollywood a dump—in the human sense of the word?

✦ They Said

Scott liked the idea of sex, for its romance and daring, but he was not strongly sexed. —Oscar Kalman, close friend

Scott will never matter to a hoot in hell until he gets rid of his wife. —H. L. Mencken, author and literary critic

If the poor guy was already an alcoholic in his college days, it's a marvel that he did as well as he did. —Raymond Chandler, author

The two things I feared most were drunkenness and insanity. With Scott, I had both. —Sheilah Graham, Hollywood gossip columnist and Fitzgerald's lover

✦ First Sexual Experience

Probably lost his virginity to a prostitute while attending college.

✦ Wives

Zelda Sayre, deranged Southern belle and writer

✦ Did You Know?

Zelda Fitzgerald frequently taunted Scott that his penis was too small. As a result, he would sometimes query complete strangers about preferred penis sizes, asking them, "Do women like a man's privates large or small?"

Fitzgerald had a fetish for women's feet, because he thought his own feet were ugly and repulsive. He also never removed his socks while having sex.

Fitzgerald was actually such a prude that his longtime lover, gossip columnist Sheilah Graham, never saw him completely naked.

Fitzgerald had a screen test in 1927, but failed it because he photographed as "too old" for movies.

Lovers, Flings, or Just Friends?

Beatrice Dance, married woman he met on holiday

Isadora Duncan, dancer

Father Cyril Sigourney Webster Fay, Roman Catholic priest

Nora Flynn, Virginia socialite

Rosalinde Fuller, British actress

Sheilah Graham, gossip columnist

Lois Moran, actress

Violet Marie "Bijou" O'Conor, English friend

Maureen O'Sullivan, actress

Dorothy Parker, writer

Dorothy Richardson, nurse

Errol Flynn 1909–1959

✦ He Said

I'm just a goddamned phallic symbol to the world.

I'm not a breast man. I'm a leg man. You can't make love to a breast.

I don't have to seduce girls. For Christ's sake, I come home and they're hiding under my bed.

I just lie there reading the trade papers while they work on me.
—Admitting how he could service so many women in his dressing room

✦ They Said

You know Flynn. He's either got to be fighting or fucking. —Jack L. Warner, head of Warner Bros., Flynn's studio

Errol was so well hung that he was famous for it all over Hollywood. He often unzipped on the set in front of everybody, whipped it out for all to see . . . just to set the record straight. —Iron Eyes Cody, Native American actor who appeared with Flynn in several films

He had, in my opinion, spent his entire life, this man over whom girls swooned, picking dogs. —Orson Welles, director-actor

You never know when he is telling the truth. He lies for the fun of it. —Lily Damita, spouse

✦ First Sexual Experience

Lost his virginity to the family maid, in Australia, when he was twelve years old.

✦ Wives

Lily Damita, French actress
Nora Eddington, eighteen-year-old cider stand worker
Patrice Wymore, actress

✦ Did You Know?

To what did Flynn attribute much of his sexual prowess? A bit of cocaine on the tip of his penis before intercourse, of course.

Flynn claimed that before she fellated him, actress Lupe Velez would always cross herself three times.

When Flynn and Tyrone Power got together, Errol was the top and Tyrone the bottom. While Errol preferred oral stimulation, Ty liked anal intercourse and often disgusted Errol with the "things" he wanted done to him.

Annoyed at his next-door neighbor, Hedda Hopper, Flynn once stomped over to her front door and masturbated, slinging semen all over it. Hedda simply stood in a window, watching and laughing.

Lovers, Flings, or Just Friends?

Beverly Aadland, actress (costar in *Cuban Rebel Girls*, '59)

Joan Bennett, actress

Linda Christian, actress

Truman Capote, author and social gadfly

Appollonio Diaz, Mexican beach-boy

Doris Duke, tobacco heiress

Edmund Goulding, director

Axel Wenner Gren, Swedish Electrolux founder

Virginia Hill, mobster moll

Rock Hudson, actor

Howard Hughes, aviation and cinema mogul

Barbara Hutton, heiress

Hedy Lamarr, actress

Carole Landis, actress (costar in *Four's a Crowd*, '38)

Laurence Olivier, actor

Eva Perón, actress-dictator

Tyrone Power, actor

Ann Sheridan, actress

Gloria Vanderbilt, heiress

Lupe Velez, actress

Shelley Winters, actress

plus Flynn once claimed that he'd had sex from twelve to fourteen thousand times in his life, which isn't surprising since he sometimes managed to entertain as many as four different "starlets" a day in his dressing room while filming

Henry Fonda 1905–1982

✦ He Said

I'm ashamed of being married so many times. It makes me seem like a fool and a failure. —Reflecting on his marital record

Will I have to take my clothes off? —Querying his daughter, Jane, who had asked him about playing a cameo in her sexually provocative film *Barbarella* ('68)

✦ They Said

A Don Juan homosexual who has to prove himself with one woman after another. —George Sanders, retorting after hearing a nasty crack Fonda had made about Sanders and Tyrone Power having a relationship

Hank could be a real bastard at times. —Josh Logan, director

I was in awe of my father. As a girl, I would do naughty things just to gain his attention. —Jane Fonda, on her frustrating relationship with her father

He was—and he was the first to admit it—a lousy husband. —Jack Lemmon, actor

✦ First Sexual Experience

Lost his virginity as a young man in an Omaha whorehouse. He called it "a horrible experience," saying, "It was just wham-bam. I was repulsed. It turned me off for quite a while."

✦ Wives

Margaret Sullavan, actress (costar in *The Moon's Our Home,* '36)
Frances Seymour Brokaw, socialite
Susan Blanchard, socialite
Afdera Franchetti, Italian socialite
Shirlee Adams, airline stewardess

✦ Did You Know?

Edward Albee wrote the play *Who's Afraid of Virginia Woolf,* about an abusive marital relationship, with Fonda in mind for George, the Milquetoast husband. Fonda's agents passed on the play without even telling him about it.

Lovers, Flings, or Just Friends?

Annabella, actress (costar in *Wings of the Morning,* '37)

Lucille Ball, actress

Diana Barrymore, actress

Imogene Coca, actress-comedienne

Joan Crawford, actress (costar in *Daisy Kenyon,* '47)

Bette Davis, actress (costar in *Jezebel,* '38)

Jeanette MacDonald, singer-actress

Glenn Ford 1916–

✦ He Said

I think escape is the reason all actors choose their profession.

If they try and rush me, I always say, I've only got one other speed, and it's slower. —Revealing his method of pacing himself when he acts

✦ They Said

Who is that son of a bitch that should say he helped me have a comeback! That shitheel wouldn't have helped me out of a sewer! —Bette Davis, actress, taking umbrage after Ford made some unwise comments about having helped Davis stage a comeback by appearing with her in the film *A Pocketful of Miracles* ('61)

He approached his craft like a twelve-year-old temperamental child. Were he mine, I would have spanked him physically. —David Swift, director, who directed him in *Love Is a Ball* ('63)

He had such an inferiority complex, it was sheer hell. —Eleanor Powell, actress-dancer, on appearing in public with her hubby back when they were first married

It is an easily won bet that in a few years he will get just like the other movie people: bored, sprawling, careless, an overly relaxed fallen angel—they are all affable boys out here, almost tramps. —Clifford Odets, playwright and screenwriter, on his first meeting with Ford

✦ First Sexual Experience

Unknown.

✦ Wives

Eleanor Powell, actress-dancer

Kathryn Hayes, actress

Cynthia Hayward, actress

Karen Johnson

Jeanne Baus

✦ Did You Know?

Ford once worked as a stableboy for homespun comedian Will Rogers.

After her divorce, when Ford started dating the former Mrs. Johnny Carson, the comedian made several cracks about him on the *Tonight Show*. Carson's antics annoyed Ford so much he contemplated suing the entertainer.

Harrison Ford 1942–

✦ He Said

I was kind of a runty thing. And I liked to hang out with the girls. That annoyed the boys.

I was the loner type.

I'm a real bore.

I believed that life was made for couples, not for single men. —On why he's the marrying type, rather than the playboy type

I was definitely not Mr. Sweetness and Light. —How he now perceives he was during his first marriage

Being normal is a kind of victory. What I really like is peace and quiet.

✦ They Said

Harrison Ford is hot. He's a man, not a little boy. —Sean Young, actress

Someday Harrison, you'll see. You'll be like Cary Grant. —Cindy Williams, actress, giving encouragement during his struggling days as an actor

Harrison can be villainous and romantic all at once. —Steven Spielberg, director, defining Ford's screen allure

✦ First Sexual Experience

It would not be unreasonable to guess that maybe Ford lost his virginity while he was a member of Sigma Nu fraternity at Ripon College, if he didn't do so while he was in high school.

✦ Wives

Mary Marquardt, student
Melissa Mathison, screenwriter

✦ Did You Know?

For those who've wondered how Ford acquired that noticeable scar on his chin that so many admirers feel adds a roguish touch to his visage, here's the real story. It came from an automobile accident when he slammed his car into a telephone pole years ago. The cause of the accident was typical for the straight-arrow Ford. He was distracted while attempting to fasten his seat belt.

Who were some of the Hollywood community who employed Ford's talents as a carpenter before he achieved superstar status in films? Richard Dreyfuss, James Caan, James Coburn, Sally Kellerman, Valerie Harper, musician Sergio Mendes, and writers Joan Didion and John Gregory Dunne rank among those who did so.

Lovers, Flings, or Just Friends?

Lesley-Anne Down, actress (costar in *Hanover Street*, '79)

Clark Gable 1901–1960

✦ He Said

When I was young I'd shack up with any female that appealed to me.

Hell, if I'd jumped on all the dames I'm supposed to have jumped on, I'd never have time to go fishing.

They're all beautiful and I've had every one of them! —Comment on seeing a group photo of MGM's leading ladies

✦ They Said

One inch less and he'd be Queen of Hollywood. —Carole Lombard, actress and spouse

I can't stand a man who has fake store teeth and doesn't keep his uncircumcised cock clean under the foreskin. I hear he shoots too soon and messes himself all the time. —Bette Davis, expressing why she never sought Gable sexually

He wasn't a satisfying lover. I often tried to distract him from the bedroom. —Joan Crawford, actress

Clark dear, the soap is to clean the cheese beneath your foreskin and the Listerine is to take away the smell. —Text of note that director George Cukor is rumored to have sent Gable, along with a cake of Lifebuoy soap and a small bottle of Listerine

✦ First Sexual Experience

Lost his virginity when he was fifteen years old in Cadiz, Ohio, to a very attractive widow in her fifties.

✦ Wives

Josephine Dillon, acting teacher
Ria Langham, Houston socialite
Carole Lombard, actress (costar in *No Man of Her Own*, '32)
Lady Sylvia Ashley, socialite
Kay Williams Spreckels, actress-socialite

✦ Did You Know?

Gable suffered from a severe case of phimosis, a condition where the foreskin refuses to retract properly or is too painful to retract. He was noted for a really bad smegma odor.

Gable had an accident while driving drunk one evening. His car crashed and killed a female pedestrian. Louis Mayer, the MGM studio boss, covered up both the accident and the woman's death to save Gable's career.

Lovers, Flings, or Just Friends?

Mary Astor, actress

Lionel Barrymore, actor

Joan Crawford (costar in *Dancing Lady*, '33)

Marion Davies, actress (costar in *Polly of the Circus*, '32)

Nancy Davis (Reagan), actress

Yvonne De Carlo, actress (costar in *Band of Angels*, '57)

Ava Gardner, actress (costar in *The Hucksters*, '47)

Paulette Goddard, actress

William "Billy" Haines, actor and interior decorator

Jean Harlow, actress (costar in *Red Dust*, '32)

Grace Kelly, actress (costar in *Mogambo*, '53)

Hedy Lamarr, actress (costar in *Boom Town*, '40)

Marilyn Monroe, actress (costar in *The Misfits*, '61)

Merle Oberon, actress

Louella Parsons, gossip columnist

Norma Shearer, actress (costar in *A Free Soul*, '31)

Adela Rogers St. Johns, writer

Lana Turner, actress (costar in *Honky Tonk*, '41)

Mamie Van Doren, actress

Lupe Velez, actress

Patricia "Honeychile" Wilder, radio actress

Shelley Winters, actress

Loretta Young, actress

John Garfield 1913–1952

✦ He Said

I was in Hollywood a week before I got laid. I don't know, that may just be a record.

I'd always been poor until I came to Hollywood, and I had a stimulating, exciting life.

✦ They Said

He loves being John Garfield because of all the pussy and the perks. —Artie Shaw, clarinetist

He had a penchant for picking up girls, sometimes two at a time, and a reputation as a demon lover. He died young, in bed, which was understandable. —Lana Turner, actress

He made love like a sexy puppy, in and out, huffing and puffing in quick gasps. —Sheilah Graham, gossip columnist

He had always had the face of a bar mitzvah boy gone just wrong enough to enhance his appeal. —Walter Bernstein, screenwriter

He was one of the nicest people I've ever known. My mother saw him just once and tried to get him into bed with her. —Truman Capote, author and social gadfly

✦ First Sexual Experience

Unknown for certain, but probably with some girl in the Bronx, where he was raised, when he was in his early teens.

✦ Wives

Roberta Seidman, salesgirl

✦ Did You Know?

When Garfield was first introduced to Joan Crawford, with whom he was to costar in *Humoresque* ('46), she extended her hand for him to shake. Instead of doing so, he reached right over and pinched her breast. Infuriated at first, Crawford gave him a knowing look and said, "You know, I think we're going to get on just fine." They did, on the set and in the sack.

Lovers, Flings, or Just Friends?

Truman Capote, author

Joan Crawford, actress (costar in *Humoresque*, '46)

Gloria Dickson, actress (costar in *They Made Me a Criminal*, '39)

Frances Farmer, actress (costar in *Flowing Gold*, '40)

Sheilah Graham, gossip columnist

Betty Grayson, actress

Hedy Lamarr, actress (costar in *Tortilla Flat*, '42)

Ida Lupino, actress (costar in *The Sea Wolf*, '41)

Eleanor Parker, actress (costar in *The Pride of the Marines*, '45)

Edith Piaf, singer

Micheline Presle, actress (costar in *Under My Skin*, '50)

Ann Sheridan, actress (costar in *They Made Me a Criminal*, '39)

Ann Shirley, actress (costar in *Saturday's Children*, '40)

Margo Stevenson, actress

Lana Turner, actress

Margaret Whiting, singer

Iris Whitney, actress-decorator

Shelley Winters, actress

plus many, many showgirls, extras, script girls, starlets, women students at the American Laboratory Theatre (when he trained in New York City), and well-known actresses

Richard Gere 1949–

✦ He Said

I'm very monogamous. When I'm with someone, I'm really with them. I've had long relationships.

Gossip has been around since the beginning of time. It's like the Twelfth Commandment: "Thou shalt gossip about everyone."

I have muscles, so I use them, just as I have a brain and I try to use it.

I'll be very disappointed in myself if I become just an actor.

✦ They Said

Richard's obviously been accused of being gay. Like when *does he have time to be gay?* —Cindy Crawford, wife

Richard Gere has taken his shirt off in every movie he's made. He's falling out of his clothes. —Christopher Reeve, actor

You expect him to be this macho kind of guy, and in fact he's Ferdinand the Bull, wandering in the meadow and smelling the flowers. —Jonathan Cott, author and longtime friend

He seems to be the Gable for the nineties. —Mark Rydell, director

✦ First Sexual Experience
Unknown.

✦ Wives
Gabrielle Lazure
Cindy Crawford, model

✦ Did You Know?
Gere was the subject of probably the most vicious rumor bandied around about any film star during the late 1980s. It all concerned a clandestine visit to an emergency room, a gerbil, and his anus. The rumor reached such wide distribution that Barbara Walters even broached the subject to Gere while interviewing him. While Walters didn't state the exact nature of the rumor, she did ask Gere if he had heard it and asked about his feelings on hearing such things discussed about himself.

Lovers, Flings, or Just Friends?

Kim Basinger, actress (costar in *No Mercy*, '86)

Barbara Carrera, actress

Tina Chow, fashion designer

Lauren Hutton, model-actress

Sylvia Martins, Brazilian artist

Penelope Milford, actress

Priscilla Presley, actress

Rachel Roberts, actress

Diana Ross, singer-actress

Susan Sarandon, actress

Dawn Steel, film executive

Barbra Streisand, actress-singer

Uma Thurman, actress

Diane von Furstenberg, fashion designer

Tuesday Weld, actress

George Gershwin 1898–1937

✦ He Said

I can't go out with you anymore because you're just a telephone operator and I'm a composer. —Dropping one of his earlier flings

They are interesting, but a movie star is a movie star. They leave you with a sort of emptiness when you say goodnight.

Hollywood is a place of great extremes—when it rains, it pours—when it's cloudy, it's cloudy the whole day—and when the sun shines, well, you know about that.

All I've got is a lot of talent and plenty of chutzpah.

✦ They Said

His chest was the hairiest since Beethoven's. I used to make fun of it. I'd say, "Cut off a lock and give it to a girl." —Oscar Levant, pianist-composer

I know stories of his womanizing were prevalent, but I never saw him go steady in any sense of that word. —Al Hirshfield, famed news caricaturist

He was so lionized that there were always people three-deep around him. —Vincente Minnelli, director

✦ First Sexual Experience

Lost his virginity when he was nine years old.

✦ Wives

Gershwin never married, although he was constantly proposing to women.

✦ Did You Know?

While in Hollywood, Gershwin, who had a receding hairline, succumbed to the movie colony's obsession with physical beauty. He purchased and used a contraption marketed by the Crosley Radio Corporation that had been recommended as a positive grower of hair. It failed to do its duty on the composer.

During a visit to Havana, Cuba, during the thirties, Gershwin ardently wooed a comely Cuban miss. When she stood him up for dinner he chastised her. The lady delivered a devastating retort. She told him, "Oh, I meant to phone and tell you, but do you know what? I couldn't remember your name."

While he was working on his masterpiece opera *Porgy and Bess,* Gershwin frequently referred to it as his "nigger opera."

Lovers, Flings, or Just Friends?

Elizabeth Allen, British actress

Adele Astaire, dancer

Grace Brown, chorus girl

Kitty Carlisle, actress

Mollie Charleston (a.k.a. Margaret Manners), chorus girl and actress

Countess de Granny, French noblewoman

Paulette Goddard, actress

Pauline Heifetz, sister of violinist Jascha Heifetz

Benita Hume, actress

Gertrude Lawrence, actress-dancer

Anita Loos, author

Marilyn Miller, actress

Aileen Pringle, actress

Luise Rainer, actress

Ginger Rogers, actress-dancer

Simone Simon, actress

Kay Swift, friend

Constance Talmadge, actress

Rosamond Walling, college student

Fay Wray, actress

Mel Gibson 1956–

✦ He Said

I believe in fidelity. It isn't a bad thing to believe in, is it?

I'm romantic but I wouldn't expect every woman to want to tear her clothes off when she meets me.

I've got a beat-up look and my nose is bent. So I'm not sure what people mean when they say I'm this great sex symbol.

Am I sexy? I'm never sure what they mean when they write that stuff.

If I've still got my pants on in the second scene, I think they've sent me the wrong script.

I get more fun out of being a family man than I get from the glitz and glamour of acting.

✦ They Said

Mel is the most gorgeous man I've ever seen. —Sigourney Weaver, actress

The guy is very married, no playing around. —Tina Turner, singer-actress

He has the roughness of McQueen, the gentleness of Montgomery Clift, the sexuality and charm of Gable. —Mark Rydell, director

He had no trouble attracting girls. But he never got carried away with it. —Phil Avalon, Australian producer, commenting on Gibson's "bachelor" days

✦ First Sexual Experience

Unknown.

✦ Wives

Robyn Denise Moore, nurse

✦ Did You Know?

Mel does have his wild side, especially back in the days when he liked to drink. During one of those sprees, Mel hid in a cabinet and burst forth naked to surprise a female fan, as a drunken practical joke. This curious, generally out-of-character romp occurred in Modesto, California, during an evening's partying with two waitresses he'd met earlier. Another party in the evening's festivities snapped candid shots of Mel sucking fingers, crotch nuzzling, and with a woman's shoe in his mouth. In 1993, a couple of years after the event, nine of those photos appeared in a tabloid, much to his displeasure.

Lovers, Flings, or Just Friends?

Angela, waitress

Shawn, waitress

Wendy Lee Klein, student

John Gilbert 1895–1936

✦ He Said

I have been on the screen for twenty years and I have managed to squeeze out of it complete unhappiness.

I love you. I love you. I love you. —The infamous words from his film *His Glorious Night* ('29), which sent audiences into gales of laughter over his speaking voice

✦ They Said

He drank with carpenters, danced with waitresses, and made love to whores and movie queens alike. —Ben Hecht, screenwriter

Every day there were propositioning letters and telephone calls at all hours. —Leatrice Joy, spouse

You're finished, Gilbert. I'll destroy you if it costs me a million dollars. —Louis B. Mayer, after being slugged by Gilbert. When Greta Garbo stood up Gilbert at the altar, Mayer, who was in attendance, taunted Gilbert by saying, "What's the matter with you, Gilbert? What do you have to marry her for? Why don't you just fuck her and forget about it?" Gilbert slugged Mayer as soon as the words were out of his mouth.

Gilbert was the type of man who would turn to the bottle at any disappointment. —Eleanor Broadman, silent film actress

He loves to impress folks with his greatness by being unpleasant to them. —Lon Chaney, actor

✦ First Sexual Experience

Possibly lost his virginity to Effie Stewart, an older actress, who took him into her home for three months as a live-in lover.

✦ Wives

Leatrice Joy, actress
Ina Claire, actress
Virginia Bruce, actress

✦ Did You Know?

Did MGM's Louis B. Mayer really destroy Gilbert's film career, and, if so, how did he do it? The most common assumption is that Mayer had the sound engineers at MGM fiddle and tamper with either the bass or treble sound levels of Gilbert's first "talking" films, thus distorting his voice and making it sound absolutely unsuitable for films.

Later in life, after his career had virtually ended, Gilbert often attended gay parties where he danced with men—frequently in the company of actor Robert Taylor.

Lovers, Flings, or Just Friends?

Enid Bennett, actress
Clara Bow, actress
Marlene Dietrich, singer-actress
Jeanne Eagels, actress
Greta Garbo, actress (costar of *Flesh and the Devil*, '27)
Mary Hay, actress
Miriam Hopkins, actress
Barbara La Marr, actress
Lila Lee, actress
Princess Liliuokolani of Hawaii
Beatrice Lillie, actress-comedienne
Carole Lombard, actress
Dorothy Parker, writer
Mary Pickford, actress
Adela Rogers St. Johns, writer
Effie Stewart, actress
Laurette Taylor, actress
Robert Taylor, actor
Lupe Velez, actress
plus many of the girls who worked at Lee Francis's exclusive Beverly Hills brothel

Jackie Gleason 1918–1987

✦ He Said

I never thought I was fat. I never worried about it.

I'm no alcoholic. I'm a drunkard. The difference is, drunkards don't go to meetings.

It was the greatest thing that could happen to you, that instant critique of laughter, better than anything, even sex. —Remembering the first time he heard applause from a live audience

✦ They Said

Gleason screwed around a lot and he wanted you to know. Some guys fuck a lot and they don't talk about it. Gleason talked. —Milton Berle, fellow comedian

He was as false as his teeth. —Betty Grable, actress

Jackie left me dozens of times. Every time he got successful, he left. —Genevieve Halford, first wife

Jackie Gleason knows he can't drown his troubles in drink, but he sure makes them swim for it! —Red Skelton, fellow comedian

✦ First Sexual Experience

Probably lost his virginity to a Brooklyn prostitute when he was in his teens.

✦ Wives

Genevieve Halford, ballerina
Beverly McKittrick, secretary
Marilyn Taylor, dancer

✦ Did You Know?

Gleason's friends tell a tale that sounds almost unbelievable: The Great One, as a prankish bet, hid under a bed with a goat in a hotel room that was occupied by a pair of newlyweds. During their lovemaking, Gleason kept squeezing the goat, causing it to make extraordinary noises—which each member of the couple thought the other was making. Once they had finished, Gleason emerged from under the bed, goat in hand, to bid them goodnight.

Gleason once vomited on Frank Sinatra at a baseball game. In fact, Gleason vomited on lots of people; it was just one of the many "stunts" he liked to pull on people.

Lovers, Flings, or Just Friends?

Joan Crawford, actress
Dorothy Loudon, actress
Honey Merrill, showgirl
Estelle Parsons, actress
Martha Raye, comedienne
Kikki Roberts, ex-girlfriend
   of mobster Legs Diamond
Ann Sheridan, actress

Elliott Gould 1938–

✦ He Said

I really don't like women. I mean, I'm attracted to them, but I don't want to be friends with them. I don't want to have a woman for a pal.

I believe that you can be lovers and not go to bed together.

It didn't help our marriage when I became known as Barbra Streisand's husband. When we met, I was the leading man, she was the newcomer.

Actors dress for effect. Actors date for effect. It all suddenly becomes real to them and they're affected.

When I'm dead, I'm not sure if I want to be burned, buried, put in a mausoleum, or eaten.

✦ They Said

He was the first person to teach me to enjoy acting. He never throws a tantrum, never gets into a snit. —Candice Bergen, actress

✦ First Sexual Experience

Has said, probably in jest, that he lost his virginity to Barbra Streisand, when he was twenty-three years old.

✦ Wives

Barbra Streisand, actress-singer
Jennifer Bogart, daughter of director Paul Bogart
Jennifer Bogart, daughter of director Paul Bogart

✦ Did You Know?

Gould must really believe in having everything handy to please his women. When he and Streisand were married there was a fridge near their bed.

Lovers, Flings, or Just Friends?

Vicki Hodge, actress
Bianca Jagger, model-actress
Jennifer O'Neill, actress
Valerie Perrine, actress
Jane Seymour, actress

Stewart Granger 1913–1993

✦ He Said

My God, I have been married three times and have four children. —Responding to insinuations of a homosexual affair with fellow British actor Michael Wilding, with whom he had a long friendship

Conversation can be as important in a relationship as sex.

✦ They Said

Now don't come too fast, will you? —Hedy Lamarr, giving Granger instructions on how to perform in bed with her

Women sense that there's a bit of the brute in him. —Deborah Kerr, actress

I have never seen anything like the way ladies with high boiling points and high intelligence are falling to pieces over Mr. Granger. —Dorothy Kilgallen, columnist

I don't think I have ever met anyone who was quite so conceited. —Grace Kelly, actress

✦ First Sexual Experience

Lost his virginity to Josette, a young French prostitute he met while in Paris for a rugby match.

✦ Wives

Elspeth March, British actress
Jean Simmons, actress (costar in *Adam and Evelyne*, '49)
Caroline Lecerf, Miss Belgium 1962

✦ Did You Know?

As a young man, Granger was invited by British actor Henry Kendall to accompany him—all expenses paid—on a seaside holiday. On the journey it became evident that Kendall was anticipating sexual favors from Granger, who was forced to inform the actor that he wasn't "that way." Kendall accepted the news gracefully, saying, "With all the beautiful young men around I had to choose a square."

Lovers, Flings, or Just Friends?

Linda Christian, actress

Deborah Kerr, actress (costar in *King Solomon's Mines*, '50)

Hedy Lamarr, actress

Minouche, French actress

Rosemary Riachi, friend of actress Merle Oberon

Vittoria, Spanish girlfriend of matador Luis Miguel Dominguin

Michael Wilding, actor

plus a French friend of his wife Elspeth, from whom he got gonorrhea

Cary Grant 1904–1986

✦ He Said

To succeed with the opposite sex, tell her you're impotent. She can't wait to disprove it.

I think making love is the best form of exercise.

There was no such thing as a Cary Grant until I invented him.

Would you like to come have lunch with me? —Spoken to Stewart Granger, at their first meeting. Granger has said he knew Grant was sexually attracted to him, but he never made any advances.

✦ They Said

They are trying to show he's a great lover, but they'll never prove it to me. —Zsa Zsa Gabor, actress and expert on male lovers

I had no feelings. He was a homosexual. —Marlene Dietrich, dismissing any chance of an involvement with Grant

I knew him when his name was Archie Leach, and that's all he ever was—a goddamn leech! —Orry-Kelly, costume designer

He could be a terrible bastard, that one. —Dudley Walker, Grant's valet

✦ First Sexual Experience

Probably with Francis Renault, a New York City female impersonator, when he was about sixteen years old.

✦ Wives

Virginia Cherrill, actress
Barbara Hutton, Woolworth heiress
Betsy Drake, actress
Dyan Cannon, actress
Barbara Harris, publicist

✦ Did You Know?

In November 1980, when asked about Grant on an NBC television talk show, Chevy Chase referred to him as a "homo" and said "Whatta gal!" Grant initially sued for $10 million, but didn't complete the legal action, probably because the truth about him would have come out.

Grant was once caught having sex with a man in a department store rest room and arrested. Due to a police payoff, he was released before being taken to the police station. In 1969, the police questioned Grant based on a complaint by a woman that he had picked up her young son on a highway and made advances to him.

Grant wore women's nylon panties, claiming they were easy to wash and hang up to dry when he was traveling.

Lovers, Flings, or Just Friends?

Mary Brian, actress (costar in *The Amazing Quest of Ernest Bliss*, '36)

Frederick Brisson, producer

Phyllis Brooks, actress

Phil Charig, composer

Gary Cooper, actor

Noël Coward, playwright-entertainer

Maureen Donaldson, British photojournalist

Doris Duke, tobacco heiress

Howard Hughes, aviation and cinema mogul

Grace Kelly, actress (costar in *To Catch a Thief*, '55)

Sophia Loren, actress (costar in *Houseboat*, '58)

Mister Blackwell, fashion designer and critic

Vicki Morgan, actress-prostitute

Kim Novak, actress

Clifford Odets, playwright

(George) Orry-Kelly, fashion designer

Jacqueline Park, starlet

Cole Porter, songwriter

Francis Renault, female impersonator

Ziva Rodann, actress

Ginger Rogers, actress-dancer (costar in *Monkey Business*, '52)

Randolph Scott, actor

Susan Strasberg, actress

Mae West, actress)

Fay Wray, actress

Lovers, Flings, or Just Friends?

Catherine, daughter of the Duchess of Bedford

Marina Cicogna, Italian jet-setter

Britt Ekland, actress

Charlotte Ford, heiress

Lynda Bird Johnson, presidential daughter

Susan Kohner, actress

Sylvia Kristel, actress

Denice Lewis, model

Imelda Marcos, codictator of the Philippines

B. D. Merrill (Sherry), daughter of Bette Davis

Jean Moreau, actress (costar in *Viva Maria!*, '65)

Julie Newmar, actress

Merle Oberon, actress

Catherine Oxenburg, actress-model

Françoise Pascal, model

Vanessa Redgrave, actress

Elizabeth Taylor, actress

Wendy Vanderbilt, socialite

Mary Wilson, singer in the Supremes

George Hamilton 1939–

✦ He Said

I like to make my women feel like ladies.

Nobody has been in the sun longer than I have—nobody.

It's an actor's lifeblood. —Referring to publicity, which he has usually garnered by being seen frequently in the company of either beautiful or exceptionally well-known women

✦ They Said

If producer Robert Evans and Tony Perkins had an affair, the result would be George. —Burt Reynolds, actor, joking about Hamilton's appearance

George is the kind of person who, if he were marooned on a desert island, would come back to civilization on a yacht with three pretty girls. —David Hamilton, his brother

The world's gone mad—Michael Jackson and George Hamilton have officially crossed lines on the pigmentation flow chart. —Dennis Miller, comedian

✦ First Sexual Experience

Unknown, but he did have sex at an early age with the same, older female store owner in Palm Beach, Florida, to whom Burt Reynolds lost his virginity.

✦ Wives

Alana Collins, stewardess-model

✦ Did You Know?

Hamilton's perpetual suntan has even made the comic strips. "Doonesbury" character Zonker once embarked on acquiring a George Hamiltonish tan, going so far as to place toothpicks between his toes to ensure he was tan even there.

Tom Hanks 1956–

✦ He Said

I've got kind of a bizarre body, a big ass and fat thighs.

I was death with women in high school—absolutely strikeout king. I was a little too geeky, a little too gangly, and much too manic.

I'm your average family Joe.

I think my first marriage broke up for many of the reasons that any other marriage breaks up. Lack of communication plays a huge part, and the basic nature of the relationship.

In some ways, I guess, I have been a classic absentee father.

✦ They Said

He's absolutely the most lovable human being on this planet. —Sally Field, actress

He was soo easy to be around. —Rita Wilson, wife, on why she fell in love with him

Tom doesn't fit into the molds of the other American icons. —Steven Spielberg, director

His idea of a big day on the town is a doubleheader at Dodger Stadium, a Diet Coke, and a hot dog. —Sandra Hanks, his sister

Lovers, Flings, or Just Friends?

Hanks has admitted to a lack of sex in high school, then met his first wife in college. They married shortly thereafter and divorced in 1987. By that time, he'd already met and fallen in love with his second wife, which certainly didn't leave much time for him to have other "involvements," if any did exist.

✦ First Sexual Experience

Because Hanks has described his high school years as being a "strikeout king," it's reasonable to assume that he lost his virginity in college, either before or after he met the woman there who would become his first wife a short time later when he was twenty.

✦ Wives

Samantha Dillingham Lewes, actress-producer
Rita Wilson, actress

✦ Did You Know?

While several acceptance speeches through the years from Oscar winners have generated controversy—usually because of political statements incorporated into them—Hanks's was the first to do so because of the sexual content. When he won his first Academy Award, he mentioned a favorite high school teacher and commented on his homosexuality. At first, he was chided for having unwittingly "outed" the man, until it was revealed that his remarks had been cleared in advance with the gentleman.

Woody Harrelson 1961–

✦ He Said

I thought I couldn't be happier than if I was having sex with a lot of women. I spent almost a decade on that hedonistic bent.

Violence was almost an aphrodisiac to me.

[Larry Flynt and I] are both white-trash hedonists who made good in the world—or made bad in the world.

I think freedom of expression should be absolute.

✦ They Said

Now we really know that Woody is a really big star. —Kristin Baer, actress and costar (*The Cowboy Way*, '94), having seen Harrelson nude during filming

✦ First Sexual Experience

Unknown.

✦ Wives

Nancy Simon, daughter of playwright Neil Simon

✦ Did You Know?

Are you familiar with Woody's father? He's in a penitentiary for a murder plot against a federal judge, but he's not idling away his time. He made an escape attempt in 1995 that was thwarted by authorities.

Woody revealed in 1995 that he's frequently been a devotee of "retention" sex—lovemaking without orgasm for the male.

Lovers, Flings, or Just Friends?

Glenn Close, actress

Carol Kane, actress

Laura Louie, personal assistant

Penelope Ann Miller, actress

Ely Pouget, actress (costar in *Cool Blue*, '88)

Ally Sheedy, actress

Brooke Shields, actress

Moon Unit Zappa, singer-actress and daughter of rock musician Frank

Jed Harris 1900–1979

✦ He Said

To be sexy, you've got to have menace.

✦ They Said

He'd fuck anything. If he got hold of a snake, he'd fuck it. —Lee Shubert, Broadway impresario

He was a man of satanic good looks. —James Mason, actor

The man I've watched treating women in the most arrogant way of all is Jed Harris. —Elia Kazan, director

Actresses swooned over him; they lived only to be directed by him and some even died as a result of it. . . . His seductions were notorious. —S. N. Behrman, writer

I don't believe there is a person walking the face of the earth who would have a good word to say for my father. —Abigail Harris, daughter

When I die, I want to be cremated and have my ashes thrown in Jed Harris's face. —George S. Kaufman, playwright

The most hurtful, arrogant, venomous little fiend that anyone could meet, let alone work for. —Laurence Olivier, actor

✦ First Sexual Experience

Probably lost his virginity during a weeklong affair while on a visit to Paris when he was about seventeen years old.

✦ Wives

Anita Green (Baum), student
Louise Platt, actress
Beatrice "Bebe" Allan, dancer

✦ Did You Know?

Harris frequently answered the door nude and often conducted meetings with playwrights and others in the theater while completely naked. At the end of one such nude encounter with Harris, playwright George S. Kaufman, praised for his sexual "expertise" in actress Mary Astor's notorious diary, paused at Harris's door, then told the director, "Your fly is open."

Lovers, Flings, or Just Friends?

Judith Anderson, actress
Enid Bagnold, author
Pat Burroughs, student
Ina Claire, actress
Constance Collier, actress
Gilda Davis, whose husband wrote the song "Baby Face"
Edna Ferber, author
Hilda Gaige, wife of a close friend
Cinda Glenn, acrobatic dancer
Ruth Gordon, actress
Lillian Hellman, playwright-author
Katharine Hepburn, actress
Wendy Hiller, actress
Peggy Jacobsen, starlet
Marilyn Miller, actress
Geraldine Morris, ex-wife of superagent William Morris
Rosamond Pinchot, socialite-actress
Margaret Sullavan, actress

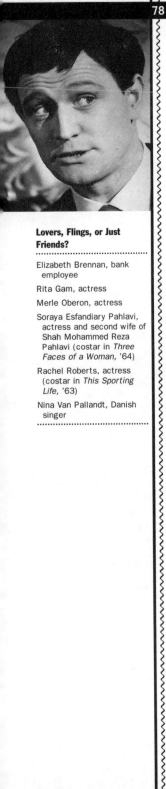

Richard Harris 1930–

✦ He Said

I always was a horny bastard.

My ideal woman is a beautiful, mute nymphomaniac who runs the local boozer.

I need a woman to haunt me, a woman to tear my insides out.

I can't tell you how disheartened I'd be if a love affair didn't end tragically.

I've no idea who I am. I'm five people, and each of them is fighting the other four.

When I'm in trouble, I'm an Irishman. When I turn in a good performance I'm an Englishman.

I found it better to wake up feeling a success than clawing, hung over, through a fog of self-disgust, wondering if I or some other feller still had the same number of teeth we went to bed with.
—Discussing his new, more sedate lifestyle

✦ They Said

Richard is very much the professional Irishman. —Charlton Heston

Richard Harris makes me look sober. —Richard Burton

✦ First Sexual Experience

Unknown.

✦ Wives

Elizabeth Rees-Williams, acting student
Ann Turkel, actress (costar in *99 and 44/100% Dead,* '74)

✦ Did You Know?

During his late teens, Harris frequently masturbated over pictures of actress Merle Oberon; years later he spent a loving night with the real item.

On the set of *Camelot* ('67), Harris, who played King Arthur, appeared for the filming of one scene with costar Vanessa Redgrave with an erection, which he proudly displayed to the cast as a joke, saying "I wanted something handmade for my queen."

Lovers, Flings, or Just Friends?

Elizabeth Brennan, bank employee

Rita Gam, actress

Merle Oberon, actress

Soraya Esfandiary Pahlavi, actress and second wife of Shah Mohammed Reza Pahlavi (costar in *Three Faces of a Woman,* '64)

Rachel Roberts, actress (costar in *This Sporting Life,* '63)

Nina Van Pallandt, Danish singer

Rex Harrison 1908–1990

✦ He Said

I vowed never to fit into the life of some woman. She has to fit into mine.

The happiest married men I know have a wife to go home to, not to go home with.

Offstage I can be far from charming. I am acid. Acid. I have a direct tongue and I say what I think is the truth and I don't give a damn for the consequences.

✦ They Said

A pompous cad and an ambitious creep. —Cesar Romero, actor

It is a melancholy fact, Rex, that between us we have supported more women than Playtex. —Alan J. Lerner, lyricist of *My Fair Lady* ('64) and also much-married

I found him very English—the perfect image of the English gentleman. Very independent, very opinionated, very judgmental, very male and arrogant, but in the best sense of the word. —Nancy Olson, actress

✦ First Sexual Experience
Unknown.

✦ Wives

Noel Marjorie Collette Thomas, fashion model
Lilli Palmer, actress
Kay Kendall, actress (costar in *The Reluctant Debutante,* '58)
Rachel Roberts, actress
Elizabeth Rees-Williams Harris, the first Mrs. Richard Harris
Mercia Tinker, socialite

✦ Did You Know?

Where did he acquire the nickname Sexy Rexy? It appears that actress Coral Browne first dubbed him with it while rejecting his advances during the play *Heroes Don't Care,* which they appeared in together early in their careers.

Lovers, Flings, or Just Friends?

Christine Barry, actress
Martine Carol, French actress
Tammy Grimes, actress
Eloise Hardt, actress
Carole Landis, actress
Vivien Leigh, actress
Merle Oberon, actress
Romy Schneider, actress
Lana Turner, actress
and a favorite black prostitute he liked to frequent as a young "gent" in Liverpool

Laurence Harvey 1928–1973

✦ He Said

I like them provided they have beauty, are slim, and dress well. I like them a bit showy and I adore the mother image. —Describing what he looked for in a woman

Dealing with women is like dealing with known thieves. It is not possible to fall into their beds without falling into their cunning little webs.

I know some people say I have used women wickedly, but it really isn't so. I've got the scars and the debts to prove it.

I've been called Florence of Lithuania for years. It has never worried me.

I never talk about anyone except myself.

Talent is nothing without a studio head or two in your pool.

✦ They Said

Larry Harvey was once accused of being such a bitch he could play Hedda Gabler. *Well, Larry replied, "Well, it is a good part."* —Sean Connery, actor

After you're lived with Laurence Harvey, nothing in life is ever really too awful again. —Hermione Baddeley, actress

He had an Oedipus complex in being attracted to older women. —Anonymous relative

✦ First Sexual Experience
Unknown.

✦ Wives
Margaret Leighton, actress
Joan Perry Cohn, widow of Columbia Pictures' Harry P. Cohn
Paulene Stone, model

✦ Did You Know?
At a party to be attended by Princess Margaret, Harvey first removed his pants, then locked himself into the ladies' rest room, where he proceeded to howl, scream, and curse. He then pranced onto the dance floor and embarrassed many folks by asking all the men to dance with him. At a later dinner for the princess, he plopped into an empty seat beside her then-husband Lord Snowden, reducing the royal consort to tears of mortification by pretending to be his female dinner companion. His most notable episode of outrageousness: grabbing actor Peter Lorre, then kissing him and practically ramming his tongue down Lorre's throat.

Lovers, Flings, or Just Friends?

Hermione Baddeley, actress (costar in *There Is Another Sun,* '51)

Siobhan McKenna, actress

Eric Portman, actor (costar in *Cairo Road,* '50)

Jimmy Woolf, producer

and lots of other women, preferably older, plus many men

Charlton Heston 1924–

✦ He Said

Nudity is never erotic, except in the bedroom.

I'm too dull, square, and protestant—in the philosophical, not the religious sense—to be a big, popular public figure; a beloved figure. I'm not a drunk. I've only had one wife. My kids aren't runaways. It's not what people expect.

The industry has created its own monsters and some of them are feminine.

Audiences like stars who seem to suffer, who are disappointed in love, always on the brink of some personal disaster. Well, I'm not like that.

✦ They Said

He is so square, he came out of a cubic womb. —Richard Harris, actor

He has an ego the size of Texas and a talent the size of South Dakota. —Sal Mineo, actor

He has a bad memory. He still thinks he's parting the Red Sea. —Barbara Stanwyck, actress

That guy Heston has to watch it. If he's not careful, he'll get actors a good name. —Frank Sinatra, singer-actor

Every family has a skeleton in its cupboard. But the Hestons let theirs out and he wants to be an actor. —Anonymous friend to Heston's wife, Lydia, when they were dating in college

✦ First Sexual Experience
Unknown.

✦ Wives
Lydia Clarke, drama student

✦ Did You Know?

Heston—despite all his renowned conservatism—was the first major American film star to show his ass in a film, when the apes stripped his tattered rags away in *Planet of the Apes* ('68).

Lovers, Flings, or Just Friends?

Grand Prix winner of the right half of the Tightly Upraised Zipper Award, since his name has never been connected "romantically" with anyone outside his marriage.

Dustin Hoffman 1937–

Lovers, Flings, or Just Friends?

Barra Gable
Kate Jackson, actress
Sally Kirkland, actress
and lots and lots of other women, if his friends are to be believed

✦ He Said

I got into acting so I could meet girls.

There used to be a time when it was impossible for me to have a woman friend if we weren't lovers.

I've [always] been attracted to women who were working behind counters—salesgirls, working girls, waitresses—rather than rich women who go shopping every day.

✦ They Said

He came up to me and said, "I'm Dustin—burp—Hoffman," and he put his hand on my breast. What an obnoxious pig, I thought. —Meryl Streep, recalling her first meeting with Hoffman at an audition for a play

Dustin has had more girls than anyone I've ever known—even more than Joe Namath ever dreamed about. —Robert Duvall, actor and close friend

These drab-looking people like Dustin Hoffman—can you believe any girl looks at Dustin Hoffman and gets a thrill? —Ruth Waterbury, columnist

I told his wife I'd never work again for an Oscar winner who was shorter than the statue. —Larry Gelbart, writer, remarking on the difficulty of working with the demanding Hoffman on *Tootsie* ('82)

✦ First Sexual Experience

Unknown.

✦ Wives

Anne Byrne, dancer
Lisa Gottesgen, attorney

✦ Did You Know?

During the making of *Marathon Man* ('76), Hoffman was going to all sorts of lengths to prepare for his scenes. For one particular scene, he kept himself awake for hours and hours. When costar Laurence Olivier queried Hoffman on what he was doing, Hoffman informed him that he was preparing for a scene in which his character was supposed to be exhausted. Olivier merely looked at Hoffman and said, "Dear boy, why don't you just *learn* to act?"

From where does Hoffman get his unusual first name? His mother named him after one of her favorite film stars: silent star Dustin Farnum (1874–1929), who appeared in Cecil B. De Mille's *The Squaw Man* ('14).

William Holden 1918–1981

✦ He Said

I had practice being a whore. When I was a young actor starting out in Hollywood, I used to service actresses who were older than me.

I'm a whore, all actors are whores. We sell our bodies to the highest bidder.

I'm going to screw a girl in every country I visit. —Snapping about his travel plans after his affair with Audrey Hepburn ended

I'm too damned old and too conservative to do a striptease. —Complaining about having to do the tattered-shirt-removal scene in *Picnic* ('55)

If the son of a bitch hadn't died, I coulda had my second Oscar. —Annoyed that *Network* ('76) costar Peter Finch died and received a posthumous Oscar for a film in which Holden was also nominated

✦ They Said

In my sixteen years of dealing with chronic drug and alcohol abusers, Bill was the sickest person I ever treated. He was the sweetest, classiest guy you could ever want to meet, but when he was strung out on drugs and alcohol, he could be a monster. —Michael Klassman, psychotherapist, who treated Holden for a number of years

Bill probably enjoyed his vices more than his virtues. —Jerry Wald, producer

✦ First Sexual Experience

Unknown for certain but probably with a prostitute in South Pasadena or San Bernardino, when he was in his late teens or early twenties.

✦ Wives

Brenda (Ardis) Marshall, actress

✦ Did You Know?

Holden, a notorious alcoholic, was once charged with drunk driving and manslaughter in Italy. His Ferrari hit a small Fiat on a superhighway, killing a man. After being found guilty, Holden received an eight-month suspended jail sentence and paid the victim's widow $80,000.

Holden was a compulsive bather—he often took as many as four showers a day.

Lovers, Flings, or Just Friends?

Lucille Ball, actress

Capucine, French actress (costar in *The Seventh Dawn*, '64)

Susan Hayward, actress (costar in *Young and Willing*, '43)

Audrey Hepburn, actress (costar in *Sabrina*, '54)

Grace Kelly, actress (costar in *The Country Girl*, '54)

Nancy Kwan, actress (costar in *The World of Suzie Wong*, '60)

Dorothy Lamour, actress (costar in *The Fleet's In*, '42)

Diana Lynn, actress

Jacqueline Kennedy Onassis, wealthy widow

Stephanie Powers, actress

Gail Russell, actress

Barbara Stanwyck, actress (costar in *Golden Boy*, '39)

Patricia Stauffer, model-divorcée

Shelley Winters, actress

Bob Hope 1903–

✦ He Said

I was lucky, you know. I always had a beautiful girl and the money was good.

I don't need to be in politics. I'm already in show business.
—Revealing to why he never considered going into politics

✦ They Said

He's a fast man with a squaw, but a slow man with a buck.
—Bing Crosby, teasing Hope about being tight-fisted with money

He fooled around with anyone who was young and nubile and guest-starred on the show. —Larry Gelbart, screenwriter and television writer

Bob bedded lots of Las Vegas showgirls, but tried to keep a low profile. —Jan King, employee

Bob Hope will go to the opening of a phone booth in a gas station in Anaheim, provided they have a camera and three people there. —Marlon Brando, actor

Hope? Hope is not a comedian. He just translates what others write for him. —Groucho Marx, who very definitely *was* a comedian

✦ First Sexual Experience

Unknown.

✦ Wives

Grace Louise Troxell, vaudeville dance partner (marriage unconfirmed, but rumored)

Dolores Reade, singer

✦ Did You Know?

During one period in Hollywood, so the rumors say, Hope so generously bestowed mink coats on starlets for services rendered that he created a minicrisis. Starlets with their own mink coats were afraid to wear them, lest others think that they had had a fling with Bob.

Lovers, Flings, or Just Friends?

Johnine Avery, Miss World 1968

Joan Billings, interior decorator

Jeanne Carmen, model

Jeannie Corbett, starlet

Gloria DeHaven, actress

Betsy Duncan, singer

Rhonda Fleming, actress

Rosemarie Frankland, Miss World winner

Paulette Goddard, actress (costar in *The Ghost Breakers*, '40)

Ursula Halloran, press agent

Joey Heatherton, actress

Betty Hutton, actress

Dorothy Lamour, actress (costar in *The Road to Bali*, '52)

Frances Langford, singer

Marilyn Maxwell, actress

Joy Monroe, starlet

Janis Paige, actress

Barbara Payton, actress

Barbara Sykes, actress

Patricia "Honeychile" Wilder, radio actress

Dennis Hopper 1936–

✦ He Said

I don't think there was a starlet around who could have been had in those days that I didn't have.

I'd rather give head to a beautiful woman than fuck her, really.

Jimmy and I were into peyote and grass when it was still something you couldn't even mention to your closest buddies. —Referring to doing drugs with his buddy James Dean

✦ They Said

[Hopper's] got one the size of an elevator button. —Howard Stern, shock-jock, after viewing Hopper's penis on-screen

I think he had a dilating brain. —Tuesday Weld, actress

We don't want you to be an actor. We want you to be something respectable. —His parents, chiding him when he told them he wanted to be an actor

✦ First Sexual Experience

Unknown.

✦ Wives

Brooke Hayward, model-actress
Michelle Phillips, singer (the marriage lasted eight days)
Daria Halprin, actress
Katherine LaNava, ballerina
Victoria Duffy, actress-socialite

✦ Did You Know?

Hopper's fabled dabbling with drugs started at a very early age. When he was a child on a farm in Kansas, he used to sniff the gasoline fumes from his grandfather's truck. He gave that up when he hallucinated badly and used a baseball bat to break out the truck's headlights and windows.

Lovers, Flings, or Just Friends?

Maria Conchita Alonzo, actress
Ursula Andress, actress
Ellen Archuletta
Joan Collins, actress
Pamela Des Barres, author and rock groupie
Caterine Milinaire, photographer-writer
Taryn Power, actress
Jean Seberg, actress
Jamie Thompson, production assistant
Natalie Wood, actress (costar in *Rebel Without a Cause*, '55)
plus lots of starlets and other assorted women

Leslie Howard 1893–1943

✦ He Said

I wasn't cut out to be an actor. I haven't the energy for acting—it's too exhausting.

The movie studios are sweatshops killing the best in actors.

✦ They Said

He was adorable. He was just a little devil and just wanted his hands on every woman around. He would have your hand while looking into your eyes and rubbing his leg on somebody else's leg at the same time, while having the gateman phone him before his wife arrived on the lot. —Joan Blondell, actress

✦ First Sexual Experience

Unknown.

✦ Wives

Ruth Evelyn Martin

✦ Did You Know?

Leslie was busy having sex with costar Merle Oberon in his dressing room during one of their films when the couple got caught. His wife walked in on them, and seeing the action, indignantly asked her husband what he was doing, to which he blithely replied, "Rehearsing."

Lovers, Flings, or Just Friends?

Ingrid Bergman, actress (costar in *Intermezzo*, '39)

Claudette Colbert, actress

Violette Cunnington, actress (costar in *Pimpernel Smith*, '41)

Marion Davies, actress (costar in *Five and Ten*, '31)

Kay Francis, actress (costar in *British Agent*, '34)

Ann Harding, actress (costar in *Devotion*, '31)

Myrna Loy, actress (costar in *The Animal Kingdom*, '32)

Baroness Miranda, Nazi spy

Merle Oberon, actress (costar in *The Scarlet Pimpernel*, '35)

Maureen O'Sullivan, actress

Mary Pickford, actress (costar in *Secrets*, '33)

Rock Hudson 1925–1985

✦ He Said

A favorite question among the fan magazines was whether or not I slept in the nude. I couldn't understand who could give a damn about my sleeping habits.

I'd think of Lana Turner, and I couldn't sleep. —An example of a typical Hollywood publicity comment, made before the real truth about Rock's sexual proclivities became common knowledge

I'm looking for happiness, but I don't think I'm quite ready for marriage yet. —Quote to a fan magazine about why he wasn't married

✦ They Said

He was mentally constipated. —Paul Lynde, comedian

The boulder his agent named him after must have been a big one. Rock was well endowed. —Mamie Van Doren, actress

What a waste of a face on a queer. You know what I could have done with that face? —John Wayne, actor

He was predatory. He flaunted it. —Joe Hyams, writer

Just because it wiggles, you don't have to fuck it. —Mark Miller, close friend, cautioning Hudson on his sex drive

✦ First Sexual Experience

Occurred with an older man on a farm he was visiting when he was in his early teens.

✦ Wives

Phyllis Gates, secretary

✦ Did You Know?

What kept Hudson's homosexuality so well protected from the "scandal" press? Rumors say that his studio, in order to kill a story about Hudson planned by *Confidential,* a sleazy exposé magazine, fed the smear-sheet information on Rory Calhoun's time in jail for burglary and auto theft when he was younger. Hudson did have a long-standing relationship with a married executive at Universal Studios, who'd fellate him in his office. Perhaps this person was the "guardian angel" who kept Hudson protected for so many years.

Mickey Rooney says that Rock put the make on him at a party once. Hudson didn't do it personally, but sent a male friend over to invite Mickey up to Rock's house later, because he was having "a few guys over." Mick declined, saying he thought Rock knew "that I liked girls."

Lovers, Flings, or Just Friends?

Betty Abbott, script girl

Paul Barresi, porn star

Claudia Cardinale, actress (costar in *Blindfold,* '66)

Marc Christian (MacGinnis), companion

Tom Clark, studio publicist

Jack Coates, companion

Joan Crawford, actress

Vera Ellen, actress

Floyd, carhop

Errol Flynn, actor

Lee Garlington, actor-stockbroker

Jon Hall, actor

Ken Hodge, radio producer

Kerry X. LeBre, hustler

Liberace, entertainer

Marilyn Maxwell, actress

Sal Mineo, actor

Jim Nabors, singer-actor

George Nader, actor

Jack Navaar, aircraft worker

Tyrone Power, actor

Bob Preble, actor

Elizabeth Taylor, actress (costar in *Giant,* '56)

Marilu Toto, Italian actress

Mamie Van Doren, actress

Henry Willson, agent

plus many, many other males and females, including lots of people not associated with the film industry

Howard Hughes 1905–1976

✦ He Said

I've found that sex is so much better, so much more intense with a new divorcée.

Today I saw the most beautiful pair of knockers I've ever seen in my life. —Gushing the first time he saw a photo of Jane Russell

✦ They Said

Howard Hughes would fuck a tree. —Joan Crawford, actress

In his heyday he boasted of deflowering two hundred virgins in Hollywood. He must have got them all. —Jimmy the Greek, gambler

Two of his girlfriends told me he wasn't worth a damn as a lover. He was just no good in the sack. They said all he wanted to do was to look and fondle. —Wilson Heller, pioneer Hollywood publicist

He'd have five or six girls a day. But it was kind of chaste because he only did it one way. —Paulette Goddard, actress

The greatest swordsman. —James Bacon, Hollywood columnist

✦ First Sexual Experience

Occurred with his paternal uncle, Rupert Hughes, when he was fifteen years old. One source believes that Hughes first had sex with a woman when he bedded his first wife shortly after their marriage.

✦ Wives

Ella Rice, Houston socialite
Terry Moore, actress
Jean Peters, actress

✦ Did You Know?

Playwright George S. Kaufman, who had been known to dip his pen into the inkwells of some Hollywood beauties, was appalled over the promotional hype for Hughes's *The Outlaw* ('43), with supermammaried Jane Russell. He said the film should have been called *A Sale of Two Titties*.

Hughes liked recently divorced women; he called them "wet decks."

Hughes's favorite kind of sex: oral, both giving and receiving.

Lovers, Flings, or Just Friends?

Gary Cooper, actor
Richard Cromwell, actor
John Darrow, actor
Bette Davis, actress
Yvonne De Carlo, actress
Olivia de Havilland, actress
Marlene Dietrich, singer-actress
Billie Dove, actress
Errol Flynn, actor
Ava Gardner, actress
Mitzi Gaynor, actress
Russel Gleason, actor
Paulette Goddard, actress
Cary Grant, actor
Kathryn Grayson, actress-singer
Jean Harlow, actress
Susan Hayward, actress
Rita Hayworth, actress
Katharine Hepburn, actress
Veronica Lake, actress
Hedy Lamarr, actress
Carole Lombard, actress
Marilyn Monroe, actress
Tyrone Power, actor
Luise Rainer, actress
Ginger Rogers, actress-dancer
Randolph Scott, actor
Norma Shearer, actress
Gene Tierney, actress
Lana Turner, actress
Shelley Winters, actress
Fay Wray, actress

William Hurt 1950–

✦ He Said

I'm embarrassed about my body. I don't bare my body easily.

I'm a basic, next-door type.

Don't treat me like a god.

I think I discovered a long time ago and rediscovered sometimes, that I am alone—not that I'm lonely, but that I am alone.

✦ They Said

What I respect about Bill is that he's not afraid to sound like an asshole. —Sigourney Weaver, actress

I never saw a man who could talk so long and so much. —Joanna Pacula, actress

The trouble with Bill is he can't stop talking. . . . As some people are compulsive eaters, Bill is a compulsive talker. When I heard he was living with a deaf lady I came to believe in the old adage some marriages are made in heaven. —Ken Russell, director

He'd have one drink and he'd have a personality change. —Sandra Jennings, in her court testimony when she sued for a "divorce" as his common-law wife

His concentration is so extreme he can make everybody around him tense. —Glenn Close, actress

He is a WASP heartthrob on whose chest the Lacoste alligator shirt was meant to be displayed. —The *New York Times*

✦ First Sexual Experience
Unknown.

✦ Wives
Mary Beth Supinger, actress
Heidi Henderson, daughter of bandleader Skitch Henderson

✦ Did You Know?
Hurt seems to have earned a reputation for making suggestive remarks to female members of the press who interview him.

When he was ten, Hurt's mother married Henry Luce III, son of Henry Luce Jr., founder of *Life* and *Time* magazines.

Hurt graduated magna cum laude from Tufts University as a theology major. He had intended to become a minister.

Lovers, Flings, or Just Friends?

Sandrine Bonnaire, French actress

Glenn Close, actress

Sandra Jennings, dancer

Marlee Matlin, actress (costar in *Children of a Lesser God*, '86)

John Huston 1906–1987

◆ He Said

Try to give them an inferiority complex. If the actress is beautiful, screw her. —Giving advice to a new director on how to handle actors

Most of us go through life searching for the unobtainable, and if we do get it, we find it's unacceptable.

◆ They Said

Warren Beatty's got broads, but John . . . he didn't miss anybody, he had every movie star you can think of. —Doris Lilly, gossip columnist, who had an affair with Huston

He was very gallant about women, he didn't talk about them. —Marietta Fitzgerald Tree, socialite

Women were so available and John was so weak, he couldn't say no to a woman. —Eloise Hardt, friend and employee

Just a drunken boy; helplessly immature. You'd see him at every party, wearing bangs, with a monkey on his shoulder. Charming. Very talented, but without an ounce of discipline in his makeup. —Henry Blanke, producer, on the young Huston

◆ First Sexual Experience

Lost his virginity to a nursemaid, who ended up being fired by his mother.

◆ Wives

A marriage while in high school
Dorothy Harvey, actress
Lesley Black, divorcée
Evelyn Keyes, actress
Enrica (Ricki) Soma, model-ballerina
Celeste (Cici) Shane, divorcée
Maricell Hernandez, Mexican maid to his fifth wife

◆ Did You Know?

During an evening of heavy drinking Huston got into an argument with producer Mike Todd, who really didn't want to argue with the temperamental director. Huston kept challenging Todd to fight, finally even blocking Todd's way as he attempted to leave. Todd gently pushed Huston out of his path, which was enough to send the drunken director to the floor. After vainly trying to rise several times, Huston finally clenched his fists and said from the floor, "If you had any kind of guts, you son of a bitch, you'd get down here and fight me like a man."

Lovers, Flings, or Just Friends?

Eiko Ando, Japanese actress (directed her in *The Barbarian and the Geisha*, '58)

Mary Astor, actress (directed her in *The Maltese Falcon*, '41)

Truman Capote, author and social gadfly

Maka Czernichew, artist

Olivia de Havilland, actress (directed her in *This Is Our Life*, '42)

Connie de Pinna, department store heiress

Suzanne Flon, French actress (directed her in *Moulin Rouge*, '52)

Ava Gardner, actress

Paulette Goddard, actress

Eloise Hardt, employee

Zita Johann, actress

Doris Lilly, gossip columnist

Leni Lynn, British actress

Marilyn Monroe, actress

Pauline Potter, dress designer

Irene Mayer Selznick, daughter of MGM's Louis B. Mayer

Marietta Fitzgerald Tree, socialite

Doris Warner, daughter of studio boss Henry Warner

Kay Wellesley, studio worker

plus a pro-Nazi woman in Britain who gave him the "clap"; a Russian princess; the wife of a southern Congressman; *and* hundreds of other women, both famous and unknown

Michael Jackson 1958–

✦ He Said

I love being around them. There always seems to be a bunch of kids over at the house, and they're always welcome. They energize me—just being around them. —Referring to his love of kids

This is a bond. It's not about sex. This is something special. —Supposedly pleading to his special friend—the pseudonymous Jamie, who later sued him—to be allowed to continue his relationship with him

✦ They Said

I was on one side of the bed and he was on the other. It was a big bed. —Brett Barnes, an eleven-year-old Australian friend of Jackson's, with whom he used to spend the night

I cannot and will not be a silent collaborator of his crimes against small innocent children. As far as his sexual preference, he never had a girlfriend—ever. —LaToya Jackson, sister, mouthing off about her brother's troubles

Even to say he's not gives people the idea that he is. People want to hear ugliness. —Jermaine Jackson, brother

He's the least weird man I've ever known. —Elizabeth Taylor, actress

His nose looked like a wax model with most of the wax melted away. —Anonymous woman who sat close to Jackson at the World Music Awards in Monaco

✦ First Sexual Experience

Unknown.

✦ Wives

Lisa Marie Presley, heiress to the Elvis legacy
Deborah Rowe, nurse

✦ Did You Know?

What were some of the things Case No. SC026226, filed in Los Angeles Superior Court on September 14, 1993, on behalf of the thirteen-year-old son of a Beverly Hills dentist, charged Jackson with? "These sexually offensive contacts include and are not limited to defendant Michael Jackson orally copulating plaintiff, defendant Michael Jackson masturbating plaintiff, defendant Michael Jackson eating the semen of plaintiff, and defendant Michael Jackson having plaintiff fondle and manipulate the breasts and nipples of Michael Jackson while defendant Michael Jackson would masturbate." The case was later settled out of court for an amount reputed to be more than $20 million.

Lovers, Flings, or Just Friends?

Brandon Adams, actor

Bubbles, a chimpanzee

Jordan Chandler, age thirteen

Macauley Culkin, age twelve, actor

Sean Lennon, actor and son of John Lennon and Yoko Ono

Emannuel Lewis, age twelve, actor

Jimmy Safechuck, age ten, whose parents received a Rolls-Royce from Jackson

and hundreds and hundreds of other extremely young "special friends"

Mick Jagger 1943–

✦ He Said

All women are groupies.

There's really no reason to have women on tour unless they've got a job to do. The only other reason is to fuck.

What really upsets people is that I'm a man and not a woman. I don't do anything more than a lot of girl dancers, but they're accepted because it's a man's world.

✦ They Said

Believe me, he's about as sexy as a pissing toad. —Truman Capote, author

The fact is that Mick doesn't like women. He never has. —Chrissie Shrimpton, model

I'm not sure about those two, you know. What do you think? —John Lennon's question to Paul McCartney, after he caught Mick and Keith Richards in bed together

The mouth is almost too large; he is beautiful and ugly, feminine and masculine. A rare phenomenon. —Cecil Beaton, British photographer and designer

✦ First Sexual Experience

Occurred, as he has put it, "with boys at school." He then moved on to women when an Italian nurse at Bexley Mental Hospital, where he was employed, pulled him into a linen closet where they had sex standing up.

✦ Wives

Bianca Perez Morena de Macais, Nicaraguan model-actress
Jerry Fay Hall, model

✦ Did You Know?

What accounts for that large bulge Jagger's pants often show onstage? Singer Etta James discovered it's padding. She was backstage after Jagger's wad had slid out of place and was almost down to his knees. According to her, Jagger was feverishly trying to reposition his mock love-bulge.

Jagger and Nureyev once positioned television personality Geraldo Rivera into a personal body sandwich between them, with Rudi at the rear and Mick in front. As Jagger fingered Rivera's chest and Rudi toyed with his hair, they commented on his "virginity," and how they could "break him in." Rivera escaped from their clutches.

Lovers, Flings, or Just Friends?

Brigitte Bardot, actress
Estelle Bennett, rock singer
David Bowie, singer-actor
Carla Bruni, Italian tire heiress
Bebe Buell, model and *Playboy* centerfold
Eric Clapton, musician
Patti D'Arbanville, actress-model
Thomas Driberg, Labor member of Parliament
Marianne Faithfull, singer
James Fox, actor
Natasha Fraser, student
Allen Ginsburg, poet
Brian Jones, musician
Nicole Kruk, model
Patti LaBelle, singer
Madonna, singer-actress
Camilla Nickerson, model
Rudolph Nureyev, ballet dancer
Andrew Oldham, business manager
Anita Pallenberg, partygirl-actress
Michelle Phillips, singer
Princess Margaret, British royalty
Keith Richards, musician
Linda Ronstadt, singer
Chrissie Shrimpton, model
Carly Simon, singer
Uma Thurman, actress
Margaret Trudeau, political wife
Andy Warhol, artist

Don Johnson 1949–

✦ He Said

Nice girls just didn't, but older girls did. And that's what I was interested in. —Explaining his attraction to older women, which he developed early

I feel you can get just as real a love from a guy as you can from a chick.

If you get a good wife, you live happily every after. If you get a bad one, you become a philosopher.

You know what they say. It's lonely at the top, but it's lonely at the bottom and in the middle, too.

And for me to be happy, I want to pack this life full. I want it all.

Was I fat and ugly as a kid? No. . . . I was pretty.

✦ They Said

His epicene looks suggest a lot of seamy living. —Judith Crist, critic

More than anything, Don wants to be a star, but I think he's really a country boy at heart. —Jennifer Lee, actress and later one of the Mrs. Richard Pryors

This man is unbearable. —Rumored remark from Mickey Rourke, who costarred with him in *Harley Davidson and the Marlboro Man* ('91)

✦ First Sexual Experience

Lost his virginity at age twelve to a seventeen-year-old baby-sitter.

✦ Wives

He married his first wife in '68 or '69; she's rumored to have been either a high school sweetheart or a dancer he met in San Francisco. They divorced after two months. The second wife is completely obscure, except that he has described her as a "bimbo."

Melanie Griffith, actress (costar in *Paradise*, '91)

Melanie Griffith, actress (costar in *Born Yesterday*, '92)

✦ Did You Know?

It was rumored that the Johnson-Streisand relationship breakup occurred because the reportedly well-endowed Johnson refused to have his uncircumcised penis "cut" for Streisand.

In 1988 Johnson won the title of world's offshore powerboat champion in a competition.

Lovers, Flings, or Just Friends?

Jannike Bjorling, ex-girlfriend of tennis ace Bjorn Borg

Patti D'Arbanville, actress

Pamela Des Barres, rock groupie and author

Pamela Loubman, fitness instructor

Sal Mineo, actor

Liz Renay, starlet-model

Susan Sarandon, actress

Anita Sorrels, college professor

Barbra Streisand, actress-singer

Tanya Tucker, singer

Marjorie Wallace, former Miss World

Livy Winsten, model

and a twenty-six-year-old cocktail waitress he lived with when he was about sixteen, *plus* lots of other women of varying ages

Lovers, Flings, or Just Friends?

Betty Boyce, showgirl

Gloria Cook, showgirl

Kitty Doner, vaudeville performer (who specialized in impersonating men)

Joanne Dru, actress

Melville Ellis, homosexual theatrical pianist-designer

Jinx Falkenberg, model-actress

Harry Richman, entertainer

Barbara Stanwyck, actress

Bunny Waters, showgirl

and lots of prostitutes, showgirls, and what were then called "colored" girls

Al Jolson 1886–1950

✦ He Said

After I go, I'll be forgotten.

I've had fame and glamour and success, but after a man passes the forty mark, they don't seem to mean the same as when he was younger.

Outside of my liking for wine, women, and racehorses, I'm just a regular husband.

✦ They Said

Words can't describe the meanness of this man. —Harry Richman, entertainer

Jolson used to steal gags from vaudeville actors and then have his lawyer write them letters saying they had stolen the jokes from him. —Milton Berle, comedian

I never liked him. —Fanny Brice, comedian, on being asked for a comment on Jolson's death

I was surprised at his delicate legs and ankles. —Clifford Odets, playwright-screenwriter

✦ First Sexual Experience

It is not known for certain, but he probably lost his virginity to some female vaudeville performer, as he started performing when he was about fourteen years old.

✦ Wives

Henrietta Keller, dancer
Ethel Delmar, showgirl
Ruby Keeler, dancer-actress
Erle Galbraith, X-ray technician

✦ Did You Know?

Jolson's sexual preference: having oral sex performed on him and having sex in unusual positions.

Jolson would do anything onstage for a laugh. He'd often break wind loudly and then call more attention to the fact by saying, "Jolie made a fartsola."

When Jolson's life was the subject of a film (*The Jolson Story,* '46), third wife Ruby Keeler refused to allow her name to be used in the picture. Why? She said she didn't want her children "to grow up and maybe see the picture and know I was married to a man like that."

Tommy Lee Jones 1946–

✦ He Said

I hang on to my memories with cat's claws.

I don't recall any great suffering, but I do recall lots of solitude.
—Reflecting on his childhood

The more we know, the better we think, the less fearful we are and the better life gets.

It's more fun than polo. It's like going undefeated in football.
—Describing the fun of making movies

✦ They Said

He is not what you think of as a dashing leading man that women swoon over. Yet women look at him. —Andy Davis, director

Tommy is like the original cactus. —Laurie McDonald, producer

✦ First Sexual Experience
Unknown.

✦ Wives
Katherine Lardner, granddaughter of writer Ring Lardner
Kimberlea Cloughley, photojournalist

✦ Did You Know?

Jones is an eighth-generation Texan, which firmly places his family roots in the state back to when it was the Republic of Texas.

Jones definitely has friends in high places. Vice President Al Gore was one of his roommates at Harvard.

Lovers, Flings, or Just Friends?

Lisa Taylor, actress-model

Danny Kaye 1913–1987

✦ He Said

She has a Fine head on my shoulders. —Referring to his wife, Sylvia Fine, who acted as a personal manager–overseer of his career

✦ They Said

Nobody wants to fuck Danny Kaye. —Sam Goldwyn, producer, on Kaye's lack of sex appeal

He's the most repressed innate homosexual I ever met. —William Haines, gay twenties actor and latter-day interior decorator

Danny was a lovely clown, in deep trouble with himself. —Mai Zetterling, actress and costar in *Knock on Wood* ('54)

Danny is a total sadist as far as his marriage is concerned. Sylvia is a total masochist. —Anonymous friend

He was the most depressed, dejected person in the world. —Jack Warner Jr., close friend

Danny is very moody. He would not have too much cheer. —Virginia Mayo, actress

Yes, he's a hog. He has to be on every moment, and everybody has to watch him. —Angela Lansbury, actress

✦ First Sexual Experience
Unknown.

✦ Wives
Sylvia Fine, songwriter, who first met Kaye when he was only fourteen years old, then married him when he was seventeen

✦ Did You Know?
Kaye frequently referred to himself as a "wife-made man," giving his wife most of the credit for his career.

Look at Kaye's legs closely in the film *The Court Jester* ('56). They appear to be quite shapely in the tights he wears, but they're not quite Kaye's actual legs. He wore "symmetricals" or "leg falsies" to give him more shapely legs in the film.

Rumors abound that Kaye, a well-known medical "buff," once assisted noted heart surgeon Dr. Michael DeBakey with an operation.

Lovers, Flings, or Just Friends?

Eve Arden, actress

Lillian Lux, vaudevillian

Marina, the Duchess of Kent

Princess Margaret, British royalty

Shirley MacLaine, actress

Laurence Olivier, actor

Joanna Simon, opera singer, sister of Carly

Gwen Verdon, dancer-actress (costar in *On the Riviera*, '50)

Joseph Frank "Buster" Keaton 1895–1966

✦ He Said

Having got two boys out of our first three years of marriage, it looked as if my work was done. Lost my amateur standing. I was moved into my own bedroom.

You are all right as long as you can drink and wake up without a hangover. —Defining his views on consuming alcohol, while ignoring the fact that he was an alcoholic

I don't feel qualified to talk about my work.

✦ They Said

Buster was very sexy, very relaxed and easy with women. —Louise Brooks, silent screen actress

If somebody had thrown their arms around him and hugged him and kissed him, he'd have been the happiest man in the world. . . . What he wanted, what he really needed, was affection. —Buster Collier, lifelong close friend

Socially, he didn't give a damn about people. He was never what I would call popular. —Irene Mayer Selznick, daughter of MGM's Louis B. Mayer

✦ First Sexual Experience

Lost his virginity when he was sixteen years old to a local girl in Muskegon, Michigan. He said that she was "dying for experience."

✦ Wives

Natalie Talmadge, sister of actresses Constance and Norma
Mae Scriven, nurse
Eleanor Norris, MGM studio dancer

✦ Did You Know?

Keaton was on such an alcoholic binge that he married his second wife without realizing it. It was several weeks after the marriage before he sobered up and discovered her in bed with him.

In an era when Hollywood stars strove to outdo each other with their automobiles, Keaton was supreme. He owned a thirty-foot land cruiser (actually a large bus) that he had acquired from the Fifth Avenue Bus Company and had specially appointed for him. It had two drawing rooms, sleeper bunks that were handy for sex, a galley, and an observation deck. Keaton often drove the vehicle himself—outfitted in an admiral's uniform lent by MGM's costume department. For several years he kept it parked—illegally—on the MGM lot, where it served as the scene of his many orgies.

Lovers, Flings, or Just Friends?

Louise Brooks, actress
Viola Dana, actress
Mae Busch, actress
Kathleen Kay, actress
Alice Lake, actress
Beatrice Lillie, comedienne-actress
Dorothy Sebastian, actress (costar in *Spite Marriage*, '29) who later married William ("Hopalong Cassidy") Boyd
Leah Clampitt Sewell, socialite
Marlyn Stuart, showgirl
and lots of girls "backstage" while touring in vaudeville

Lovers, Flings, or Just Friends?

Sandra (Sandi) Grant Bennett, ex-wife of singer Tony Bennett

Helene Marlowe, dancer

Vincente Minnelli, director (directed him in *The Pirate*, '47)

Gene Kelly 1912–1996

✦ He Said

It was all right when I was playing football with them and being one of the gang. But when they saw me all dressed up on the stage—singing and dancing—that was a different story. —Reminiscing about how his childhood playmates reacted to his other side

I wouldn't work for you even if I had to dance in the street for pennies. —From an angry letter to Louis B. Mayer of MGM, who'd promised him a screen test and then didn't deliver

✦ They Said

Every chorus boy has a crush on him. —Jack Cole, choreographer

What struck you most was his charm and his clean-cut good looks. You didn't think of him as a dancer at all. —Adolph Green, Broadway composer

For me, he was Hollywood. The way I'd imagined it as a child. —Catherine Deneuve, actress and costar in *The Young Girls of Rochefort* ('68)

✦ First Sexual Experience
Unknown.

✦ Wives
Betsy Blair, dancer-actress
Jeane Coyne, dancer
Patricia Ward, writer

✦ Did You Know?
Kelly, once a devout Catholic, turned into an agnostic after a 1939 trip across the Southwestern United States and Mexico. His change in religious belief was triggered when he saw the poverty of Mexican peasants alongside the churches where they worshiped, which were full of artifacts worth a fortune. He couldn't fathom how a church could place a higher value on its material possessions than the welfare of its adherents.

John F. Kennedy 1917–1963

✦ He Said

I'm not finished with a woman until I've had her three ways.

I'm not interested—once I get a woman. I'm not interested in carrying on, for the most part. I like the conquest.

✦ They Said

I know a lot about cocks—I've seen an awful lot of them—and if you put all the Kennedys together, you wouldn't have a good one. I used to see Jack in Palm Beach. . . . He used to come down so he could swim in the nude. He had absolutely *nothing.* —Truman Capote, author

Jack always had his mind between his legs. —Lady May Lawford, mother of actor Peter

One of the great cunt men of all times, except for me. —Jerry Lewis, actor

No one was off-limits to Jack. Not your wife, your mother, your sister. —George Smathers, former U.S. senator and a close friend

He was terrible in bed. . . . He did not perceive women as human beings or even as objects of affection. —Anonymous former lover

Because of his bad back he preferred making love with the girl on top. —Susan Imhoff, former friend

I don't think he was a ladies' man. . . . He always felt they were a useful thing to have when you wanted them, but when you didn't want them, put them back. —Charles Houghton, Harvard roommate

✦ First Sexual Experience

Lost his virginity when he was seventeen years old in a Harlem whorehouse to a black prostitute.

✦ Wives

Jacqueline Bouvier, socialite-reporter

There are rumors of a first marriage to one Durrie Malcolm, a socialite. They've never been definitely proven or disproven; Ms. Malcolm denies a marital connection to Kennedy.

✦ Did You Know?

Kennedy was the frequent recipient of nonreciprocal fellatio from longtime close friend LeMoyne Billings.

Kennedy ended the festivities of his Inauguration Day by having a ménage à trois with two starlets imported from Hollywood by his brother-in-law, actor Peter Lawford. The two were chosen by the president from among the six Lawford brought along.

Lovers, Flings, or Just Friends?

June Allyson, actress

LeMoyne Billings, school roommate

Florinda Bolkan, Brazilian actress

Judith Campbell, lady friend of mobster Sam Giancana

Joan Crawford, actress

Peggy Cummins, actress

Arlene Dahl, actress

Nancy Dickerson, telejournalist

Angie Dickinson, actress

Marlene Dietrich, singer-actress

Rhonda Fleming, actress

Zsa Zsa Gabor, actress

Susan Hayward, actress

Sonja Henie, ice skater–actress

Audrey Hepburn, actress

Hedy Lamarr, actress

Janet Leigh, actress

Sophia Loren, actress

Jayne Mansfield, actress

Marilyn Monroe, actress

Kim Novak, actress

Lee Radziwill, socialite and sister of his wife

Lee Remick, actress

Jean Simmons, actress

Blaze Starr, stripper

Tempest Storm, stripper

Gene Tierney, actress

Lana Turner, actress

Tennessee Williams, playwright

John F. Kennedy Jr. 1960–1999

✦ He Said

Women keep calling to invite me to dinner and I keep turning them down. —Revealing how popular he was—and how he reacted to it—while attending Brown University

I don't plan to make acting my profession, although I do love it. —Commenting on his appearances in several school and collegiate productions. His uncle, actor Peter Lawford, did encourage him to become a professional actor, but his mother was dead set against the notion.

✦ They Said

I'm afraid he's going to grow up to be a fruit. —Jacqueline Onassis, worried about her son's fatherless upbringing

Well, he's kinda naive, like a young boy. —Madonna, supposedly commenting on his expertise in bed

✦ First Sexual Experience

Unknown.

✦ Wives

Carolyne Bessette, public relations director

✦ Did You Know?

At least one good frontal nude photo of Kennedy exists. It was snapped on the island of St. Barts, after he'd doffed his swimsuit, by a female travel agent on vacation. She's thus far rejected all offers to buy it, preferring to keep the viewing pleasure personal.

Kennedy seemed so proud of his body that, while he was in college, some friends joked that he went through college wrapped in a towel to show off his assets.

While attending Andover, Kennedy seems to have experimented with marijuana. He was caught smoking by a campus security officer on one occasion, necessitating, as per school rules, that his mother be notified.

Not many people are aware that Kennedy appeared in at least one film: a low-budget, 1988 feature titled *A Matter of Degree*.

Lovers, Flings, or Just Friends?

Julie Baker, model

Sonia Braga, actress

Jenny Christian, student

Melanie Griffith, actress

Christina Haag, acting student

Darryl Hannah, actress

Madonna, singer-actress

Sally Munro, student

Christina Onassis, shipping heiress and stepsister

Sarah Jessica Parker, actress

Ashley Richardson, model

Julia Roberts, actress

Kelly Squier, socialite–office worker

Sharon Stone, actress

Joseph P. Kennedy 1888–1969

✦ He Said

We want winners. We don't want losers around here. —An oft-spoken comment to his family

Look at that bunch of pants-pressers in Hollywood making themselves millionaires. I could take the whole business away from them.

If there's anything I'd hate as a son-in-law, it's an actor. And if there's anything I think I'd hate more than an actor as a son-in-law, it's an English actor. —Uttered shortly before daughter Patricia married English actor Peter Lawford

✦ They Said

The old man had an eye out for every woman that walked. In the Kennedy's sense of morality that was all right. —Oleg Cassini, fashion designer

Joe Kennedy represented the height of vulgarity. He was horny, that's all he was. —Doris Lilly, columnist

He had three interests: politics, golf, and women. —Slim Aarons, photographer

He's one of the biggest crooks who ever lived. —Sam Giancana, mob boss

✦ First Sexual Experience

Unknown.

✦ Wives

Rose Fitzgerald, daughter of Boston mayor

✦ Did You Know?

When he was ambassador to Great Britain, Kennedy once showed his complete uncouthness by referring to the then–Queen Elizabeth (the present Queen Mum) as a "cute trick."

Whenever Kennedy gave Gloria Swanson jewelry, he made certain it was charged to her personal account. His largesse with her riches extended to others. A playwright who had suggested the title for a film received a Cadillac from Kennedy. It, too, had been charged to Swanson. When she brought the incident to his attention, he terminated their affair immediately. On being told of Kennedy's stroke in the early sixties, Swanson commented, "I hope he suffers."

According to one Boston newspaper, the largest private phone bill in 1929 America belonged to Kennedy because of his transcontinental calls to Swanson in Hollywood.

Lovers, Flings, or Just Friends?

Constance Bennett, actress

Evelyn Brent, actress

Nancy Carroll, actress

Pamela Digby Churchill (Hayward Harriman), socialite

Betty Compson, silent screen actress

Viola Dana, silent screen actress

Marion Davies, actress

Janet Des Rosiers, personal secretary

Marlene Dietrich, actress

Greta Garbo, actress

Phyllis Haver, actress

Sonja Henie, ice skater–actress

Clare Booth Luce, playwright and journalist

Marina, the Duchess of Kent, British royalty

Gloria Swanson, actress

and lots of young women, many of whom he "swapped" with his sons, *plus* lots of call girls, young actresses, and dancers

Aly Khan 1911–1960

✦ He Said

I only think of the woman's pleasure when I am in love.

I must have women around me. . . . Life means nothing without them.

They called me a bloody nigger and I paid them back by winning all their women.

✦ They Said

Aly had only two real interests, horses and woman. I don't know anything about horses and Aly never discussed his women. —Otto Preminger, director

When he first had a date, he would give them a cigarette case with one emerald in it. When he fucked them, he'd give them [a] bracelet. —Don Richardson, drama instructor

I don't know who didn't have an affair with Aly. —Juliette Greco, singer-actress

When he fell in love with a woman, it was madly and deeply. The only thing, it might last only one night. —Elsa Maxwell, gossip columnist and society gadabout

You weren't in the swim, and you were really déclassé, démodé, nothing, you hardly counted if you'd not been to bed with Aly. —Anonymous friend

✦ First Sexual Experience
Unknown.

✦ Wives
Joan Yarde-Buller, British aristocrat
Rita Hayworth, actress

✦ Did You Know?
What was the secret of Aly's sexual success with so many women? It seems to have been his "staying" power. He was reputed to be able to have almost constant intercourse for hours and hours. He supposedly had been trained in an Arabic sexual technique called *Imsák* as a young teenager in Egypt. He was also rumored to keep a bucket of ice on each side of the bed. When he was about to climax, he'd thrust his arms into them to delay his ejaculation.

Oleg Cassini said that Khan was famed for his skill as a cunnilinguist; he supposedly practiced it three times a day on whichever woman he was then involved with.

Lovers, Flings, or Just Friends?

Lia Amanda, Italian actress

Simone Bodin, model (a.k.a. Bettina)

Lise Bourdin, French actress

Yvonne De Carlo, actress

Danièle Delorme, French actress

Louise de Valmorin, socialite

Joan Fontaine, actress

Lady Thelma Furness, socialite

Zsa Zsa Gabor, actress

Juliette Greco, singer-actress

Pamela Digby Churchill (Hayward Harriman), socialite

Clara Margherita Kelly, model

Virginia Lang, actress

Nicole Largille, French student

Corinne Luchaire, French actress

Lois Maxwell, Canadian singer

Kim Novak, actress

Merle Oberon, actress

Irene Pappas, actress

Gene Tierney, actress

Pamela Turnure, socialite

Margaret Whigham, socialite

plus lots and lots of other women from all walks of life

Alan Ladd 1913–1964

✦ He Said

I have the face of an aging choirboy and the build of an undernourished featherweight. If you can figure out my success on the screen you're a better man than I.

Maybe I thought too much about picking up the money and not enough about the really good parts.

✦ They Said

He looked like a young Greek god, and he was unforgettable. —Sue Carol (Ladd), describing the first time she saw Ladd when he walked into her agency office

What a complex Alan had about his height. —Eve Arden, actress

The whole problem with Alan's psyche was his inability to recognize he was a big star. —Virginia Mayo, who costarred with Ladd in *The Iron Mistress* ('52)

Alan was a marvelous person in his simplicity. —Veronica Lake, his costar in several films

He always seemed to have a large measure of reserve and dignity. —George Stevens, who directed Ladd in his greatest film, *Shane* ('53)

✦ First Sexual Experience
Unknown.

✦ Wives
Marjorie (Midge) Jane Harrold, student
Sue Carol, agent-manager

✦ Did You Know?
Due to his height (variously described as anywhere from 5'3" to 5'6"), most of Ladd's female costars were required to walk in ditches beside him, wear flat shoes, or have him to stand on a box to kiss them. Shelley Winters got particularly annoyed at being required to walk in a ditch while filming *Saskatchewan* ('54), complaining that she keep tripping and nearly fell several times.

Ladd's wife, Sue, was both his agent and his manager. She attended the shooting of all his films, usually never leaving the camera area when he was present. Sue also watched every scene and setup shot to ensure it favored her husband.

Lovers, Flings, or Just Friends?

June Allyson, actress (costar in *The McConnell Story,* '55)

Fernando Lamas 1915–1982

✦ He Said

The difference between Latin and American men is that the Latins give you a little more of everything, I think. More headaches, more temper, more tenderness.

I got into movies because it was a great way to meet broads.

I don't mind. I am a handsome Latin and a wonderful lover!
—Stating his view on being typecast as a Latin lover

✦ They Said

He was a beautiful man. Very much in love with himself. —Cesar Romero, actor

Come back in ten years, you've got a lot of fucking to do. —Esther Williams, aquatic actress, when she first met Lamas and he began expressing an interest in her. He did, and they were later married.

✦ First Sexual Experience
Unknown.

✦ Wives
Pearla Mux, Argentine actress
Lydia Babchi, Uruguayan socialite
Arlene Dahl, actress (costar in *The Diamond Queen,* '53)
Esther Williams, actress (costar in *Dangerous When Wet,* '53)

✦ Did You Know?
Lamas and costar Ethel Merman got into a feud during the run of their Broadway show *Happy Hunting.* The plot called for a passionate kiss between the stars. One night, after the kiss, Lamas walked to the edge of the stage and wiped his mouth, which infuriated Merman. When asked about it later, he described kissing her as "somewhere between kissing your uncle and a Sherman tank."

Lovers, Flings, or Just Friends?

Ava Gardner, actress
Lana Turner, actress (costar in *The Merry Widow,* '52)

Burt Lancaster 1913–1994

✦ He Said

I guess I'm the guy who went to bed with the girl—even if it was after the movie had finished.

I know what you've heard about me, that I am difficult and grab all the broads. It's not true. I'm difficult only some of the time and grab only some of the broads.

[Running] is one way of getting my heart started in the morning. Other people use masturbation.

Don't bother me with any of these creepy newspaper people.

✦ They Said

He loved to go to bed with his leading ladies. —Jackie Bone, long-time companion

In Italy Burt is known as a bisexual. —Idalah Luria, Italian dialogue coach

Masculinity was oozing from every pore. —Sheilah Graham, gossip columnist, describing her first sight of Lancaster

He had tremendous intensity and was the kind of macho man who says nothing but takes the girl by the hand and leads her off to his lair. —Yvonne De Carlo, actress

A big bag of wind and the most unctuous man I've ever met. —Montgomery Clift, actor

✦ First Sexual Experience
Unknown.

✦ Wives
June Ernst, circus acrobat
Norma Anderson, stenographer
Susie Scherer, film coordinator

✦ Did You Know?

Lancaster evidently liked his sex with something luxurious underneath. Yvonne De Carlo said she and Burt had sex on a mink coat under a backyard oleander bush. The first time he had sex with Shelley Winters it was on a blue and white bedspread covering a thick white rug.

Lancaster has always evoked strong opinions from those who've worked with him. For instance, consider French actress Jean Moreau: "Burt Lancaster! Before he can pick up an ashtray, he discusses his motivation for an hour or two. You want to say, Just pick up the ashtray, and shut up!"

Lovers, Flings, or Just Friends?

Jackie Bone, hairdresser

Delores, a Katherine Dunham dancer

Yvonne De Carlo, actress (costar in *Brute Force*, '47)

Francesca de Scaffa, wife of actor Bruce Cabot

Marlene Dietrich, singer-actress

Zina Rachevasky, playwright

Liz Renay, model

Shelley Winters, actress

Lovers, Flings, or Just Friends?

Zsa Zsa Gabor, actress (costar in *For the First Time*, '59)

Judy Garland, singer-actress

Maria Margelli, secretary to singer Ezio Pinza

Rita Moreno, actress

and many, many starstruck female fans who followed him everywhere and flooded his fan mail with suggestive letters containing photographs of them in pornographic poses

Mario Lanza 1921–1959

✦ He Said

It's all sex when I'm singing. That's me. It comes right out of my balls. —Replying to a query on the secret of his singing ability

The more I lay other women, the better I am as a husband.

I am a movie star, and I should live like one. Nobody wants movie stars to be like the guy next door.

✦ They Said

He was the only man who had pubic hair on his head. He used to pee on his leading lady. —Leonard Spigelgrass, producer

He keeps ramming his tongue down my throat. It's the crudest thing I've ever been exposed to. —Kathryn Grayson, costar, complaining about his unwanted amorous advances

He recognized no authority, no discipline, no frontiers, except his own gigantic appetite for food, drink, and women. —Hedda Hopper, gossip columnist

He was neurotic and you never knew if he'd turn up on time. I had to keep flattering him, telling him how wonderful he was. —Sir Lew Grade, producer

✦ First Sexual Experience
Unknown.

✦ Wives
Betty Hicks, sister of a friend from his stint in the U.S. army

✦ Did You Know?
During his time in service at Texas Air Base in Marfa, Texas, Lanza made a bet with some of his buddies that he could have sex with twelve women consecutively. They solicited the twelve women, and Lanza won the bet—with a circle of his buddies cheering him on—while performing on the floor of a local garage.

During the making of *That Midnight Kiss* ('49), his first film, Lanza kept French-kissing costar Kathryn Grayson, much to her disgust. She and costume designer Helen Rose devised a nice method of retaliation. Rose sewed brass knuckles into all of Grayson's costumes. At their next kiss, Grayson fisted Lanza in the crotch when she felt his tongue try to enter her mouth. He quickly ceased his unwanted amorous attentions.

Lanza told another female costar, "You've got to be more sexy. Push up to me; let me feel your pussy next to my cock."

Charles Laughton 1899–1962

✦ He Said

I don't know if you know, and I don't know if you care, and I don't care if you know, but there is a strong streak of homosexuality in me. —Comment made to Robert Mitchum, while driving to the set of *Night of the Hunter* ('55), in which Laughton was directing Mitchum

I have a face like the behind of an elephant.

✦ They Said

If I had known all this before we were married it might have been very different, one way or another. But the deception is what hurt so deeply. —Elsa Lanchester, who always believed her husband was straight until a policeman appeared with him in tow. Laughton had been compromised by a male prostitute. He wasn't charged, and was released.

Gary [Cooper] is a divine *man, but you,* Charlotte, *are a repulsive, fat mess of glop!* —Tallulah Bankhead, snarling away bitchily at Laughton during the filming of *Devil and the Deep* ('32). She also refused to shake hands with him because of his dirty fingernails.

The only actor I ever knew who was a genius was Charles Laughton. Maybe that's why he was so difficult. —Laurence Olivier

✦ First Sexual Experience
Unknown.

✦ Wives
Elsa Lanchester, actress (costar in *Witness for the Prosecution,* '57)

✦ Did You Know?
During the making of the uncompleted film *I, Claudius* ('37), one scene called for Laughton to enter a room by being almost thrown into it and falling on his knees. Take after take was tried with Laughton seemingly unable to master the proper entrance. He then suggested to the director that perhaps someone needed to physically kick him into the room. The director agreed to try, and Laughton selected one of the handsomest extras to perform the task. He still required many takes to do the scene. Costar Merle Oberon said it was obvious Laughton was thoroughly enjoying the physical abuse from the extra and was deliberately spoiling the takes.

Laughton had a brother, Frank, who was also a homosexual.

Director Leo McCarey once asked the star, "Jesus, Charles, do you have to be so nancy?" Laughton replied, "But, my dear fellow, after eight o'clock a bit of it is bound to show!"

Lovers, Flings, or Just Friends?

Terry Jenkins, photographer's model

Bill Phipps, actor

Erich Pommer, studio executive at Germany's UFA

Tyrone Power, actor (costar in *Witness for the Prosecution,* '57)

plus lots of "rent boys" from Piccadilly Circus, chauffeurs, masseurs, barmen, and other furtive encounters

Peter Lawford 1923–1984

✦ He Said

I have frightening depressions. I have great days, then one like death. Why? I have everything.

I'm just trying to do my bit for the generation gap. —Commenting on the twenty-seven-year age difference between him and his second wife

✦ They Said

He was into oral sex. He could and did do the other, but he preferred oral sex. —Molly Dunne, sex partner

Peter was not a good lover—not at all. —George Cukor, director

He's the world's worst actor. —Anita Loos, playwright-author

✦ First Sexual Experience

Occurred at age ten when a thirty-five-year-old governess fellated him to climax. Later, other governesses also used Lawford for their sexual purposes.

✦ Wives

Patricia Kennedy, heiress
Mary Rowan, daughter of comedian Dan Rowan
Deborah Gould, actress
Patricia Seaton, actress

✦ Did You Know?

Lawford's mother, Lady May Lawford, once called on her son's boss, MGM studio head Louis B. Mayer, and told him she suspected that Peter was a homosexual. She asked Mayer to find out the truth and perhaps have him given "treatment." Mayer did talk to Lawford, but needed the reassurance of Lana Turner, before he believed that Peter was straight.

Lawford was regarded as a fairly lousy lover. Intercourse didn't interest him that much, due to his predilection for oral sex.

Lovers, Flings, or Just Friends?

June Allyson, actress
(costar in *Good News*, '47)
Lucille Ball, actress
Anne Baxter, actress
Noël Coward, playwright-entertainer
George Cukor, director
Dorothy Dandridge, singer-actress
Sharman Douglas, socialite
Tom Drake, actor
Rhonda Fleming, actress
Ava Gardner, actress
Judy Garland, singer-actress
Rita Hayworth, actress
Judy Holliday, actress
Van Johnson, actor
Janet Leigh, actress
Marilyn Maxwell, actress
Sal Mineo, actor
Kim Novak, actress
Nancy Davis (Reagan), actress
Lee Remick, actress
Elizabeth Taylor, actress
Lana Turner, actress
Robert Walker, actor
Clifton Webb, actor
Jane Wyman, actress
Keenan Wynn, actor

plus lots of college girls, starlets, "beach bunnies" he met while surfing, and prostitutes who knew Lawford as an excellent $50 oral sex trick; *and* "call boys," male hustlers, young male extras, and studio messengers

Jerry Lewis 1926–

✦ He Said

I'm more than a great movie star. I'm also a neurotic, temperamental imbecile.

You never had a handsome man and a monkey. Sex and slapstick, that's what we were. —Describing what made the team of Martin and Lewis unique

I'm a multifaceted, talented, wealthy, internationally famous genius. I have an IQ of 190—that's supposed to be a genius.

✦ They Said

Although he is serious about his flirting, from a woman's point of view it is funnier than his pratfalls. —Judith Campbell, one of John F. Kennedy's girlfriends

Through the years I've seen him turn into this arrogant, sour, ceremonial, piously chauvinistic egomaniac. I'm just amazed at his behavior. —Elliot Gould, actor

He couldn't direct traffic. —Dean Martin, putting down Lewis's ambitions as a film director

✦ First Sexual Experience

Lost his virginity during a burlesque tour with his father in the winter of 1937–38, when he was between eleven and thirteen years old, to a stripper, named Marlene, in her dressing room.

✦ Wives

Patti Palmer (Esther Calonico), singer
Sandra Pitnick

✦ Did You Know?

Party girl and sometime-actress Liz Renay tattled that Lewis had a unique method for remaining faithful to his wife. According to her, he carried around a small rug. He'd place it on the floor, then masturbate onto the rug while watching females—such as her—"perform" for him. That way, he could say he'd never touched another woman. She also rated him as a 1 on her 1 to 10 sex scale.

Tallulah Bankhead once slugged Lewis so hard it nearly broke his jaw. He (and partner Dean Martin) were scheduled to appear on her radio show. The duo showed up minutes before airtime, with Lewis bare-chested and pretending to be shaving with an electric razor, which he'd plugged into his navel and secured there with tape. When Tallulah asked what they thought they were doing, Lewis replied, "I'm shaving, Mama."

Lovers, Flings, or Just Friends?

Judith Campbell, lady friend of President Kennedy and mobster Sam Giancana

Gloria DeHaven, actress-singer

Liz Renay, model

Stella Stevens, actress (costar in *The Nutty Professor*, '63)

plus many, many other women from various occupations

Liberace 1919–1987

✦ He Said

Men are my kind of people.

Some people say fucking saps your creative energy, but I don't believe that. I think it's a very healthy thing. A healthy sex life keeps you young and vital.

I want to thank my mother, who made all this possible.
—Comment that he always made, at some point, during every performance

I don't want to be remembered as an old queen who died of AIDS. —Moaning on his deathbed

✦ They Said

This deadly, winking, sniggering, snuggling, chromium-plated, scent-impregnated, luminous, quivering, giggling, fruit-flavored, mincing, ice-covered heap of mother love. . . —Comments from a review in London's *Daily Mirror*, which resulted in a lawsuit from Liberace

✦ First Sexual Experience

Lost his virginity at age sixteen (he often claimed it was thirteen) to a big-chested, red-haired blues singer he accompanied on the piano at Rick's Club Madrid, a Wisconsin roadhouse. She began, as Liberace put it, by "gobbling him," then moved on to conventional sex. The result: Liberace was no longer a virgin—but he ended up with bright red lipstick smears on his white pants. He also claimed that the first man he ever had sex with was a member of the Green Bay Packers.

✦ Wives

Claimed (to the press) that he was engaged three times.

✦ Did You Know?

Liberace, famed for his bizarre collections of things, once met someone with an even stranger collection. In Louisville, Kentucky, he encountered a chambermaid who proudly showed him an assortment of pubic hairs from famous people, which she kept in matchboxes.

Liberace committed perjury during his libel suit against a British newspaper that had implied he was gay. When asked, "Have you ever indulged in homosexual practice?" he answered, "No sir, not in my life. I am against the practice because it offends convention, and it offends society." After his death, London's *Daily Mirror* requested a refund of the $24,000 libel settlement they had been forced to pay the Glitter Fairy back in 1959.

Lovers, Flings, or Just Friends?

Leonard Bernstein, composer-conductor

Sonja Henie, ice skater–actress

Rock Hudson, actor

Cary James, companion

Gregory Scortenu, houseboy

Scott Thorson, companion-chauffeur

and lots of young men in New York City during 1941, and in the Hollywood–Long Beach area during 1942, *plus* many, many blond, blue-eyed young men with strong physiques

Rob Lowe 1964–

✦ He Said

It was just one of those quirky, sort of naughty, sort of wild, sort of, you know, drunken things that people will do from time to time. —On his sexual videotape

What really angers me is that in Europe no one would have persecuted me like this. They'd have said, "You were involved in a sex scandal? Really? Great!"

Show me someone who hasn't done that and I'll show you someone who's been so sheltered they're gonna be dull. —On people making personal sex videos

It's just a label. . . . It's helped my career up to a point. But it's something I'd prefer to play down now. —On being a sex symbol

✦ They Said

Having Rob Lowe lecturing our children on morals is like inviting Hitler to a Jewish wedding. —A teacher commenting on Lowe's sentence after the sex video scandal

✦ First Sexual Experience

Lost his virginity on his fifteenth birthday as a present from a neighborhood girl.

✦ Wives

Sheryl Birkhoff, makeup artist

✦ Did You Know?

It has been estimated that underground entrepreneurs have earned close to a million dollars from copies of Lowe's sex video.

In 1990 rumors flew that Lowe had entered the Sierra Tucson Rehabilitation Clinic in Arizona. What was his problem? It was reported that he stood in front of the other patients and described himself as addicted to women.

Lovers, Flings, or Just Friends?

Linda Buchanan, model

Melissa Gilbert, actress

Fawn Hall, ex-secretary of Oliver North

Nastassja Kinski, actress (costar in *The Hotel New Hampshire,* '84)

Demi Moore, actress

Brigitte Nielsen, actress

Jan Parsons, student

Tara Seburt, student

Brooke Shields, actress-model

Princess Stephanie of Monaco

Steve McQueen 1913–1980

✦ He Said

I want my wife barefoot, pregnant, and in the kitchen.

I live for myself and I answer to nobody. The last thing I wanted to do was fall in love with any broad.

Don't ever tell anyone I am seeing a shrink. I don't want anyone to think I am weak. —Cautioning Ali MacGraw about his fears

✦ They Said

One thing about Steve, he didn't like for the women in his life to have balls. —Ali MacGraw, one-time spouse

Steve was the world's champ at getting laid in the bathroom of an airplane. —Elmer Valentine, close friend and sexual confidant

Steve liked to fuck blondes, but he married brunettes. —Neile Adams McQueen, wife, who said that McQueen would come home and share the details of his sexual conquests with her

✦ First Sexual Experience

Unknown, probably in his very early teens, either on the streets during the time he was running with a gang or to another boy when he was in reform school.

✦ Wives

Neile Adams, dancer-actress
Ali MacGraw, actress (costar in *The Getaway,* '72)
Barbara Minty, model

✦ Did You Know?

When he lived in New York City's Greenwich Village, McQueen wore Bermuda shorts constantly, which brought him supposedly unwanted attention from the neighborhood's gay element. He was always annoyed when they propositioned him, angrily rejecting their advances. But, as his girlfriend at the time has noted, he continued to wear the shorts.

McQueen liked having sex with more than one woman at a time. He also enjoyed it when several males—including himself—had sex with the same woman at once. As one close friend has said, "He enjoyed making love to a woman who was still warm, at it were, from sex with his buddies."

McQueen frequently suffered from inflamed hemorrhoids, which years of motorcycle riding aggravated, and he often wore two sanitary napkins when riding.

Lovers, Flings, or Just Friends?

Ann-Margret, actress (costar in *The Cincinnati Kid,* '65)

Jacqueline Bisset, actress (costar in *Bullitt,* '68)

Judy Carne, actress

Faye Dunaway, actress (costar in *The Thomas Crown Affair,* '68)

Louise Edlind, actress

Peggy Fleury, actress

Lauren Hutton, actress-model

Barbara Leigh, actress (costar in *Junior Bonner,* '71)

Lita Milan, actress

Lee Remick, actress

Gia Scala, actress

Barbra Streisand, actress-singer

Sharon Tate, actress

Mamie Van Doren, actress

Tuesday Weld, actress

Mary Wilson, singer in the Supremes

Natalie Wood, actress

plus sampling the wares of a whorehouse in the Dominican Republic, where he worked for eight weeks as a towel boy, *and* lots of women, from all professions, whom he picked up in various places, *plus* McQueen always boasted that he'd slept with all of his costars, but first wife Neile has said that's untrue, that in reality he "missed" a couple of them

Fredric March 1897–1975

✦ He Said

I do not believe in matrimonial vacations. I am conservative, perhaps old-fashioned, domestically speaking. I like being married.
—A strange, out-of-character comment from a man regarded as one of the most lecherous fanny-grabbers in films

✦ They Said

He was able to do a very emotional scene with tears in his eyes and pinch my fanny at the same time. —Shelley Winters, describing acting with March

The man is shameless! —Charles Laughton, actor, professing outrage because March wore no underwear beneath his ultratight, crotch-hugging trousers in *The Barretts of Wimpole Street* ('34)

He treated me like dirt under his talented feet. —Veronica Lake, actress and costar in *I Married a Witch* ('42)

His overacting is admirable. To overact as he does requires skill. —Ray Milland, actor

✦ First Sexual Experience
Unknown.

✦ Wives
Ellis Baker, actress
Florence Eldridge, actress

✦ Did You Know?

March was such a determined womanizer that one female hairdresser has stated that she refused to go to his dressing room to fit him with a wig unless she was accompanied by a makeup man. But he once got a taste of his own medicine. March became thoroughly annoyed at homosexual costar Charles Laughton while they were filming *The Sign of the Cross* ('32). Why? Because Laughton kept trying to look up March's toga to get a glimpse of his genitals.

Lovers, Flings, or Just Friends?

Tallulah Bankhead, actress (costar in *My Sin*, '31)

Clara Bow, actress

Olivia de Havilland, actress

Ann Harding, actress (costar in *Paris Bound*, '27)

Miriam Hopkins, actress (costar in *Dr. Jekyll and Mr. Hyde*, '31)

Dean Martin 1917–1995

✦ He Said

In Hollywood, if a guy's wife looks like a new woman, she probably is.

To me this isn't a love affair. This is a big business. —Remarking on the Martin and Lewis partnership

You wanna talk, see a priest. —Common line he used to women who wanted him to talk to them after enjoying their favors

I'm the only singer around who has 10 percent of four gangsters. —Joking about his supposed mob connections

✦ They Said

The most beautiful broads went crazy for Dean. In truth, I fucked more than he did; but it was always like they wanted to burp me. —Jerry Lewis, on Martin's sex appeal

He was a bastard; all wine and candlelight, then a pat on the ass in the morning. —An early Ohio ladylove, describing the Martin technique

✦ First Sexual Experience

Unknown at this time, but probably lost his virginity in a whorehouse in Steubenville, Ohio, the town where he grew up.

✦ Wives

Elizabeth Anne McDonald, student
Jeanne Biegger, model
Catherine Mae "Kathy" Hawn, receptionist
Joni Andersen, model

✦ Did You Know?

Lou Costello, part of another famous duo, Abbott and Costello, advanced Martin the money for his first nose job, but the crooner wasted it all on something else first. Later, two other friends advanced him more money to have the operation.

For several years Martin was a heavy user of Percodan, an addictive narcotic with an effect on the central nervous system similar to morphine. He's said those years were "blurred."

Lovers, Flings, or Just Friends?

June Allyson, actress
Pier Angeli, actress
Jacqueline Bisset, actress
Andre Boyer, college student
Judith Campbell, lady friend of President Kennedy and mobster Sam Giancana
Peggy Crosby, restaurant hostess
Phyllis Elizabeth Davis, actress
Catherine Deneuve, actress
Gloria DeHaven, actress
Miriam LaVelle, dancer
Dorothy Malone, actress
Marilyn Monroe, actress
Lori Nelson, actress (costar in *Pardners*, '56)
Gail Renshaw, model–beauty queen
Ann Sheridan, actress
Gregg Sherwood, chorus girl
Jill St. John, actress
Lana Turner, actress

Steve Martin 1945–

✦ He Said

I don't want the way I live to get out to the world. Once private things get into print, your private life is over. Everybody knows exactly who you are, and it makes you dull.

We have got to keep in our world something private. Otherwise you feel like you get up to go to the bathroom and it becomes a possible anecdote for an interview.

Anyone who is arrogant in the arts is just plain ludicrous.

Well, Excuuuuuuse Meeeee!

✦ They Said

Oddly enough, in private Steve is shy and reserved, while in public he never shuts up. —Rachel Ward, actress

He was really a screwball in school. —John Flory, a high school classmate

✦ First Sexual Experience

Unknown.

✦ Wives

Victoria Tennant, actress (costar in *All of Me,* '84)

✦ Did You Know?

Is Steve a wild and crazy guy? A swinger? Or a straight arrow? Whichever he is now, he started out really, really normal. While in junior high school in Inglewood, California, Steve was president of the Square Dance Club. In high school he was head cheerleader and king of the senior prom.

Lovers, Flings, or Just Friends?

Diane Keaton, actress (costar in *Father of the Bride, Part II,* '95)

Bernadette Peters, actress (costar in *Pennies From Heaven,* '81)

Linda Ronstadt, singer

Lovers, Flings, or Just Friends?

Jean Moreau, French
  actress (costar in *Monte
  Walsh*, '70)

Michelle Triola, singer-
  starlet

Lee Marvin 1924–1987

✦ He Said

There's an old adage in the business. Never shack up with anyone with lower billing than you.

I bet you got the prettiest little pink clittie in the room. —Drunken comment to a seventyish British woman at an elegant dinner party in London

Love is a matter of degrees. I think of a gas tank with the empty and full positions.

I don't exactly look like the type of guy women throw themselves off the cliffs to get at.

When I was young I never got my share of the action.

✦ They Said

If I could generalize, I'd say Lee's basically an antiwoman man. He's happiest hanging around bars talking with other guys. —Betty Ebeling, first wife

Not since Attila the Hun swept across Europe, leaving five hundred years of total blackness, has there been a man like Lee Marvin. —Josh Logan, who directed Marvin in *Paint Your Wagon* ('69)

More male than anyone I've ever acted with. —Jean Moreau, French actress

✦ First Sexual Experience

Unknown.

✦ Wives

Betty Ebeling, music major
Pamela Feeley, childhood sweetheart

✦ Did You Know?

'What was Marvin's favorite entertainment when he was doing his legendary drinking? To don a hairnet and his favorite red, yellow, and black striped bathrobe; grab his gun; and go out shooting up the mailboxes in his neighborhood. When he was out of town on location for a film, his antics could be a little milder. During the filming of *Donovan's Reef* ('63) in Hawaii, Marvin got drunk one night, stripped completely, and performed the hula on the bar of the Kawaii Hotel.

James Mason 1909–1984

✦ He Said

There have been ups and downs in my life, though the downs do seem to have been more frequent than the ups.

To be a successful film star as opposed to a successful film actor, you should settle for an image and polish it forever; I somehow could never quite bring myself to do that.

✦ They Said

His icy English smile froze my heart. —Micheál Mac Líammóir, Irish actor

James always found himself drawn in marriage to very strong and dominant women, but inside himself he was, I think, a little afraid of life, so he tended to float through it trying to avoid trouble whenever possible. —Ann Todd, actress and ex-lover

He had that curious quality of a man with an eternal secret. —Geraldine Fitzgerald, actress

He was a loyal man, shy and desperate to avoid any confrontation in public or private. —Vivian Cox, writer

The curious thing about him is that he always remained secretive and solitary. —Phyllis Calvert, actress

✦ First Sexual Experience

Unknown at this time, but one rumor alleges that Mason remained a virgin until he was twenty-six years old and met his first wife, Pamela, who was then married to a cameraman.

✦ Wives

Pamela Ostrer Kellino, former child actress
Clarissa Kaye, Australian actress

✦ Did You Know?

Despite being an actor never widely acclaimed for his looks, Mason certainly had his avid female fans. One watched his house almost constantly, then disappeared one day never to be seen again. She did take Mason's cat with her as a memento of her obsession. Another female fan used to rummage through his garbage, taking only the scraps of paper on which his handwriting appeared.

Mason's contract for the Disney film *20,000 Leagues Under the Sea* ('54) contained one of the most curious "vanity" clauses of any film contract. It permitted Mason to take home prints of any Disney movie his daughter Portland chose to watch for a weekend.

Lovers, Flings, or Just Friends?

Countess Vivi Crespi (Vivi Stokes), American-born Italian socialite

Judy Garland, actress (costar in *A Star Is Born*, '54)

Donna Greenberg, ex-munchkin from *The Wizard of Oz* ('39)

Vera Miles, actress (costar in *A Touch of Larceny*, '59)

Ann Todd, actress (costar in *The Seventh Veil*, '45)

Kaye Webb, children's writer

Yasuko Yama, Japanese actress

Marcello Mastroianni 1924–1996

Lovers, Flings, or Just Friends?

Anouk Aimée, actress (costar in 8½, '63)

Ursula Andress, actress (costar in *The Tenth Victim*, '65)

Carla Bruni, model-heiress

Catherine Deneuve, actress (costar in *It Only Happens to Others*, '72)

Faye Dunaway, actress (costar in *A Place for Lovers*, '68)

Nastassja Kinski, actress (costar in *Stay as You Are*, '78)

Jean Moreau, actress (costar in *La Notte*, '61)

Susan Strasberg, actress

Anna Maria Totò, television director

✦ He Said

Well, to tell you the truth, I'm not a great fucker. —Replying to Dick Cavett's questioning about his reputation as a Latin lover

I'm too old to be a Latin lover. . . . At my age [mid-60s], if you have sex, you go to bed and rest for three days.

Acting is a pleasure, like making love. No, wait a minute, not always; lovemaking is often an ordeal.

One must love one's costar. Otherwise how will the audience believe it?

They come for you in the morning in a limousine; they take you to the studio; they stick a pretty girl in your arms. . . . They call that a profession? Come on!

✦ They Said

Marcello is a man who thinks like a man, talks like a man—is a man! He has so much magnetism, he brings out the very soul in a woman. —Sophia Loren, frequent costar

Marcello represents a kind of ideal man. He is the man every woman would want. —Federico Fellini, director

I wanted a child by him. He gave one to Catherine Deneuve instead. —Faye Dunaway, actress

✦ First Sexual Experience

Unknown.

✦ Wives

Flora Carabella, actress

✦ Did You Know?

How far back does Mastroianni's association with director Federico Fellini go? Well, they met while both were involved in theatrics during college. Perhaps that's why both men were rumored by those who knew them well to share a strange lovemaking habit. Supposedly both Mastroianni and Fellini preferred to keep their socks on during sex.

Victor Mature 1913–1999

✦ He Said

The trouble is I can't get along without a wife, and, when I have one, I can't live with her.

I can't help it I've got a good set of muscles. I want to prove I've got something more. I'm tired of being nothing but a male striptease.

I can't act, but what I've got that the others don't is this.
—Referring to his muscular body

✦ They Said

I love Victor because he's such a crazy, attractive, friendly son of a gun. —Sheilah Graham, gossip columnist

I never like a movie where the hero's tits are bigger than the heroine's. —Groucho Marx, quipping about Mature's appearance in *Samson and Delilah* ('49)

You are my favorite male star and muscleman in the white race.
—Don Blackman, black light-heavyweight wrestling champion

✦ First Sexual Experience
Unknown.

✦ Wives
Frances Evans, acting student
Martha Stephenson Kemp, widow
Dorothy Stanford Berry, divorcée
Adrienne Joy Urwick, actress
Yvonne Huston, model

✦ Did You Know?
Mature placed the imprint of his bare buttocks on a slab of concrete that resided outside his dressing room door to show his annoyance at not being invited to place the more conventional imprints of his hands and feet in the cement outside Graumann's Chinese Theatre.

Lovers, Flings, or Just Friends?

Wendy Barrie, actress
Phyllis Brooks, actress
Buffy Cobb Chapman, divorcée
Alice Faye, actress-singer
Betty Grable, actress (costar in *I Wake Up Screaming*, '41)
Sheilah Graham, gossip columnist
June Haver, actress
Rita Hayworth, actress (costar in *My Gal Sal*, '42)
Betty Hutton, actress (costar in *Red, Hot and Blue*, '49)
Veronica Lake, actress
Carole Landis, actress (costar in *One Million B.C.*, '40)
Bernice Parks, entertainer
Anne Shirley, actress
K. T. Stevens, actress
Elizabeth Taylor, actress
Gene Tierney, actress
Lana Turner, actress (costar in *Betrayed*, '54)
Vera Zorina, ballerina-actress

Louis B. Mayer 1882–1957

✦ He Said

A woman's ass is for her husband, not theatergoers.

I worship good women, honorable men, and saintly mothers.

Here we are making you a big star, and you tell me that you don't want to be one. You ungrateful little bitch! —Snapping at Kathryn Grayson, age eleven, who had just told him that what she really wanted was to train for the operatic stage

You be nice to me and I'll be nice to you. —Mayer's oft-repeated phrase to the actors—and especially actresses—under contract to his studio

I can't make love to a girl I really don't care for.

If God chose me for this post, it was because he wanted a man who's just like everybody else. —Being pompous about his position as head of MGM

✦ They Said

He couldn't get laid in a whorehouse! —Lew Wertheimer, a friend, joking about Mayer's often fumbling attempts at sex

He could play the part of any star in the studio and play it better. —Adela Rogers St. Johns

He has the memory of an elephant and the hide of an elephant. The only difference is that elephants are vegetarians and Mayer's diet is his fellow man. —Herman J. Manckiewicz, screenwriter

✦ First Sexual Experience

Unknown.

✦ Wives

Margaret Shenberg, bookkeeper
Lorena James Danker, actress-showgirl

✦ Did You Know?

When he first arrived in Hollywood, former junk peddler Mayer had a thick, almost unintelligible Yiddish accent. He hired actor Conrad Nagel to teach him how to speak properly. Nagel succeeded, and Mayer lost all trace of his former accent. How did Mayer repay Nagel? By practically driving him out of films, probably in order to keep his voice training of Mayer a secret.

Under Mayer, MGM maintained an in-house abortionist, presumably to ensure that unwanted pregnancies among his female stars didn't compromise either their reputations or the shooting schedules of the studio's films.

Lovers, Flings, or Just Friends?

Mabel Cooper, mother of child star Jackie Cooper

Joan Crawford, actress

Jean Howard, actress

Betty Jaynes, starlet

Myrna Loy, actress

Jeanette MacDonald, singer-actress

Dr. Jeanne Marmonston, physician

Ilona Massey, actress

Ann Miller, actress-dancer

Grace Moore, singer-actress

Gladys O'Brien, mother of child star Margaret O'Brien

Beatrice Roberts, starlet

Adeline Schulberg, agency head

Jenny (Ginny) Sims, starlet-vocalist

Mabel Walker Willebrandt, MGM lobbyist and attorney

plus lots and lots of stars, starlets, and their mothers

Burgess Meredith 1908–1997

✦ He Said

God knows I was not a dashing swain, but in a kind of mongrel way I chased the foxes.

✦ They Said

Meredith's extraordinary success on stage has practically nothing to do with what he looks like. —Wolcott Gibbs, critic

✦ First Sexual Experience

Unknown.

✦ Wives

Helen Derby, divorcée

Margaret Perry, daughter of Antoinette Perry, for whom Broadway's Tony Awards are named

Paulette Goddard, actress (who was earlier the third Mrs. Charlie Chaplin)

Kaja Sundsten, dancer

✦ Did You Know?

During sex with Tallulah Bankhead, the eminently quotable actress shrieked out at Meredith, "For God's sake, don't come *inside* me! I'm engaged to Jock Whitney."

Lovers, Flings, or Just Friends?

Peggy Ashcroft, actress

Tallulah Bankhead, actress

Ingrid Bergman, actress

Olivia de Havilland, actress

Marlene Dietrich, singer-actress

Hedy Lamarr, actress

Gussie Moran, tennis player

Ginger Rogers, actress-dancer (costar in *Tom, Dick, and Harry,* '41)

Norma Shearer, actress

and a ménage à trois with a rich German lady and her lesbian lover

Lovers, Flings, or Just Friends?

Jewel Hart

Rita Hayworth, actress

Mercedes McCambridge, actress

Gary Merrill 1914–1990

✦ He Said

I was not good with sex—partly because I was afraid. If I stumbled across it, fine. —Describing his sex life in his earlier years

✦ They Said

Poor Gary, you are in for trouble with your wife. So are the children. Be careful. —A close female friend after meeting Bette Davis, his wife at the time

Gary liked to drink more than he liked to act. —Walter Bernstein, screenwriter

✦ First Sexual Experience

Lost his virginity in his mid-teens to an older married woman, with a four-year-old son, for whom he baby-sat in Windsor, Connecticut. Their relationship ended when the woman's husband contacted Merrill and advised him to cease "fooling around with my wife."

✦ Wives

Barbara Leeds, actress
Bette Davis, actress (costar in *All About Eve,* '50)

✦ Did You Know?

While Merrill and Bette Davis were performing in San Francisco, he took her to see the show at Finocchio's, a famous transvestite club featuring male performers in drag. Davis refused to believe they were men until they went backstage to meet them. Then, she claimed she'd never seen—or heard of—such performers, even though she was almost fifty at the time.

Merrill ran for the Republican nomination to the U.S. House of Representatives from Maine's first congressional district in 1968. He placed last of the three candidates in the race.

Ray Milland 1905–1986

✦ He Said

I didn't know what a test was. I thought you had to urinate in a bottle or something. —Mistaking the term *screen test* for something else

I never concerned myself with Hollywood and movies. I just stayed home, and I never really got over the feeling that I was psychologically and emotionally not cut out to be an actor.

I don't believe that most of the men columnists were failed actors, but most of the women gossips took out their frustrations on the beautiful actresses who became stars. —Delivering his view on Hollywood's gossip columnists

✦ They Said

Ray Milland was not careful of his personal hygiene—he stank! —Marlene Dietrich, costar in *Golden Earrings* ('47), who feuded constantly with Milland during filming

A shit! —Bette Davis, actress

✦ First Sexual Experience

Lost his virginity in an empty stable stall one evening when he was almost fifteen, to a "determined" blonde, who was two years older.

✦ Wives

Malvina Muriel Weber, college student

✦ Did You Know?

Want to catch Milland indulging in some water sports? Watch his film *The Jungle Princess* ('36), with Dorothy Lamour, because he urinates in the swimming pool while they're necking together. Milland told the story on himself during a visit to the *Tonight Show,* saying "I thought, Oh God, not now! but the cold water of the pool did its work on me."

Milland claimed he lost his hair prematurely because of the heavy doses of women's permanents and electric curlers used to give him curly hair for his role in *Reap the Wild Wind* ('42).

Thought of as a mild man, Milland could be merciless when provoked. *Beau Geste* ('39) costar Brian Donlevy annoyed Milland so intensely during filming that he sought an unusual revenge. During a fencing sequence, Milland deliberately nicked Donlevy's unpadded penis, drawing blood. The bothersome actor promptly fainted, which caused the crew to give Milland a burst of applause.

Lovers, Flings, or Just Friends?

Margaret Banks, dancer

Estelle Brody, actress

Esperanza Baur Diaz Ceballos, actress

Mona Gaye, British actress (costar in *The Lady From the Sea,* '29)

Grace Kelly, actress (costar in *Dial M for Murder,* '54)

Lovers, Flings, or Just Friends?

James Dean, actor (costar in *Rebel Without a Cause,* '55)

Jill Haworth, actress (costar in *Exodus,* '60)

Joey Heatherton, dancer-actress

Rock Hudson, actor

Don Johnson, actor

Peter Lawford, actor

Tina Louise, actress

Nicholas Ray, director (directed him in *Rebel Without a Cause,* '55)

Bobby Sherman, singer

Gregg Tyler, author-actor

Tuesday Weld, actress

Sal Mineo 1939–1976

✦ He Said

I like them all—men, I mean. And a few chicks now and then.

Everyone's supposed to be bi. . . . Besides, what's wrong with being bi?

I've got a girl in every port—and a couple of guys, too.

Where you start is pretty much how you wind up. I mean, you get typed in the first thing that clicks, then they don't give you no more fucking chances. Hollywood don't flex its muscle brain.

Call me a sissy and you're dead. —Remarking about his dancing classes

✦ They Said

Sal had some strange tastes, but he was totally unaffected by them. —Peter Bogdanovich, director and friend

He was gay, by his own admission, but I don't know that he was completely gay, because he was also with women. —Don Johnson, actor

He was simply a bundle of nerves. —Gregg Tyler, author-actor

I can't say I ever felt any love for Sal. I didn't like or dislike him. I thought he was scary . . . a bit weird. —Polly Platt, production designer

He was such a fine young man. —Mickey Cohen, underworld figure

✦ First Sexual Experience

Unknown.

✦ Wives

Mineo never married.

✦ Did You Know?

When he became a star, Mineo purchased a $200,000, twenty-room mansion for his parents in Mamaroneck in New York's Westchester County. It was originally built for actress Mary Pickford, and D. W. Griffith shot part of *Birth of a Nation* at the estate.

Sal certainly had the girls fooled about his preferring men to women. In his heyday, when the *Dick Clark American Bandstand* show ran a contest on "Why I'd like to have dinner with Sal Mineo," more than twenty-seven thousand responses were received in three days.

Robert Mitchum 1917–1997

✦ He Said

I started out to be a sex fiend but I couldn't pass the physical.

I get drunk, follow pretty broads, make a fool of myself, and stagger home. —Answering a psychiatrist's question, when he was arrested for a marijuana bust, on what he did when he attended parties

People think I have a sexy walk. Hell, I'm just trying to hold my gut in.

I agree with the guy who wrote that I look like a shark with a broken nose.

✦ They Said

There's not a dame around who won't drop her britches for him, and to make it worse, he don't give a damn. —Howard Hughes

He should watch his bad breath and he is a lousy kisser. —Marilyn Monroe, actress

I married a character. —Dorothy Spence, spouse

You know you can't act. If you hadn't been good-looking, you would never have gotten a picture. —Katharine Hepburn, annoyed at Mitchum's shenanigans on an early film

You're either the lousiest actor in the world or the best. I can't make up my mind which. —Mervyn LeRoy, who directed Mitchum in *Undercurrent* ('46)

✦ First Sexual Experience
Unknown.

✦ Wives
Dorothy Spence, student

✦ Did You Know?

During the early 1940s, Mitchum was a sheetmetal worker at a Lockheed Aircraft facility. The guy who used the locker next to his was one James Dougherty, who used to show Mitchum pinup photos of his young wife, Norma Jean Baker Dougherty, who later became Marilyn Monroe.

While many people are familiar with Mitchum's recording of *Thunder Road*, the theme from his film of the same name, he's also made other recordings. In March 1957, he recorded an album of calypso vocals for Capitol Records called *Robert Mitchum— Calypso Is Like So!* Mitchum developed his facility singing calypso in Trinidad during the making of *Fire Down Below* ('57).

Lovers, Flings, or Just Friends?

Carroll Baker, actress (costar in *Mister Moses*, '65)

Lucille Ball, actress

Ava Gardner, actress (costar in *My Forbidden Past*, '51)

Gloria Grahame, actress (costar in *Crossfire*, '47)

Jane Greer, actress (costar in *Out of the Past*, '47)

Rita Hayworth, actress (costar in *Fire Down Below*, '57)

Helen Keller, starlet

Lila Leeds, starlet

Shirley MacLaine, actress (costar in *Two for the Seesaw*, '62)

Sarah Miles, actress (costar in *Ryan's Daughter*, '70)

Marilyn Monroe, actress (costar in *The River of No Return*, '54)

Betty Rice, starlet

Jane Russell, actress (costar in *Macao*, '52)

Jean Simmons, actress

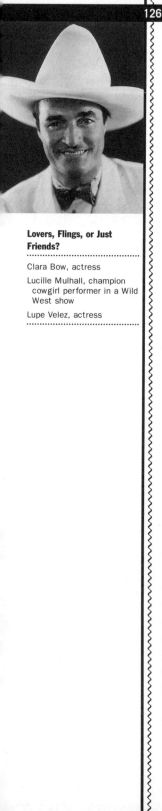

Tom Mix 1880–1940

✦ He Said

When a man's been married a half a dozen times, any sentiment about anniversaries is as cold as the ashes of last year's campfire. Payin' all them alimonies sorta drowns out the romance.

If God was good enough to give me a full head of hair, the least I can do is to keep it dyed.

My desire was to be a top-notch sheriff in the West where a man has to be a man. I dreamed and imagined that way of life as far back as I can remember.

✦ They Said

Tom's one fellow who'll never have to worry about being shot for being too modest. —Anonymous reporter, commenting on Mix's propensity to overexaggerate everything about his life

He can't act, but he can ride like hell and everybody loves him. —D. W. Griffith, director

As a boy, Tom was just a big devil, too busy playing with guns to learn much. —Elizabeth Smith Mix, his mother

✦ First Sexual Experience
Unknown.

✦ Wives
Grace I. Allin, schoolteacher
Kitty Jewel Perrine, hotel owner's daughter
Olive Stokes, rancher's daughter
Victoria Forde, star of silent Westerns
Mabel Hubbard Ward, circus aerialist

✦ Did You Know?
Mix, quite unlike his screen characters, was a rogue. He claimed to have been wounded critically four times, even offering photos and drawings of the exact spot for sale to his fans. He also boasted of having been both a federal marshal and a Texas Ranger in his career; he was neither. One fact he did not boast about: He had gone AWOL from the U.S. army when young, and they'd supposedly never missed him. The fact that he was never pursued always puzzled those close to him who knew about it.

Mix was a pallbearer at the funeral in Los Angeles in 1929 of the famed Wyatt Earp.

Robert Montgomery 1904–1981

✦ He Said

My advice to you concerning applause is this: Enjoy it, but never quite believe it.

A picture may fail and a play may fail, but an audience has never failed.

If you were a younger man, Mr. Mayer, I'd give you a beating.
—Delivered during an argument with Louis B. Mayer

I'd love to be in Congress, but nobody's asked me.

✦ They Said

He always looked like a naughty boy who's just swallowed a canary and isn't going to tell. —Norma Shearer, actress

The march of trade is yearning for young men like you, and my advice to you is to get out and stay out of the theater. —William Faversham, theatrical critic

✦ First Sexual Experience
Unknown.

✦ Wives
Elizabeth Bryan Allen, actress
Elizabeth Grant Harkness, socialite

✦ Did You Know?

When given his first screen test, by Samuel Goldwyn's company, the report said that Montgomery's neck was too long. Cagey producer Goldwyn solved the problem when he said, "His neck is not too long, his collars are too short." Outfitted with new collars, Montgomery was tested again, but MGM signed him up before Goldwyn could get his name on a contract.

After losing a dispute with MGM's Louis B. Mayer for an increased salary, the studio mogul gave Montgomery a most prestigious consolation prize: A barber's chair was installed in his private dressing room.

Lovers, Flings, or Just Friends?

Tallulah Bankhead, actress
(costar in *Faithless*, '32)

Miriam Hopkins, actress

Norma Shearer, actress
(costar in *The Divorcée*, '30)

Audie Murphy 1924–1971

✦ He Said

Sometimes I have very little faith in most men, and none at all in women.

I need the money. —On why he went to Hollywood to cash in on his hero status after World War II

I'm working with a handicap. I have no talent.

I don't mind being an actor as long as I don't have to live up to a reputation you don't have.

✦ They Said

Few women could resist him. They seemed to all want to mother him. —David McClure, close friend and associate of gossip columnist Hedda Hopper

He'd pull a little-boy act and they'd feel sorry for him and they'd have to let him have some. —Casey Tibbs, close friend, on Murphy's success with women

In spite of his baby face, he had the most frightening eyes of anyone I've ever known. —Fred De Cordova, director (directed him in *Column South*, '53)

Audie was a loose pistol, not really a cannon, but a pistol. —John Saxon, actor

A very nice kid—that's all. —Jane Wyatt, actress

✦ First Sexual Experience
Unknown.

✦ Wives
Wanda "Dixie" Hendrix, actress
Pamela Archer, airline stewardess

✦ Did You Know?
Murphy was missing most of one buttock—it was shot off during combat in World War II.

While Murphy was the most decorated soldier who came out of World War II and made his way to Hollywood stardom, two other war heroes also tried his feat with varying degrees of success: Neville Brand and Aldo Ray.

Liam Neeson 1952–

✦ He Said

I love women! Every shape, size, and color created. They are the better sex.

I've never been very promiscuous, even though this profession is renowned for changing relationships.

A major part of how successful you're going to be as an actor in Hollywood rests on how you look stripped to the waist.

Is this what it's going to say on my tombstone? He dated Julia Roberts and Barbra Streisand.

I loved and feared the nakedness of it, the purity of it. There's nothing to hide behind. —Remembering his boxing days

✦ They Said

If you put Willem [Dafoe], Liam Neeson, and Jimmy [James] Woods in a room together, there wouldn't be room for anyone else. —Dana Delaney, actress, referring to their sexual endowments. She said her statement was "purely conjecture," meant as a compliment, and that she hadn't had sex with "all of them."

When you're with Liam, don't even think about being looked at by a woman. —Tim Roth, actor

Liam has this gentleness and strength. He can cry like a baby and fight like a bear. —Natasha Richardson, actress

He said we were to be married, but I never had a diamond ring on my finger from him. —Brooke Shields, actress-model

Liam has a deep romanticism, mixed with a real hardness of being. —Michael Caton-Jones, director

✦ First Sexual Experience

Based on comments he's made, one can assume that Neeson lost his virginity while in college.

✦ Wives

Natasha Richardson, actress, daughter of Vanessa Redgrave

✦ Did You Know?

One of the first places women got to see Liam in all his physical glory was during the run of the play *Streamers*. His role required a naked sprint across the stage from him. As word of his appearance got around, more and more women began attending.

As a young man, Neeson was a Northern Ireland boxing champion for three consecutive years.

Lovers, Flings, or Just Friends?

Jennifer Grey, actress

Diane Keaton, actress (costar in *The Good Mother*, '88)

Helen Mirren, actress

Sinead O'Connor, singer

Julia Roberts, actress (costar in *Satisfaction*, '88)

Ruth, one of his many Dublin conquests

Brooke Shields, actress-model

Barbra Streisand, actress-singer

Uma Thurman, actress

Lovers, Flings, or Just Friends?

Grand Prix winner of the left half of the Tightly Upraised Zipper Award, since his name has never been connected "romantically" with anyone outside his marriage to Woodward.

Paul Newman 1925–

✦ He Said

I'm really a very ordinary guy.

Is that all they think of me? Are they going to write on my tombstone, "Here lies Paul Newman, who died a failure . . . because his eyes turned brown"?

They don't see you as a person but as an icon or object.

Sure, I drank whiskey a lot. For a while it really screwed me up. There are periods in my life in which I don't take any particular pride.

I'm not very good at revealing myself. I cover for it by telling terrible dirty jokes.

To be a good actor you have to be a child.

✦ They Said

Paul Newman's a great-looking ice cube. —Sal Mineo, actor

He's an oddity in this business. He really loves his wife. —Otto Preminger, director, who directed Newman in *Exodus* ('60)

I hated him on sight, but he was so funny and pretty and neat. —Joanne Woodward, actress and spouse, on their first meeting

I used to call him "grabby-fist" because every time you'd see him after the show, he had a beer in his mitt. —James Gregory, actor, on Newman's drinking

✦ First Sexual Experience
Unknown.

✦ Wives
Jacqueline Witte, student
Joanne Woodward, actress (costar in *WUSA*, '70)

✦ Did You Know?
Newman once had sometime-costar Robert Redford's face printed on 150 cartons of toilet paper as a joke gift—but he chickened out and never presented the items to Redford.

Newman, on occasion, has run some interesting newspaper ads. In July 1969 he ran a $2,000 ad in the *Los Angeles Times* entitled "We Are Not Breaking Up," detailing why he and Woodward were not separating. He also ran ads to apologize for having appeared in the film *The Silver Chalice* ('54) when it was shown on television.

Jack Nicholson 1937–

✦ He Said

Since my overnight stardom I can't go around picking up stray pussy anymore.

I've balled all the women. I've done all the drugs. I've drunk every drink.

I'd love to be able to say I've balled everyone, indulged in every kind of shit, gone everywhere, although I haven't.

Sometimes I think that maleness is a quality in men that's expressed in wanting all women.

I knew how to be friends with women before I knew how to be sexy with them.

I say monogamy doesn't make any difference; women suspect you whether it's true or not.

✦ They Said

No one, and I mean no one, can compare with Jack in the sack. —Karen Mayo-Chandler, ex-girlfriend

He's a serious artist—I think he's a master. —Meryl Streep, actress

I'm fed up with people telling me how good Jack Nicholson is. —Jane Fonda, actress, declining the opportunity to costar with him

I actually don't think he's that bright—not as good as Robert De Niro, for example. —Marlon Brando

✦ First Sexual Experience

Unknown, but probably with someone in Neptune City, New Jersey, where he was raised.

✦ Wives

Sandra Knight, actress

✦ Did You Know?

Jack is illegitimate: He was raised believing his real mother, June, was his older sister. Years later, after he found out, he said, "I have my own favorite downtrodden minority and it's not women. It's the bastard, the illegitimately born."

Jack was a premature ejaculator, until he overcame the problem.

Rumors say that Jack was filmed sporting a full erection—or "stinger," as he calls it—for some scenes in *The Postman Always Rings Twice* ('81). Gossips on the set further claimed that he kept a video of the scenes to play for friends.

Jack is one of the top private art collectors in the U.S.

Lovers, Flings, or Just Friends?

Susan Anspach, actress (costar in *Five Easy Pieces,* '70)

Candice Bergen, actress (costar in *Carnal Knowledge,* '71)

Rebecca Broussard, actress

Princess Caroline of Monaco

Georgianna Carter, actress (costar in *The Wild Wide,* '60)

Lois Chiles, actress

Julie Delpy, actress

Catherine Deneuve, actress

Faye Dunaway, actress

Sabrina Guinness, socialite and beverage heiress

Jerry Hall, model

Anjelica Huston, actress (costar in *Prizzi's Honor,* '85)

Lauren Hutton, model-actress

Diane Keaton, actress

Jessica Lange, actress (costar in *The Postman Always Rings Twice,* '81)

Kelly Le Brock, actress

Mimi Machu, model-actress

Madonna, singer-actress

Karen Mayo-Chandler, actress

Joni Mitchell, singer

Christina Onassis, shipping heiress

Michelle Phillips, singer-actress

Maria Schneider, actress

Margaret Trudeau, political wife

David Niven 1909–1983

✦ He Said

Bumping around for long periods in motorcars, trains, or planes has always had a strangely exuberant effect on my sexual ambitions.

Hollywood was hardly a nursery for intellectuals. It was a hotbed of false values, it harbored an unattractive percentage of small-time crooks and con artists.

✦ They Said

If you want sophistication, go have lunch with David Niven.
—Burt Reynolds, actor

He was a model of how people who are famous and who enjoy the terrific privilege of stardom or public acclaim should behave.
—John Mortimer, British critic

✦ First Sexual Experience

Lost his virginity at age fourteen to Nessie, a Piccadilly prostitute, with whom he kept frequent company thereafter.

✦ Wives

Primrose "Primmie" Rollo, British military officer
Hjordis Paulina Tersmeden, Swedish model

✦ Did You Know?

During a visit to Prince Rainier and Princess Grace in Monaco, Niven was asked by the prince who was the most satisfying of all the Hollywood beauties he'd bedded. Forgetting to whom he was speaking, Niven enthusiastically replied "Grace!" Then, suddenly catching the astounded expression on her husband's face, he stammered to add "Er . . . Gracie . . . I mean, Gracie Fields."

Niven and priapic Errol Flynn used to stage weekend boating trips on Flynn's yacht, the notorious *Sirocco*. Naturally they were always accompanied by a bevy of comely young ladies. The standard routine was that the guys would furnish the booze, while the girls supplied the food. Niven noted that one winsome beauty's "contribution consisted of nothing but a loaf of bread and a douche bag."

Lovers, Flings, or Just Friends?

Virginia Bruce, actress
Doris Duke, tobacco heiress
Alice Faye, singer-actress
Ava Gardner, actress
Paulette Goddard, actress
Rita Hayworth, actress
Barbara Hutton, heiress
Grace Kelly, actress
Deborah Kerr, actress (costar in *Bonjour Tristesse*, '58)
Evelyn Keyes, actress
Hedy Lamarr, actress
Carole Lombard, actress
Ida Lupino, actress
Merle Oberon, actress
Ginger Rogers, actress
Norma Shearer, actress
Ann Sheridan, actress
Simone Simon, actress
Ann Todd, actress
Loretta Young, actress (costar in *The Bishop's Wife*, '47)
Mae West, actress

Nick Nolte 1941–

✦ He Said

No, I've had a testicle tuck. It makes the penis look bigger.
—Commenting on the supposed body work he'd had done

There haven't been many women who've been able to live with me very long. I'm an extremist.

My ex-wives used to threaten to shoot me with a tranquilizer gun.

✦ They Said

He's got much more sex appeal than I do. —Warren Beatty, actor

I hear you've been dead drunk in every gutter in town, and it has to stop. —Katharine Hepburn, chiding him on his lifestyle

He loved me to pretend to be a doll so he could undress me.
—One ex-lover remembering some fond moments

✦ First Sexual Experience
Unknown.

✦ Wives
Sheila Page, actress
Sharyn Haddad, dancer
Rebecca Leigh Linger, model

✦ Did You Know?

When he was about ten years old, Nolte accidentally impaled himself on a neighbor's picket fence. He managed not to castrate himself, but the accident did cause him to grow extra skin in his groin area, which made it appear as if he had a third testicle until he had surgery. True or not? Nolte has told the tale on himself. But then, he's also told about accidentally leaving his dead father's artificial leg in a bar.

During his college years, Nolte had a bad experience with the legal arm of the U.S. Justice Department. He was fined $45,000 and sentenced to seventy-five years in prison for selling fake draft cards. His sentence was finally reduced to five years on probation.

One of Nolte's ex-wives smashed him in the head with a telephone during an argument. She also tossed all his clothes into the swimming pool, and then him.

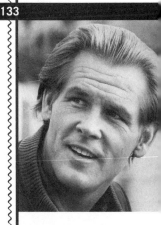

Lovers, Flings, or Just Friends?

Karen Eklund, actress

Vicki Lewis, actress

Lucy Saroyan, daughter of author William Saroyan

Debra Winger, actress (costar in *Cannery Row*, '82)

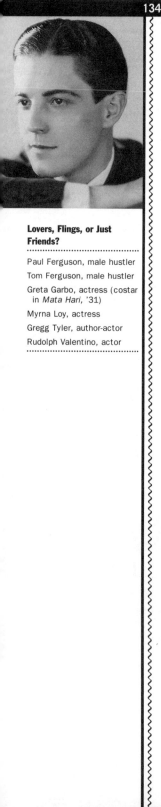

Ramon Novarro 1899–1968

✦ He Said
I tried to become a Jesuit, but they said I was too old, and, of course, they were right. Then I contemplated the life of a Trappist monk. Can you imagine an actor taking a vow of silence!

✦ They Said
Women were crazy about him, but of course Ramon preferred another personal lifestyle, which in those days was kept very much in a secret closet. —Lina Basquette, silent film actress

He had great discretion. It was whispered that he was homosexual, which was without doubt true. —Micheline Presle, actress

Poor Raymond, he was a very unhappy and sensitive fellow, and a rather lost one. —William "Billy" Haines, fellow actor and homosexual, who once took Novarro to a male brothel on Wilshire Boulevard. Louis B. Mayer got wind of their escapade and nearly fired him for it. Finally, Mayer had the police close the place to keep some of his other stars away from temptation.

✦ First Sexual Experience
Unknown.

✦ Wives
Novarro never married.

✦ Did You Know?
During the last six months of his life Novarro wrote more than 130 checks to male hustlers—for services rendered. One of his tricks, prostitute-actor Gregg Tyler, revealed that Novarro fellated him while he stood beside a coffin in which the silent-screen star reposed.

Valentino presented Novarro with a black lead dildo, inscribed with his signature in silver, which was a replica of his own penis. Many years later it figured prominently in Novarro's death, when it was rammed down his throat during the sex and murder spree the Ferguson brothers, Paul and Tom, conducted at Novarro's home on Halloween, October 31, 1968.

Novarro was the first film star to seek anonymity in public by wearing dark glasses.

Rudolph Nureyev 1938–1993

✦ He Said

I know what it is like to make love as a man and a woman.

It is not wonderful for everybody to come out of their closets. Not everybody is a good asset to gays.

Myths are like measles. If you don't keep them indoors, they spread.

Everybody wants to be a movie star.

✦ They Said

Rudolph had a sex life that was probably as wide-ranging as anyone's in this century. —James Toback, film director and close friend

He liked street boys, toughs, the lowest of the low. —Monique Van Vooren, actress

In many ways Nureyev reminded me of Greta, the same wild untamed quality of genius. —Cecil Beaton, comparing the dancer to Greta Garbo

When you've known Nijinsky, you don't want to see Nureyev. —Gabrielle "Coco" Chanel, couturier, who knew Nijinsky

He constantly complained about his legs, which be considered to be too short. —Marlene Dietrich

We want Rudi—especially in the nudi! —Popular chant of his fans

✦ First Sexual Experience

Unknown.

✦ Wives

Nureyev never married, although he formed several relationships with men; some lasted for several years.

✦ Did You Know?

Nureyev claimed that he and a prominent politician once shared the favors of a sex partner, a young American soldier. Who was the famed politician? Robert Kennedy.

While filming a scene in *Valentino* ('77), Nureyev got into an argument over the size of his penis with director Ken Russell. The scene portrayed Valentino urinating in his pants and was to be accomplished with a hose pipe stuffed into Nureyev's pants. The Russian kept insisting that the hose be pushed farther and farther down his pants leg until, as Russell put it, "It looked as though Rudy was wrestling with a snake halfway down his pants."

Lovers, Flings, or Just Friends?

Cecil Beaton, photographer-designer

Leonard Bernstein, composer-conductor

Erik Bruhn, Danish ballet dancer

Luis Falco, choreographer

Dame Margot Fonteyn, ballerina

Talitha Pol Getty, daughter-in-law of oilman J. Paul Getty

Roy Halston, fashion designer

Mick Jagger, singer-actor

Robert Mapplethorpe, artist

Freddie Mercury, singer

Anthony Perkins, actor

Michelle Phillips, singer

Wallace Potts, lover

Alexander Pushkin, ballet teacher

Lee Radziwll, socialite sister of Jackie O.

Giorgio Sant'Angelo, fashion designer

Maria Tallchief, ballerina

Robert Tracy, lover

Ultra Violet, actress

Monique Van Vooren, actress

Laurence Olivier 1907–1989

✦ He Said

I am prepared to believe that the sense of romance in those of our brothers and sisters who incline toward love of their own sex is heightened to a more blazing pitch than in those who think of themselves as normal.

The only time I ever really feel alive is when I'm acting.

✦ They Said

He would have slept with anyone. —David Lewis, producer

Noël adored Larry, there is no other word for it. —Larry Cole, a close friend of Coward's

This actor is the ugliest actor in pictures! This actor will ruin me! —Samuel Goldwyn, on seeing the daily rushes of Olivier in *Wuthering Heights* ('39)

✦ First Sexual Experience

Occurred at age fourteen with another boy. Olivier's homosexual experiences continued to dominate until his late teens. It was rumored that he was going to include his homosexual affairs—then and later—in his autobiography, until some family members objected, feeling that the revelations would be too embarrassing to them.

✦ Wives

Jill Esmond, actress
Vivien Leigh, actress (costar in *Fire Over England*, '36)
Joan Plowright, actress

✦ Did You Know?

Jill Esmond, Olivier's first wife, was a lesbian and their marriage remained unconsummated for a long time.

Olivier had a long-running affair with Danny Kaye, before dropping him abruptly. Kaye, who called Olivier Lally or Lala, once played an embarrassing joke on his lover. He disguised himself as a customs officer and had Olivier waylaid at New York's Idlewild Airport. Olivier was taken, by Kaye, into a secluded room, forced to submit to a strip-search and humiliating full body cavity probe. Once the joke was over, the couple scooted off to spend the night together in a New York hotel room.

Lovers, Flings, or Just Friends?

Maxine Audley, actress

Claire Bloom, actress (costar in *Richard III*, '56)

Richard Burton, actor

Noël Coward, playwright-entertainer

Lily Damita, actress

Errol Flynn, actor

Greer Garson, actress

Danny Kaye, actor (whose moods of depression reminded Olivier of his second wife, Vivien Leigh)

Elissa Landi, actress (costar in *The Yellow Ticket*, '31)

Sarah Miles, actress (costar in *Term of Trial*, '62)

Jean Simmons, actress (costar in *Hamlet*, '48)

Dorothy Tutin, actress (costar in *The Beggar's Opera*, '52)

Kenneth Tynan, British theater critic

Jane Welsh, actress

James Whale, director

Aristotle Onassis 1906–1975

✦ He Said

All Greek husbands, I tell you, all Greek men without exception, beat their wives. It's good for them.

I approach every woman as a potential mistress.

Beautiful women cannot bear moderation. They need an inexhaustible supply of excess.

You must let your nearest and dearest go to hell when they are no longer of service to you.

✦ They Said

He is obsessed with famous women. He was obsessed with me because I was famous. —Maria Callas, opera diva

Celebrities are important to Ari. All his fantasies are connected with them. —Tina Onassis, spouse

Like most wealthy people, he has very few friends. There were a whole lot of people who were just hangers-on, and others who were merely there to profit from him in every manner. —His Serene Highness Rainier III, sovereign prince of Monaco and husband of Grace Kelly

✦ First Sexual Experience

Lost his virginity at age twelve to an "attractive and buxom" French tutor.

✦ Wives

Athina (Tina) Livanos, shipping heiress
Jacqueline Bouvier Kennedy, JFK's widow

✦ Did You Know?

Greta Garbo, one of Onassis's close friends, once rebuffed his only sexual overture to her by saying, "Go to sleep, Ari. Don't ruin our friendship."

Onassis was reputedly responsible for Monaco's Prince Rainier marrying an American film star. The wily Greek recommended that such a marriage would be good for business in Monaco—the tourist business, that is. His first suggested mate for the prince? Marilyn Monroe, but she wasn't interested because she was out to "hook" Arthur Miller, so Grace Kelly got the nod instead.

Despite the worldly, cultured circle he moved in, Onassis retained a strong streak of peasant ignorance within himself. For example, he thought the Impressionist school of painters were artists who liked to impress people. He also believed in mermaids.

Lovers, Flings, or Just Friends?

Maria Callas, opera diva

Maria Constantinesco, German spy

Ingebord Dedichen, socialite, whose toes he liked to lick between

Doris Duke, tobacco heiress

Paulette Goddard, actress

Pamela Digby Churchill Hayward Harriman, socialite

Veronica Lake, actress

Claudia Muzio, opera diva

Eva Perón, actress-dictator, who made him scrambled eggs after their liaison

Lee Radziwill, socialite sister of Jackie O.

Jeanne Rhinelander, close friend of wife Tina's

Simone Simon, French actress

Geraldine Spreckels, sugar heiress

Gloria Swanson, actress

and a Russian ballerina with the Anna Pavlova Swan Ballet company *plus* a young Turkish lieutenant when he was a teenager

Lovers, Flings, or Just Friends?

Isabelle Adjani, actress

Marisa Berenson, actress (costar in *Barry Lyndon*, '75)

Jacqueline Bisset, actress

Oona Chaplin, widow of Charlie

Joan Collins, actress

Britt Ekland, actress

Mia Farrow, actress

Melanie Griffith, actress

Anjelica Huston, actress

Bianca Jagger, ex-spouse of rocker Mick

Carole King, singer-composer

Jennifer Lee, actress

Peggy Lipton, actress

Ali MacGraw, actress (costar in *Love Story*, '70)

Liza Minnelli, actress-singer

Joni Mitchell, singer

Barbara Parkins, actress

Michelle Phillips, singer-actress

Polly Platt, production designer

Linda Ronstadt, singer

Diana Ross, singer-actress

Leslie Stefanson, actress

Barbra Streisand, actress-singer (costar in *What's Up Doc?*, '72)

Margaret Trudeau, political wife

Lana Wood, actress and sister of Natalie

Ryan O'Neal 1941–

✦ He Said
I'm as moody and complex and private as anyone I ever knew.

If things ever get real bad, I can live off her. —Describing the success of his daughter Tatum, who won an Oscar for their costarring film *Paper Moon* ('73)

✦ They Said
He is an incredible lover, totally devoted to giving a woman pleasure. —Joanna Moore, first wife and mother of his two oldest children

A girl should get the best she deserves on her birthday. And he was. —Joan Collins, describing a birthday she spent with Ryan

Yeah, he's good-looking, but he's no Einstein. —Barbra Streisand

Man's got the whitest damn teeth I ever seen in my life. —Berry Gordy, record mogul and competitor for the attentions of Diana Ross

✦ First Sexual Experience
Unknown.

✦ Wives
Joanna Moore, actress
Leigh Taylor-Young, actress (costar in *The Big Bounce*, '69)
Farrah Fawcett, actress

✦ Did You Know?
Both O'Neal and his father have certainly been objects of male lust. Charles "Blackie" O'Neal, Ryan's father, was pursued relentlessly one summer by two flamboyant homosexuals, Hilton Edwards and Micheál Mac Líammoír. The two Irishmen were friends of Orson Welles, and part of an acting troupe he had assembled in a small Illinois town. O'Neal was there accompanying an actress friend who was part of the same troupe. Years later, Ryan, his son, played a role in a film with John Hurt—*Partners* ('82)—where he was a straight man, a cop, thrust into a homosexual setting where he became a desirable homosexual love object.

Peter O'Toole 1932–

✦ He Said

There is nothing on earth as good as a man and a woman.

For me, life has been either a wake or a wedding.

I never really cared how I looked. It was the other people—they cared. So I had to care because if I looked untidy, it was an obstacle to making money.

Stardom is insidious. It creeps through your toes. You don't realize what's happening until it reaches your nut. And that's when it becomes dangerous.

✦ They Said

If you had been any prettier, it would have been Florence of Arabia. —Noël Coward, reflecting on O'Toole's angelic appearance in *Lawrence of Arabia* ('62)

[O'Toole] is supposed to be a disreputably ugly rake who captivates women by the sheer power of the life force within him. —Herbert Kretzmer, British critic

The very prototype of the ham. —Omar Sharif, costar

Peter O'Toole looks like he's walking around just to save funeral expenses. —John Huston, director-actor

✦ First Sexual Experience

At age twelve, while a schoolboy in Leeds at St. Anne's, he was a member of a group called the MM, the Mutual Masturbation Society. O'Toole has said, "It was considered a healthy alternative to ordinary sex." He first had sex with a woman, a prostitute, at age fifteen.

✦ Wives

Siân Phillips, actress

✦ Did You Know?

O'Toole once passed out (in an alcoholic daze) on Johnny Carson's *Tonight* show.

O'Toole was personally barred by Prince Sihanouk from ever visiting Cambodia again. While there filming *Lord Jim*, O'Toole came to loathe the country, and didn't mind making his feelings known, which infuriated Sihanouk.

O'Toole is known for his salty tongue. During a *Playboy* interview, he said, "Given a good play and a decent set, you could chain a blue-arsed baboon in a stall and get what is known as a production."

Lovers, Flings, or Just Friends?

Ursula Andress, actress (costar in *What's New, Pussycat?*, '65)

April Ashley, British transsexual

Karen Brown, actress

Jodie Foster, actress (costar in *Svengali*, '83)

Audrey Hepburn, actress (costar in *How to Steal a Million*, '66)

Barbara Steele, British horror film queen

Malinche Verdugo, Mexican waitress

plus lots and lots of other women from all occupations, usually met during O'Toole's legendary drinking forays

Lovers, Flings, or Just Friends?

Jill Clayburgh, actress

Lyndall Hobbs, Australian director

Carol Kane, actress

Diane Keaton, actress (costar in *The Godfather*, '72)

Marthe Keller, actress (costar in *Bobby Deerfield*, '77)

Penelope Ann Miller, actress (costar in *Carlito's Way*, '93)

Michelle Pfeiffer, actress (costar in *Frankie and Johnny*, '91)

Annie Praeger, close friend of another of Pacino's lady friends

Kathleen Quinlan, actress

Maureen Springer, beauty salon owner

Jan Tarrant, acting teacher

Susan Tyrell, actress

Tuesday Weld, actress (costar in *Author! Author!*, '82)

Debra Winger, actress

Al Pacino 1940–

✦ He Said
Sure, there are starfuckers. My experience is that you can go with something like that, it can be very tempting. But I take a relationship *seriously.*

I love work because it keeps sex in perspective.

I'm a notorious pacifist. My favorite color is passive.

✦ They Said
He's the kind of man who takes you to great heights of ecstasy and knows what to do when he gets you there. —Anonymous lover

Pacino is a schmuck. —Oliver Stone, director

Al is so gentle, he won't even kill a cockroach. —Jill Clayburgh, actress

✦ First Sexual Experience
Lost his virginity at about nine or ten years old.

✦ Wives
Pacino has never been married.

✦ Did You Know?
Was Pacino the father of the baby that Diane Keaton supposedly miscarried in 1988? While the miscarriage was confirmed, neither Pacino nor Keaton would confirm whether he was the father.

Do struggling actors ever really prostitute themselves? Well, Pacino did—at least once. He went home with an older lady who offered him food and lodging in return for sex.

Mohammed Reza Pahlavi (Shah of Iran) 1919–1980

✦ He Said

Women are important in a man's life only *if they're beautiful and charming and keep their femininity.*

I myself have never been adverse to a bit of good old-fashioned lust.

I can tell you that the only reason was that I thought I would have fewer problems with a foreign wife: To begin with, her family would not be breathing down my neck all the time. —On why he'd pursued Princess Maria Gabriella of Italy as a potential spouse

✦ They Said

Even when he finds a companion, however attractive she may be, he sooner or later tires of her. Work alone commands his absolute devotion. —Asadollah Alan, minister of the shah's court

He was extraordinary. Attentive, virile, patient. —Trischa Tristan, lover

They looked like a gang of South Americans, not of very high standing. —Cecil Beaton, on the Shah's family

✦ First Sexual Experience

Lost his virginity to a chambermaid at Le Rosey, the exclusive Swiss boarding school he attended. She was dismissed for having sex with him.

✦ Wives

Princess Fawzieh, sister of Egypt's King Farouk
Soraya Esfandiary, daughter of an Iranian diplomat
Farah Diba, Iranian architecture student

✦ Did You Know?

How imperial could the Light of the Aryans be when confronted with female trouble? Very. When a young woman who he'd "met a few times" mentioned their liaisons, he sent her a stern warning. He was quite succinct, saying, "Warn her that unless she puts a stop to her tittle-tattle, she will end up behind bars."

What's the Shah's connection to Elvis Presley? Elvis rented and lived in a house the Shah owned on Perugia Way in Beverly Hills during November 1960, while he was making the film *Flaming Star* ('60).

Lovers, Flings, or Just Friends?

Ann-Margret, actress-singer
Helga Andersen, German actress
Brigitte Bardot, actress
Parvin Ghaffari, Iranian actress
Rita Hayworth, actress
Grace Kelly, actress and later a princess in her own right
Marisa Mell, actress
Karin Schubert, Swedish actress turned porn queen
Trischa Tristan, drama student and starlet
plus a reputed selection of comely professionals—preferably leggy and blond—from the establishment of Madame Claud's in Paris; *and* some of his countrymen

Gregory Peck 1916–

✦ He Said

It's all rather second-rate to expose one's insides to the public view. I'm not interested by the vogue for actors to tell all. I think it's in poor taste. My performances are the only forms of self-revelation that I go in for.

I didn't feel like a little tin god because people wrote and asked me for my autograph. It was just part of the business.

✦ They Said

Poor Greg! I like him a lot but he'll never make a film in his life. One of his ears is larger than the other. —Katherine Cornell, who gave Peck his first big break on the New York stage

That guy's so nice he'll be tripping over his halo if he isn't careful. —Lauren Bacall, actress

He has never allowed fame to lessen his natural quality of greatness. —Hedda Hopper, Hollywood gossip columnist

✦ First Sexual Experience

Unknown for certain, but possibly lost his virginity while attending the University of California at Berkeley.

✦ Wives

Greta Konen (Kukkonen), hairdresser
Veronique Passani, French journalist

✦ Did You Know?

Peck was scheduled to star with Marilyn Monroe in *Let's Make Love* ('60), an unusual singing and dancing role for him. Then Arthur Miller, Marilyn's hubby, rewrote the script, downgrading Peck's part and building up Marilyn's. Peck dropped out of the film and was replaced by French singer Yves Montand, who promptly also launched into a heavy affair with Monroe.

Lovers, Flings, or Just Friends?

Ingrid Bergman, actress (costar in *Spellbound*, '45)

Barbara Payton, actress (costar in *Only the Valiant*, '52)

Ann Todd, actress (costar in *The Paradine Case*, '47)

Sean Penn 1960–

✦ He Said

I wish I had AIDS so I could shoot you.

You take my picture and I'll break your fucking back with this rock! —Displaying the charming side of his character when confronted with photographers trying to take his picture

✦ They Said

Having Sean Penn as a marriage counselor is like taking sailing lessons from the captain of the Titanic. —Debra Winger, actress, annoyed that then-husband Timothy Hutton would go to his friend Penn for advice when the couple argued

Sean is the perfect American male to me. I'm inspired and shocked by him at the same time. —Madonna, singer-actress

✦ First Sexual Experience
Unknown.

✦ Wives

Madonna, singer-actress (costar in *Shanghai Surprise,* '86)
Robin Wright, actress (costar in *State of Grace,* '90)

✦ Did You Know?

What home videos—if they exist—would be hotter than the Rob Lowe sex tapes? The videos that Madonna and Sean reportedly shot of themselves having sex.

Penn once intimidated a female reporter by threatening her with a urine-filled water gun.

Penn goes beyond being a "method" actor. To help himself "find" his character (a dopey surfer) in *Fast Times at Ridgemont High* ('82), Penn stubbed out a cigarette on his palm.

Lovers, Flings, or Just Friends?

Maria Conchita Alonzo, actress

Valerie Golina, actress

Joyce Hyser, actress

Jewel Kilcher, pop singer

Elizabeth McGovern, actress (costar in *Racing With the Moon,* '84)

Elle Macpherson, model

Pamela Springsteen, actress (costar in *Fast Times at Ridgemont High,* '82)

and lots of tall, leggy blondes

**Lovers, Flings, or Just
Friends?**

René Clement, director
   (directed him in *This Bitter
   Earth,* '58)

Grover Dale, dancer-
   choreographer

Timmy Everett, actor

Robert Francis, actor

Alan Helms, model

Tab Hunter, actor

Kerry X. LeBre, hustler

Christopher Makos, photographer

Norma Moore, actress

Rudolph Nureyev, ballet
   dancer

Arthur Teno Pollick, actor

Victoria Principal, actress
   (costar in *The Life and
   Times of Judge Roy Bean,*
   '72)

Cynthia Rogers, actress

plus lots of hustlers, male
   prostitutes, young Thais,
   and lots of tall, thin
   dancers

Anthony Perkins 1932–1992

✦ He Said

*Well, I guess they'll give me a hundred thousand bucks for every
dick I say I sucked.* —Commenting on writing his autobiography

*Why is it that today's actors look like male hookers? Alec Bald-
win, Richard Grieco, Kiefer Sutherland. . . . They look like they
haven't slept for days—except maybe for money.*

*Movie stars in the fifties never had to discuss their personal lives
and I see no reason why I should now.* —Snapping about his refusal to
talk about his personal life, which was quite gay at the time

✦ They Said

He loved being pissed on. —One of Perkins's anonymous tricks

Tony isn't exactly Norman Bates, but he is kinky. —(Roy) Halston,
designer

*I don't like blood, and Tony's a sadist. He likes to see blood. I
mean, he is Norman Bates.* —Truman Capote, author and social gadfly

Incredibly closeted. —Alan Helms, model

*It was a wonderful love affair. If anything else was going down,
I certainly didn't know about it and I don't think he intended to
hurt me in any way.* —Berry Berenson, Perkins's widow

✦ First Sexual Experience

Perkins reportedly lost his virginity at thirty-nine to actress
Victoria Principal, but it could have been much earlier, maybe in
the winter of 1951, to a friend, older actress Cynthia Rogers.

✦ Wives

Berinthia "Berry" Berenson, model-actress (and granddaughter
of fashion designer Elsa Schiaparelli)

✦ Did You Know?

Andy Warhol said that in Perkins's "gay" days, he'd pay hustlers
to climb through his window, tie him up, and then "rape" him.

Hot sex tip from Perkins: Fill your mouth with warm water
before fellating a penis. He referred to it as giving someone a "hot
flash."

Perkins was contemplating suing the *National Enquirer* after it
wrote that he had tested positive for the AIDS virus. But he soon
learned that the story was true. Unknown to him, the results of a
blood test he'd taken for Bell's palsy, a facial disorder, were leaked
to the paper, probably by a lab technician. He, in fact, did have
AIDS, and died two years later.

River Phoenix 1970–1993

✦ He Said

I'm the monogamous type. I believe romance is important in sex.

I haven't really fucked a lot of people, five or six.

People just aren't at ease with their sexuality.

I'm so straight I don't eat meat and even my dogs are vegetarians.

The Devil is so pretty and tempting.

✦ They Said

If he loved somebody, male or female, he felt he should check it out. —Suzanne Solgot, friend

This may be the greatest story of lost virginity I've ever heard. —Rob Reiner, director, on hearing how River lost his virginity

He has the look of someone who has secrets. —Peter Weir, director

He really liked getting drunk and high, but he didn't have a gauge for when to stop. —Martha Plimpton, actress

River had a definite fascination with the dark side. —Anthony Campanaro, friend

Lovers, Flings, or Just Friends?

Samantha Mathis, actress (costar in *This Thing Called Love,* '93)

Martha Plimpton, actress (costar in *The Mosquito Coast,* '86)

Suzanne Solgot, rock singer

and a male cast member who played a minor part in *Dogfight* ('91)

✦ First Sexual Experience

River was regularly molested from the time he was four years old until he was about ten by some members of a religious sect. He lost his virginity to an eighteen-year-old female friend of his family. His parents treated the event as very special, setting up a tent in their backyard for River and his love partner.

✦ Wives

Phoenix had not married before his untimely death.

✦ Did You Know?

Phoenix prepared for his role as a street hustler in *My Own Private Idaho* ('91) by getting a little experience himself. He got into the cars of men hunting for sex and dickered for the price of his services with them. There are differences of opinion on whether he ever followed through on any of his sexual business adventures.

Brad Pitt 1963–

✦ He Said

Heartthrobs are a dime a dozen.

My attitude is get it out of your system before you take the plunge.

I'm not about to settle down with one woman. I don't care what they say about me—it's my love life.

It's a long day when you're running around with a patch on your personals. —His view on filming nude scenes

I'm most comfortable in my boxers and wearing my hair natural.

✦ They Said

We all agree he could change a woman's mind. —Lesbian singer Melissa Etheridge, speaking for some of her type of ladies

✦ First Sexual Experience

Probably lost his virginity to a schoolmate at the high school he attended in Springfield, Missouri.

✦ Wives

Pitt has yet to marry.

✦ Did You Know?

Who is Brad's fantasy woman? One tabloid claimed that he's obsessed with Farrah Fawcett, and quoted an unnamed friend as saying that Pitt had an "extensive collection of memorabilia" relating to the actress. How extensive? Well, according to their story, a pair of her underpants is included.

Lovers, Flings, or Just Friends?

Geena Davis, actress (costar in *Thelma and Louise,* '91)

Robin Givens, actress

Juliette Lewis, actress (costar in *Too Young to Die,* '90)

Courtney Love, musician-actress

Shalane McCall, actress

Gwyneth Paltrow, actress (costar in *Seven,* '95)

Jitka Pohlodek, actress

Jill Schoelen, actress (costar in *Cutting Class,* '89)

Uma Thurman, actress

Sidney Poitier 1924–

✦ He Said

I'm an American first and foremost. Then, I'm an actor. Finally, if you like, I'm a Negro.

✦ They Said

An awful lot is expected of that man, and for no reason except that he is black. —Harry Belafonte, singer, actor, and close friend

His whole being was so unashamedly sexual *that I was totally overtaken by the moment.* —Diahann Carroll, actress

✦ First Sexual Experience

Lost his virginity when he was thirteen years old to a woman in her late twenties, to whom he paid some money for sex. She gave him the sex—and also a dose of gonorrhea.

✦ Wives

Juanita Marie Hardy, model-dancer
Joanna Shimkus, actress (costar in *The Lost Man,* '69)

✦ Did You Know?

Poitier had an interesting sexual experience with a chicken when he was a child of less than ten years old. He had already attempted to have a sex with a young female relative near his own age, but failed to achieve an erection. Worried about how he'd ever be able to have sex unless he could get an erection, Poitier tried an experiment. He captured a chicken and took it under his house on Cat Island in the Bahamas. He failed with the chicken, too.

Lovers, Flings, or Just Friends?

Diahann Carroll, actress (costar in *Paris Blues,* '61)
Michelle Clark, airline worker
Anne Gurdine
Y. A. Janey, actress
and a nurse in Philadelphia

Roman Polanski 1933–

✦ He Said

I am widely regarded, I know, as an evil, profligate dwarf. My friends—and the women in my life—know better.

I've never met an intelligent woman who wasn't a castrating bitch.

I have never hidden the fact I love young girls and I will say it once and for all, I love very young girls.

All I was interested in was to fuck a girl and move on. —Reflecting on the period between his first and second marriages

Sometimes I'm charmed by the fact that there are some women with whom you can discuss the molecular theory of light all evening, and at the end they will ask you what is your birth sign.

✦ They Said

The four-foot Pole you wouldn't want to touch with a ten-foot pole. —Kenneth Tynan, critic-writer

He yearns to be the center of attention at all times, jumping up and down to make a point. —Jennifer Lee, actress

I always felt that Roman was exiled because his wife had the bad taste to be murdered in the newspapers. —Jack Nicholson, actor and close friend

✦ First Sexual Experience

Lost his virginity when he was ten years old, to a thirteen-year-old girl, while he was hiding from the Nazis in his native Poland. During their encounter, they knocked over a candle and set fire to the barn where they were having sex.

✦ Wives

Basia (Barbara) Kwiatkowska (a.k.a. Barbara Lass), Polish actress
Sharon Tate, actress
Emmanuelle Seigner, actress (directed her in *Frantic,* '88)

✦ Did You Know?

Did Polanski make videos of himself and wife Sharon Tate making love? Evidently he did, because they surfaced during the aftermath of the investigation into her murder by the Manson Family. Some rumors said that the diminutive director and his wife amused party guests by showing them their amorous carousing.

One former bedmate has said that Polanski was "unhappy with his sexual equipment." She also said that he "was ashamed to be looked at unless he was aroused."

Lovers, Flings, or Just Friends?

Isabelle Adjani, actress

Francesca Annis, actress (directed her in *Macbeth,* '71)

Catherine Deneuve, actress (he directed her in *Repulsion,* '65)

Eva, a Swedish model

Mia Farrow, actress

Fiona, an English actress

Monique Hugot, French actress

Soraya Khashoggi, wife of billionaire Adnan Khashoggi

Nastassja Kinski, actress (he directed her in *Tess,* '80)

Jennifer Lee, actress

Charlotte Lewis, actress (directed her in *Pirates,* '85)

Marina, Duchess della Rovere, Italian nobility

Marisa Mell, actress

Myrna, a Nigerian stewardess

Michelle Phillips, singer-actress

Jane Seymour, actress

and Samantha Gailey, the young lady who said he raped her, which caused him to flee to Europe from the United States during the 1970s

Cole Porter 1891–1964

✦ He Said

They say I'm a practicing homosexual. I say I'm perfect.

Hollywood? It's rather like living on the moon, isn't it?

When I first came here they told me "You'll be so bored, you'll die. Nobody wants to talk about anything but pictures." After a week, I discovered I didn't want to talk about anything else myself.
—Remarking about how he viewed his life in Hollywood

Oh, well, they made me look like Cary Grant—and that was a bonus. —Referring to his ludicrous, sanitized Hollywood film biography (*Night and Day,* '46)

It just goes to show that fifty million Frenchman can't be wrong. They eat horses instead of riding them. —Making light of the horseback-riding accident that shattered his legs and left him in pain for the rest of his life

✦ They Said

He used to describe his sex life in great detail—I think it excited him. —Truman Capote, author and gossip maven

He was extremely polite and affable, but his demeanor made you feel he never heard what you said. —Vincente Minnelli, director

Cole's opening-night behavior is as indecent as that of a bridegroom who has a good time at his own wedding. —Russell Crouse, librettist, joking about how Porter always immensely enjoyed the opening night of his shows

✦ First Sexual Experience
Unknown.

✦ Wives
Linda Lee Thomas, divorcée

✦ Did You Know?
Porter once invited a New York maitre d', a wine expert, who he had heard possessed a legendary endowment and was "available," for a visit, ostensibly to survey Porter's wine cellar. Periodically during their conversation, Porter would place his hand on a different part of the man's anatomy. Each time he did so, the maitre d' would reply matter-of-factly that "it" would cost a certain amount of money. When Porter finally grabbed his visitor's genitals, he was quoted around $2,000. Porter then strolled to his desk and wrote out a check for the original sum he'd agreed upon for the consultation. He handed the check to his visitor with the comment, "Miss Otis regrets she's unable to lunch today."

Lovers, Flings, or Just Friends?

John Vernou "Black Jack" Bouvier III, father of Jacqueline Kennedy and Lee Radziwill

Robert "Bob" Bray, actor

Jack Cassidy, actor

Cary Grant, actor

Leslie A. "Hutch" Hutchison, musician

Ray Kelly, male nurse/companion

Boris Kochno, ballet enthusiast

plus lots of longshoremen, sailors, truck drivers, Hollywood "chorus boys," rough trade types, and male prostitutes supplied by Milton "Doc" Bender, an agent, and Clint Moore, a pimp who ran a notorious male brothel in Harlem staffed by young black men

Dick Powell 1904–1963

✦ He Said

I began with two assets—a voice that didn't drive people into the streets and a determination to make money.

The best thing about being a director is that you don't have to shave or hold your stomach in anymore.

✦ They Said

Dick didn't make much noise about his acting, or his marriage troubles, or even his losing fight with cancer. —Lucille Ball, actress

Failure was a word he did not accept. He couldn't stand the idea of failure. He had to succeed. —June Allyson, actress and spouse

✦ First Sexual Experience

Unknown.

✦ Wives

Mildred Maund, childhood friend
Joan Blondell, actress
June Allyson, actress (costar in *The Reformer and the Redhead,* '50)

✦ Did You Know?

One rumor says that Powell was born without a sphincter, the muscle that controls the bowels. Because he lacked normal control, he was forced to go through life using two alternating doses of medication: One would induce constipation, then, when he was "full," he'd purge himself with laxatives.

William Powell 1892–1984

✦ He Said

You don't marry someone half of America wants to sleep with.

Matrimony, monogamy, seems to be the best system we have evolved out of our occidental civilization: a compromise between sentiment and sex.

A motion picture director is a man who hears no evil, sees no evil, and speaks no evil—of his own work. —An example of Powell's famed Hollywood wit

Money is the aphrodisiac which fate brings you to cloak the pain of living.

✦ They Said

He had a big mouth and quite a sexual appetite. —Bette Davis, actress

The son of a bitch is acting even when he takes his pajamas off. —Carole Lombard, actress and ex-spouse

He was a brilliant actor, a delightful companion, a great friend, and, above all, a true gentleman. —Myrna Loy, frequent costar

He was always modest, good-humored, and a hard worker—invariably one of the best-liked men on the lot. —Adolph Zukor, head of Paramount Pictures

They said if you looked up the word gentleman *in the dictionary, you'd find his picture.* —Fred De Cordova, producer-director

✦ First Sexual Experience

Unknown.

✦ Wives

Eileen Wilson, stage actress
Carole Lombard, actress who was also the third Mrs. Clark Gable
Diana Lewis, starlet

✦ Did You Know?

Always thought of as a dapper and debonair man, Powell cared so little for clothes that he frequently wandered around his home stark naked when he was alone.

Lovers, Flings, or Just Friends?

Bebe Daniels, actress (costar in *Señorita*, '27)

Kay Francis, actress (costar in *Street of Chance*, '30)

Jean Harlow, actress (costar in *Reckless*, '35)

Gertrude Lawrence, actress

Myrna Loy, actress (costar in *The Thin Man*, '34)

Maureen O'Sullivan, actress

Judith Wood, actress

Lovers, Flings, or Just Friends?

Gilmor Brown, theatrical teacher

Noël Coward, entertainer

Joan Crawford, actress

Weldon "Ty" Culhane, actor

Doris Day, actress

Marlene Dietrich, singer-actress (costar in *Witness for the Prosecution*, '57)

Errol Flynn, actor

Eva Gabor, actress

Judy Garland, singer-actress

Edmund Goulding, director (directed him in *Nightmare Alley*, '47)

Betty Grable, actress (costar in *A Yank in the RAF*, '41)

Lorenz Hart, songwriter

Rita Hayworth, actress (costar in *Blood and Sand*, '41)

Sonja Henie, ice skater–actress (costar in *Thin Ice*, '37)

Rock Hudson, actor

Dorothy Kilgallen, columnist

Charles Laughton, actor (costar in *Witness for the Prosecution*, '57)

Mister Blackwell, fashion designer and critic

Eva Perón, actress-dictator

Cesar Romero, actor (costar in *Captain From Castile*, '47)

Robert Taylor, actor

Lana Turner, actress

Loretta Young, actress (costar in *Suez*, '38)

Tyrone Power 1913–1958

✦ He Said

Why frustrate people? If I'm feeling horny at the time and I like them, I'll oblige them. —Answering Henry Fonda's query on why he was reputed to have round heels

Couldn't get away from them, caught, always caught. I paid gladly to get out of their grasping clutches, but it still hurts my guts, when I think that I'm fucking well furnishing houses all over the world which I shall never live in, not even visit; and I'm keeping their lovers as well. —Reflecting on his divorces, and how he paid for them

For anyone truly interested in the theater [like me], it's a tragedy to be born handsome.

✦ They Said

Miss Roundheels. —George Sanders, costar in *Solomon and Sheba* ('59), nastily nicknaming Power

As heterosexual as you might be, it was impossible to be totally impervious to that kind of charm. —Billy Wilder, musing on how Power affected even straight men

There were two reasons: First, he never asked me, and, second, he liked boys too much. —Alice Faye, actress, on why she never married Tyrone Power

✦ First Sexual Experience

Unknown.

✦ Wives

Annabella, French actress (costar in *Suez*, '38)

Linda Christian, actress

Deborah Minardos, actress

✦ Did You Know?

Henry Fonda joked that Power's death by heart attack (while filming *Solomon and Sheba*, '59) was probably caused by costar (and fellow bisexual) George Sanders wearing him out in the sack as well as on the set. Sanders was not amused and delivered a withering comment about Fonda's own sexuality.

One European version of *Hollywood Babylon* suggested that Power like to indulge in coprophagia (feces eating). His longtime "trick" Smitty Hanson says it isn't so. "Ty was never way out in what he wanted to do." He also believes that Power was basically a homosexual who "married girls from time to time."

Otto Preminger 1906–1986

✦ He Said

I have a reputation with women which is not entirely deserved, though it is true that I had my share of them, some of them stars.

I am the man with no hair who shoves around the people with hair.

I am not a difficult man. I am a misunderstood man.

✦ They Said

A very difficult and unreasonable man. I thank God that neither I nor any member of my family will ever be so hard up that we will have to work for Otto Preminger. —Lana Turner, who dropped out of his film *Anatomy of a Murder* ('59)

Otto had the sense of humor of a guillotine. —Vincent Price, actor

He loves to embarrass actors in front of other people to tear down their egos. He's only happy if everyone else is miserable. Still, if you can keep his paranoia from beating you down, you can learn a lot from the guy. —Michael Caine, who was directed by Preminger in *Hurry, Sundown* ('67)

✦ First Sexual Experience

Lost his virginity at age fourteen to a similarly aged young lady he met in dancing class. The duo studied an anatomy textbook in order to discover how to have sex, because, as he said, "It is not easy for two virgins to determine where all the limbs go."

✦ Wives

Marion Mill, Hungarian actress
Mary Gardiner, divorcée
Hope Bryce, model–fashion designer

✦ Did You Know?

Preminger took LSD with famed drug guru Timothy Leary. He did it for research on a possible film he was considering about young people and the drug.

Preminger's family, who were Jewish, fled Austria and came to the United States when the Nazis took over their country. Special circumstances were needed to extend their visitors' visas, when Tallulah Bankhead stepped in to help. She persuaded her father and uncle—speaker of the U.S. House of Representatives and senator from Alabama, respectively—to sponsor a private bill permitting the Premingers to stay in the United States.

Lovers, Flings, or Just Friends?

Dorothy Dandridge, actress (directed her in *Carmen Jones*, '54)

Marlene Dietrich, singer-actress

Hedy Lamarr, actress

Gypsy Rose Lee, stripper

plus many, many tall, long-legged Hollywood beauties

Lovers, Flings, or Just Friends?

Nick Adams, actor

Ginger Alden, actress

Ann-Margret, singer-actress (costar in *Viva Las Vegas*, '64)

Carol Connors, songwriter

Jackie DeShannon, singer-songwriter

Diana Dors, actress

Doris Duke, tobacco heiress

Anne Helm, actress (costar in *Follow That Dream*, '62)

Peggy Lipton, actress

Phyllis McGuire, singer

Jayne Mansfield, actress

Mary Ann Mobley, actress (costar in *Harum Scarum*, '65)

Joanna Moore, actress

Rita Moreno, actress

Gladys Presley, mother

Juliet Prowse, dancer

Cybill Shepherd, actress

Nancy Sinatra, actress

Connie Stevens, actress

Tempest Storm, stripper

Barbra Streisand, singer-actress

Mamie Van Doren, actress

Deborah Walley, actress

Tuesday Weld, actress

Natalie Wood, actress

plus probably thousands of girls and women from all walks of life he met in various situations, especially since he told his stepmother that he'd slept with more than 1,000 women *before* his marriage

Elvis Presley 1935–1977

✦ He Said

You had your chance. —Presley's standard put-down line to any woman who rejected him and later tried to get back into his favor

If my aunt had nuts, she'd be my uncle. —A frequently repeated sample of Presley's wit

I'm gone to take a shit, honey. —His final words before his death in a bathroom

A show really wears me out, but if I get to 'em, that's what really counts.

✦ They Said

He was a very sexual man, but I truly believe in the beginning it wasn't meant to be sexual, it just was because that was the way he felt when he played. —Barbara Eden, actress

Elvis Presley wound up looking on the outside like what he was on the inside—an overrated slob. —Joan Blondell, actress

He never contributed a damn thing to music! —Bing Crosby, singer-actor

✦ First Sexual Experience

He lost his virginity to Laura, a woman he met in Hernando's Hideaway, a seedy Memphis clip joint.

✦ Wives

Priscilla Ann Beaulieu, student

✦ Did You Know?

Elvis wasn't all that fond of penetration. He was uncircumcised and often his foreskin would tear, causing him to bleed.

Elvis had an erotic fetish for women in white panties. When he undressed a woman, he always hoped she was wearing white panties. The sight of pubic hairs peeping and curling underneath white panties was his ultimate sexual excitement.

Elvis loathed making love to a woman who had borne a child. For him, such a woman was almost a complete turnoff. After Priscilla became pregnant, he ceased having sexual relations with her and didn't resume after the birth of their child.

Want to see Elvis with an erection? Then watch *Girls! Girls! Girls!* ('62). Look for the scene where he's singing and dancing in an apartment with costar Laurel Goodwin. He's wearing black pants. Notice his pants very, very carefully and you'll see that Elvis is sporting an erection during the latter part of the scene.

Richard Pryor 1940–

✦ He Said

I used to jack off so much, I knew pussy couldn't be as good as my hand.

When a man hits a woman one of two things happens: either she hauls ass in the opposite direction or she becomes yours.

This one woman let me give her head, which was a revelation, something that changed my life, because until then, my family only fucked in one position—up and down.

I want people to be able to recognize me by just looking at a caricature of me that has no name on it.

✦ They Said

Boy, don't you ever kiss no pussy. I mean that. Whatever you do in life, don't kiss no pussy. —Advice Pryor claimed an uncle gave him

Very often when people rise they forget their roots. Richard has never forgotten. There is something about him that is exemplary and unusual. —Juliette Whittaker, one of his early teachers

✦ First Sexual Experience

Pryor lost his virginity in his teens to a girl he said reminded him of Ava Gardner.

✦ Wives

An early marriage
Shelley Bonus, heiress
Deborah McGuire, model-actress
Jennifer Lee, actress
Flynn BeLaine
Flynn BeLaine

✦ Did You Know?

Maybe one reason Pryor has disparaged gays is because at six years old he was forced to give a teenage boy a blowjob. He had another, more pleasurable session with a man later in life, however. He spent two weeks having sex with a transvestite named Mitrasha.

Both Pryor's mother and his grandmother ran whorehouses in Peoria, Illinois.

Entertainer Rudy Vallee was responsible for giving Pryor's career its first national television exposure. He hired the comic in 1964 to appear on his program *On Broadway Tonight*.

Pryor said that when his fling with actress Margot Kidder ran out, she cut up all the clothes in his closet.

Lovers, Flings, or Just Friends?

Pam Grier, actress (costar in *Greased Lightning*, '77)

Margot Kidder, actress (costar in *Some Kind of Hero*, '82)

Geraldine Mason, actress

Lucy Saroyan, daughter of author William Saroyan

Maxine Silverman, legal secretary

Lovers, Flings, or Just Friends?

Suzan Ball, actress (costar in *City Beneath the Sea*, '53)

Kathy Benvin, personal secretary

Ingrid Bergman, actress (costar in *A Walk in the Spring Rain*, '69)

Claire Bloom, actress

George Cukor, director

Rita Hayworth, actress (costar in *Blood and Sand*, '41)

Virginia Hill, mobster moll and close friend of Bugsy Siegel

Evelyn Keyes, actress

Margaret Leighton, actress

Pia Lindstrom, daughter of Ingrid Bergman

Carole Lombard, actress

Maureen O'Hara, actress (costar in *Sinbad the Sailor*, '47)

Dominique Sanda, actress (costar in *The Inheritance*, '75)

Barbara Steele, horror film queen

Inger Stevens, actress (costar in *A Dream of Kings*, '69)

Estelle Taylor, actress

Viviane Ventura, actress-author

Ruth Warrick, actress

Mae West, actress

Shelley Winters, actress

Anthony Quinn 1915–

✦ He said

If there was not a young starlet, or a companionable makeup girl, there was always a lovely local lady to take her place beside me in bed.

I've never really felt a man's masculinity was in his penis.

✦ They Said

There was simply too much of Tony. Yes, down there, too.
—Evelyn Keyes, actress

"I want to impregnate every woman in the world" he once told me, though I didn't realize till later how literally he meant it. —Ruth Warrick, actress

Women can understand why Tony is so easy to fall in love with. He is the perfect embodiment of the virile man that all women subconsciously seek. —Inger Stevens, actress

✦ First Sexual Experience

When he was fourteen, a girl three or four years older fellated him to climax at Seal Beach. Quinn had passed out from drinking homemade beer and awoke while she was licking his penis. He pretended to be asleep, but climaxed in her mouth. Two years later, he was seduced by a woman in her mid-twenties he had partnered in a dance contest.

✦ Wives

Katherine De Mille, daughter of director Cecil B. De Mille
Jolanda Addolari, wardrobe mistress

✦ Did You Know?

Quinn fathered his latest child in 1993—at age seventy-eight—with a woman reported to be his secretary. He had already fathered four children by his first wife, three by his second, and three others by various other women, according to the *New York Times*.

George Raft 1903–1980

✦ He Said

I could have been the first X-rated dancer. I was very erotic. I used to caress myself as I danced.

The cops questioned me whenever somebody lost an umbrella.
—Commenting on how the police perceived his ties to gangsters

✦ They Said

George was probably a latent homosexual. —Betty Grable, who claimed that her later affair with Raft was chaste—he never touched her except to beat her up

Screwing was his only game. He could get up in the morning and put in a whole day at it. He was a sports-screwer. For year after year after year, George averaged two different women a day. —Mack Grey, longtime close friend

The Black Snake —Sexual nickname given to Raft by many of the starlets and hookers he went to bed with

George had a certain unique look—and he kept it in most of his movies. —Howard Hawks, who directed Raft in *Scarface: Shame of a Nation* ('32)

✦ First Sexual Experience

Lost his virginity at age twelve to an attractive nurse who was about seven years older, on a sofa in the cellar under the stoop of his family's apartment house. George has said, "She was a pretty good teacher, and I must have been a good student."

✦ Wives

Grayce Mulrooney, social worker

✦ Did You Know?

Raft used to work as a gigolo-dancer, along with Rudolph Valentino, in what were called "tea rooms." Female patrons would be served tea, then discreetly choose one of the men to dance with them. In many cases, the dancing led to greater intimacies. In recalling those days Raft said, "I had affairs and slept with a lot of women." He was so popular, one woman fell in love with him and finally stabbed him because he was being "unfaithful" to her.

Lovers, Flings, or Just Friends?

Lucille Ball, actress

Marlene Dietrich, singer-actress (costar in *Manpower*, '41)

Billie Dove, actress

Ann Dvorak, actress (costar in *Scarface*, '32)

Hilda Ferguson, Ziegfeld showgirl

Betty Furness, actress

Betty Grable, actress

Texas Guinan, nightclub owner

Virginia Hill, mobster moll

Marjorie King, actress

Winnie Lightner, singer-dancer (costar in *Gold Diggers of 1933*, '33)

Carole Lombard, actress (costar in *Bolero*, '34)

Lee Marquis, singer

Helen Morgan, torch singer

Liz Renay, model

Norma Shearer, actress

Ann Sheridan, actress

Lana Turner, actress

Mae West, actress (costar in *Night After Night*, '32)

plus hundreds of hookers, showgirls, and women served during a period he worked as a gigolo

Lovers, Flings, or Just Friends?

Jean Abrams (Evans), writer

Joan Crawford, actress (directed her in *Johnny Guitar,* '54)

James Dean, actor (directed him in *Rebel Without a Cause,* '55)

Connie Ernst, actress

Libby Holman, singer

Leslie Levinson, dancer-actress

Jayne Mansfield, actress

Marilyn Monroe, actress

Natalie Wood, actress (directed her in *Rebel Without a Cause,* '55)

Nicholas Ray 1911–1979

✦ He Said
You can only learn filmmaking by making films.

✦ They Said
He was a potential homosexual with a deep, passionate, and constant need for female love in his life. This made him attractive to women, for whom the chance to save him from his own self-destructive habits proved an irresistible attraction. —John Houseman, actor-producer

Every time I've seen him in my whole life, I always wondered if he wasn't just about ready to crack up. —Robert Parrish, director

I want you to know that Nicholas Ray is a drunkard and you should never employ him. —Paul Graetz, financier-producer, after working with Ray on *Bitter Victory* ('57)

✦ First Sexual Experience
Unknown.

✦ Wives
Gloria Grahame, actress
Elizabeth Utey, actress
Susan Schwartz, student

✦ Did You Know?
Ray was a heroin addict, who also liked to shoot speed, smoke hash, take LSD, and snort coke, in addition to consuming vast quantities of alcohol.

Ray was fascinated by pornographic films, in which he "discovered" Marilyn Chambers. He thought she was a great actress and fitfully made plans to star her in a large-budget, high-scale porno epic.

Ronald Reagan 1911–

✦ He Said

In my early Hollywood days I was too busy and too scared to collect phone numbers.

I think that some of our less stable glamour peddlers with a frequent repeat pattern have given the public an impression that it isn't tragic here. —Remarking on how some people in Hollywood divorce frequently with no apparent damage

✦ They Said

He's about as good in bed as he was on the screen. —Jane Wyman, actress and ex-spouse

I can't stand the sight of Ronnie Reagan. I'd like to stick my Oscar up his arse. —Gloria Grahame, Oscar winner for Best Supporting Actress in *The Bad and the Beautiful* ('52)

This would never have happened if Hollywood had given him better parts. —Lauren Bacall, on the eve of his inauguration

Of course not. I said I've known him for a long time. —Richard Widmark, answering if he'd voted for Reagan for president

Jane Wyman seemed more upset with her husband's obsession with politics than I. I tried to make her laugh. "He'll outgrow it," I told her. —June Allyson, whose husband Dick Powell was also interested in Republican politics

Don't ask Ronnie what time it is because he will tell you how a watch is made. —Jane Wyman

✦ First Sexual Experience

Unknown, but probably lost his virginity while attending Eureka College.

✦ Wives

Jane Wyman, actress (costar in *Tugboat Annie Sails Again*, '40)
Nancy Davis, actress (costar in *Hellcats of the Navy*, '57)

✦ Did You Know?

In his autobiography *Where's the Rest of Me*, Reagan only mentions first wife Jane Wyman by name three times. He dedicated the book "To Honey with Love," meaning presumably second wife, Nancy Davis "Mommie" Reagan.

When rumors started that wife Jane Wyman was having an affair with her costar Lew Ayres (*Johnny Belinda*, '48), Reagan actually seemed to condone it, saying, "Jane very much needs to have a fling and I intend to let her have it."

Lovers, Flings, or Just Friends?

Ila Davis, actress (costar in *Secret Service of the Air*, '39)
Doris Day, actress (costar in *Storm Warning*, '51)
Penny Edwards, actress
Susan Hayward, actress
Adele Jurgens, actress
Evelyn Knight, actress
Christine Larson, actress
Piper Laurie, actress
Monica Lewis, actress
Doris Lilly, author-columnist
Jacqueline Park, starlet
Ruth Roman, actress
Dorothy Shay, actress
Ann Sothern, actress
Kay Stewart, actress
Peggy Stewart, actress
June Travis, actress (costar in *Love Is on the Air*, '37)
Betty Underwood, model
Selene Walters, actress

Robert Redford 1937–

✦ He Said

Of course I like women, but I'm not interested in loveless sex or sexless love.

I don't feel that I might have missed something. I did all my fooling around as a teenager.

All my life I've been dogged by guilt because I feel there is this difference between the way I look and the way I feel inside.

I can't stand confinement. I don't like people who are too devoted, imposing, and tying as friends. I feel most comfortable in relationships that leave you free.

✦ They Said

He's even more handsome in the flesh, but he's such a normal man, not like a movie star. —Melanie Griffith, actress

I could watch him simply filling in tax forms for hours on end. —Marlene Dietrich, singer-actress

Robert Redford's the very best kisser I ever met. —Meryl Streep, actress, who was bussed by him in *Out of Africa* ('85)

Well, at least he has finally found his true love—what a pity he can't marry himself. —Frank Sinatra, singer-actor

Redford does not want to be an actor, he wants to be a movie star. —Arthur Laurents, who worked briefly on *The Way We Were* ('73)

Redford is a dangerous man to let loose on the streets. He has holes in his head and should be arrested. —George Roy Hill, who directed him in *Butch Cassidy and the Sundance Kid* ('69)

✦ First Sexual Experience
Unknown.

✦ Wives
Lola Van Wagenen, student

✦ Did You Know?
Redford once successfully prevented the Lorillard Tobacco Company from issuing a new cigarette with the brand name of Redford.

When Redford was nineteen, he was in a Rome nightclub on New Year's Eve, where he spotted Ava Gardner. He decided that at midnight he'd go to her table and try to get a kiss. He finally got up his courage and approached her table. Suddenly, Gardner looked up, said, "Happy New Year, soldier," then pulled him down for a kiss.

Lovers, Flings, or Just Friends?

Kim Basinger, actress (costar in *The Natural*, '84)

Sonia Braga, actress (directed her in *The Milagro Beanfield War*, '88)

Kathy O'Rear, costume designer

Barbra Streisand, actress-singer (costar in *The Way We Were*, '73)

Burt Reynolds 1936–

✦ He Said

I'm not a superstud, though I'm labeled as one. The reason I get myself into these kinds of situations is because I talk too much.

I believe in good marriages. I also believe in the tooth fairy.

Posing nude for Cosmopolitan *was calculated. I couldn't do that now, but when I first started being noticed, I realized I'd have to develop a character the public would buy.*

When I die, what they're going to write on my tombstone is: Here Lies Burt Reynolds, The First Guy to Pose Nude in a Magazine.

I can go for years with a woman, then suddenly I run out of steam and I can't go any further. I try, but I can't remain friends. When I think of the real love of my life, I treasure the memories. But I wasn't meant to be with one person for the rest of my days.

✦ They Said

Burt and I are too much alike to be involved. We both wear wigs and high heels, and we both have a roll around the middle. —Dolly Parton, singer-actress

It's true, he has the most divine little ass. —Judy Carne, actress and former spouse

A toupee and lifts—the man's an impostor. —Sarah Miles, actress

At first he would get angry and only push me around. Next he started slapping me and then finally actually punching me. —Judy Carne

✦ First Sexual Experience

Lost his virginity when he was fourteen to a wealthy, much older woman in Palm Beach, Florida, who owned a store he frequented.

✦ Wives

Judy Carne, actress
Loni Anderson, actress

✦ Did You Know?

During an interview with then-girlfriend Sally Field, Oprah Winfrey asked the actress if Reynolds wore his toupee while lovemaking. The actress laughed, but didn't reveal the answer.

Burt Reynolds wasn't the first choice for the now-famous *Cosmopolitan* centerfold, he was just the first to realize what a positive impact posing might have on his career. Rumors say the men who declined the honor included Joe Namath, Steve McQueen, and Clint Eastwood.

Lovers, Flings, or Just Friends?

Lucie Arnaz, actress

Adrienne Barbeau, actress

Kim Basinger, actress (costar in *The Man Who Loved Women*, '83)

Candice Bergen, actress (costar in *Starting Over*, '79)

Susan Clark, actress

Jill Clayburgh, actress (costar in *Semi-Tough*, '77)

Catherine Deneuve, actress (costar in *Hustle*, '76)

Lesley-Anne Down, actress (costar in *Rough Cut*, '80)

Chris Evert, tennis pro

Farrah Fawcett, actress (costar in *Cannonball Run*, '81)

Sally Field, actress (costar in *Smokey and the Bandit*, '77)

Marilu Henner, actress (costar in *The Man Who Loved Women*, '83)

Lauren Hutton, model-actress

Madeline Kahn, actress (costar in *At Long Last Love*, '75)

Lorna Luft, singer

Sarah Miles, actress

Dolly Parton, singer-actress

Pam Seals, Florida cocktail waitress

Cybill Shepherd, actress

Dinah Shore, singer-actress

Elizabeth Taylor, actress

Mamie Van Doren, actress

Tammy Wynette, singer

Paul Robeson 1898–1976

✦ He Said

The white man has made a fetish of intellect and worships the God of thought; the Negro feels rather than thinks.

I came up an idealist, interested in human values, certain all races, all peoples are not nearly as different one from the other as textbooks would have it.

✦ They Said

Paul was adored by all the women he ever met. Women absolutely swooned over Paul. Paul was pursued, and sometimes caught. —Anthony Salemmé, sculptor, who sculpted a nine-foot nude statue of Robeson

✦ First Sexual Experience

Unknown.

✦ Wives

Eslanda Cardozo Goode, pathology technician

✦ Did You Know?

While Robeson and Uta Hagen were conducting their affair, she was married to actor José Ferrer. Ferrer maintained a gentle calm about their relationship, even whistling loudly outside the door to rooms the couple occupied to alert them he was about to enter. During this period, Hagen also slept with Ferrer and managed to become pregnant by him. When Robeson discovered that fact, he hit Hagen, probably causing her a miscarriage.

Lovers, Flings, or Just Friends?

Peggy Ashcroft, British actress

Louise Bransten, socialite–left-wing activist

Nilla Cook, young actress with the Provincetown Playhouse Players

Nancy Cunard, British heiress

Freda Diamond, young daughter of a revolutionary family

Emma Goldman, anarchist

Uta Hagen, actress

Nora Holt (Ray), singer

Lena Horne, singer-actress

Yolande Jackson, British actress

Nina Mae McKinney, actress (costar in *Sanders of the River,* '35)

Edwina Mountbatten, Prince Phillip's aunt

Geraldine Maimie Neale, student

Betty Salemmé, sculptor's wife

Mrs. Niles Spencer, artist's wife

Edward G. Robinson 1893–1973

✦ He Said

My whole life has been lived for women, and I've never ceased being frightened by them. They have a weapon against which there is no defense—unpredictability.

If I were a little bit taller and I was a little more handsome or something like that, I could have played all the roles that I have played and played many more.

Some people have youth, others beauty. I have menace.

Most people don't live. They worry about the afterlife and they haven't really lived here.

✦ They Said

I'm not a trained psychologist, but I don't think Eddie was very sexually oriented. —Aben Kandell, screenwriter

Eddie's attack, his vigor, his electric energy, made you forget he was a small and ugly man. —Hal Wallis, producer

He turned into a great star overnight. —Jack L. Warner, referring to Robinson's appearance in *Little Caesar* ('30)

He was a genius in everything he did. —Mervyn LeRoy, producer

✦ First Sexual Experience

Lost his virginity when he was about twenty years old to an unknown female.

✦ Wives

Gladys Cassell Lloyd, divorcée-actress
Jane Bodenheimer Adler, fashion director

✦ Did You Know?

Robinson's home was the typical palatial Hollywood estate, with one exception—he didn't have a swimming pool because he had a dreadful fear of water. Why? His son, Edward Jr., at age seven had tried to drown his mother, Robinson's first wife.

Robinson was one of the celebrity contestants who appeared on the scandal-tinged television quiz show *The $64,000 Question*. His category: art. His opponent: Vincent Price.

Lovers, Flings, or Just Friends?

Mrs. Leslie Carter, actress

Marlene Dietrich, singer-actress

Bessie Mona Lasky, artist and wife of studio head Jesse Lasky

Lupe Velez, actress (costar in *East Is West*, '30)

Mickey Rooney 1920–

✦ He Said

I had money in my jeans. If I wanted to get laid, I just went out and got laid, with no romantic illusions.

I'm the only man who has a marriage license made out "To Whom It May Concern."

I was a fourteen-year-old boy for thirty years.

✦ They Said

You're Andy Hardy! You're the United States! You're the Stars and Stripes! Behave yourself! You're a symbol! —Louis B. Mayer, shouting at Rooney, after finding out that his sixteen-year-old star was having an affair with thirty-six-year-old Norma Shearer, widow of MGM wunderkind Irving Thalberg

If you ever knock me up, you little son of a bitch, I'll kill you. —Ava Gardner, determined not to get pregnant by Rooney

He never got over her. I think that's why he got married so many times. He was always looking for another one just like Ava. —Jimmy Cook, army buddy and friend, speaking about Ava Gardner

✦ First Sexual Experience

Lost his virginity at age ten to an eleven year old named Ann he knew from Vine Street Elementary School in Los Angeles.

✦ Wives

Ava Gardner, actress
Betty Jane Rase, Miss Alabama 1944
Martha Vickers, actress
Elaine Mahnken, actress–beauty queen
Barbara Ann Thomason, model
Margie Lane, realtor
Carolyn Hockett, secretary
Jan Chamberlin, singer

✦ Did You Know?

While he was in the army and separated from Ava Gardner, Rooney once went AWOL. He heard that Ava was "dating" Howard Hughes, so he left Fort Riley, Kansas, and flew back to Los Angeles. When he arrived in California, MPs were waiting to take him back. MGM interceded and was able to use its influence to have desertion charges dropped and keep the incident covered up.

Lovers, Flings, or Just Friends?

Kay Brown, starlet

Gloria DeHaven, actress

Diane Garrett, starlet

Betty Grable, actress

Jeri Green, actress

Peggy Lloyd, daughter of comedian Harold Lloyd

Erin O'Brien, actress

Norma Shearer, actress

Tempest Storm, stripper

Gene Tierney, actress

Lana Turner, actress (costar in *Love Finds Andy Hardy,* '38)

Martha Vickers, actress

and a DuPont heiress, who told him in her upper-crust accent, "I love your bools [balls]"

and sixteen Japanese women in an orgy with actor Donald "Red" Barry

plus many, many other women

Billy Rose 1899–1966

✦ He Said

Maybe I ain't cut out to be a husband, but I'm a sucker for the best two-dollar buy in town—a marriage license.

✦ They Said

An animated slime. —Tallulah Bankhead, actress

Billy always manages to let you know what enormous income taxes he is paying, how gifted he is, how altogether attractive he is. —Clifford Odets, playwright-screenwriter

What's Billy up to these days? Answer: My waist. —Common joke around Broadway during the diminutive showman's heyday

✦ First Sexual Experience

Unknown.

✦ Wives

Fannie Brice, comedienne-actress
Eleanor Holm, Olympic swimmer
Joyce Mathews, who had already married and divorced Milton Berle twice
Joyce Mathews
Doris Warner LeRoy Vidor, divorcée

✦ Did You Know?

Rose, who was sharing the charms of a young lady with a fellow producer, once negotiated a most unusual deal. Although exceptionally beautiful, the woman had small breasts. He arranged and paid for an operation to enlarge them, but on completion of the surgery began brooding. He had paid for all the expense, yet he was only enjoying half her time. He phoned the other gentleman friend, explained how he felt, and ended up convincing the other man to pay for half of the operation. The way Rose looked at the situation, since they shared her, each one should pay for one breast.

Lovers, Flings, or Just Friends?

Dorothy Appleby, actress
Joan Crawford, actress
Gloria DeHaven, actress
Rhonda Fleming, actress
Gypsy Rose Lee, stripper
Rikki Olander, muralist
Monique Van Vooren, entertainer
and lots and lots of his showgirls

Lovers, Flings, or Just Friends?

Joan Crawford, actress
Dolores Del Rio, actress
Brenda Frazier, socialite
Zsa Zsa Gabor, actress
Ava Gardner, actress
Susan Hayward, actress
Eartha Kitt, singer-actress
Veronica Lake, actress
Patricia Kennedy Lawford, presidential sister
Manouche, French restaurant owner
Jayne Mansfield, actress
Marilyn Monroe, actress
Kim Novak, actress
Athina "Tina" Onassis, wife of Aristotle Onassis
Soraya Esfandiary Pahlavi, ex-wife of Iran's Shah
Eva Perón, actress-dictator
and hundreds, probably thousands, of other women ranging from chambermaids to the upper crust of international society and royalty

Porfirio Rubirosa 1909–1965

✦ He Said

I consider a day in which I make love only once as virtually wasted.

I do not boast of my conquests. I never reveal what you might call bedroom secrets.

Never paw a woman. A woman does not like to be pawed. She likes to be—ah, liked.

✦ They Said

It was the most magnificent penis that I had ever seen. —Doris Duke, heiress and third spouse

It was long and pointed and it hurt. It was never hard and never soft. It was nothing for Rubi to take on two or three women in a night. By late at night when he was good and drunk, he didn't give a damn what kind of legs were opening. —Manouche, friend

It looks like Yul Brynner in a black turtleneck sweater. —Jerome Zerbe, society photographer, supposedly quipping about Rubi's love equipment

✦ First Sexual Experience

Unknown.

✦ Wives

Flor de Oro Trujillo, daughter of Dominican Republic dictator Trujillo
Danielle Darrieux, French actress
Doris Duke, tobacco heiress
Barbara Hutton, Woolworth heiress
Odile Rodin (Odile Bérard), French starlet

✦ Did You Know?

Rubirosa, according to those who saw him, was described as possessing a sex organ that was "eleven inches long and thick as a beer can." His fame was so great in Paris that in restaurants throughout the city, giant peppermills were commonly called Rubirosas. Many wits among the city's society dubbed him Rubber Hosa.

A drunk once asked him at a urinal how large his equipment became when it was erect. Rubirosa replied, "I really don't know. It takes so much blood to get it up, I always pass out." Those who know have said that it was six inches in circumference, not diameter, as others have reported. Rubi could balance a chair with a telephone book on it on the tip of his erection. For virility he drank Japanese mushroom tea.

George Sanders 1906–1972

✦ He Said

I don't like nightclubs, and I don't like women. They bore me.

Hollywood girls are too beautiful—so beautiful you can't actually believe that they are real. And how in the world could a person fall in love with anyone who is unbelievable?

There's no greater aphrodisiac than money.

I find it so pleasant to be unpleasant.

I was beastly but I was never coarse.

Dear World, I am leaving because I am bored. I feel I have lived long enough. I am leaving you with your worries in this sweet cesspool. —Sanders's suicide note

✦ They Said

He had the best legs in Hollywood—of which he was very proud. He was careful to keep them in good shape. —Diana de Rosso, writer

George Sanders has always been my ideal. I've always admired his looks, his acting, and have always wanted to be like him. —Clint Eastwood, supposedly, to Zsa Zsa Gabor

He was ashamed of being an actor. —Zsa Zsa Gabor

✦ First Sexual Experience
Unknown.

✦ Wives
Susan Larson (Elsie Poole), actress
Zsa Zsa Gabor, actress (costar in *Death of a Scoundrel,* '56)
Benita Hume Colman, widow of actor Ronald Colman
Magda Gabor, older sister of Zsa Zsa Gabor

✦ Did You Know?
As a young man in Chile, Sanders fought a duel and wounded his opponent, which resulted in his being expelled from the country. It seems he was caught in bed with his landlady, an attractive widow, by her fiancé, who instigated the duel.

Lovers, Flings, or Just Friends?

Lucille Ball, actress (costar in *Lured,* '47)

Lorraine Chanel, Mexican actress

Dolores Del Rio, actress (costar in *Lancer Spy,* '37)

Doris Duke, tobacco heiress

Hedy Lamarr, actress (costar in *The Strange Woman,* '46)

Helga Maray, author

Marilyn Monroe, actress

Gene Tierney, actress (costar in *Sundown,* '41)

plus lots of other women, about whom Sanders kept very quiet

Arnold Schwarzenegger 1947–

✦ He Said

If you told me that if I ate a kilo of shit I would put on muscles, I would eat it. —Remark attributed to him while describing his early enthusiasm for bodybuilding

A lot of people think we are homosexuals because we attract them. Because to them, you know, we are heaven. —Commenting on some people's attitude toward bodybuilders

When a homosexual looks at a bodybuilder, I don't have anything against that. If I see a girl with big tits, I'm going to stare and stare.

Many times when I was getting laid, in my head I was doing a business deal.

Good things don't happen by coincidence. Every dream carries with it certain risks, especially the risk of failure.

✦ They Said

Arnold Schwarzenegger looks like a condom full of walnuts. —Clive James, author-critic

Waiting for Arnold to win an Oscar is like leaving the porch light on for Jimmy Hoffa. —Milton Berle, comedian

Charming, he's simply charming. —Diana Vreeland, *Vogue* magazine's doyenne of fashion and good taste

Arnold was a great lover. —Sue Maray, former lover

✦ First Sexual Experience
Unknown.

✦ Wives
Maria Shriver, telejournalist and Kennedy family member

✦ Did You Know?
In 1976 Arnold supposedly agreed to appear nude in a *Cosmopolitan* centerfold. He posed for the photographs, then changed his mind.

What technique did Arnold use to charm women into sleeping with him when he was a bachelor? According to friends, he'd approach any female who caught his fancy and simply say, "I want to fuck you."

Lovers, Flings, or Just Friends?

Dianne Bennett, publisher of *Bodybuilder*

Sally Kirkland, actress

Sue Maray, hairstylist

Brigitte Nielsen, actress (costar in *Red Sonja*, '85)

Barbara Outland, student-waitress

and lots and lots of other women

George C. Scott 1927–1999

✦ He Said

I became an actor to escape my personality.

The biggest mistake an actor can make is to try and resolve all the differences between himself and the characters he plays.

✦ They Said

George C. Scott. Fine actor. Big drinker. Wife beater. What else would you like to know? —Colleen Dewhurst, actress and ex-spouse

One of the best actors alive. But my opinion of him as an actor is much higher than my opinion of him as a man. —John Huston, director

✦ First Sexual Experience

Unknown.

✦ Wives

Carolyn Hughes
Patricia Reed
Colleen Dewhurst, actress
Colleen Dewhurst, actress
Trish Van Devere, actress (costar in *The Savage Is Loose*, '74)

✦ Did You Know?

Scott's nose was broken at least five times—all in barroom brawls.

Lovers, Flings, or Just Friends?

Ava Gardner, actress (costar in *The Bible*, '66)

Randolph Scott 1898–1987

✦ He Said

If a man is for men, and it's in most walks of life, I can buy that.
—Inarticulate rambling about homosexuality

I suppose I was good-looking—not spectacular.

I'm not a good person to ask about today's movies because I don't go to them.

✦ They Said

He looks like an Adonis. —L. B. Mayer, on first seeing Scott's screen test

Randolph Scott was tall, blond, and handsome. Who cares if he was Cary Grant's better half or not? —Anne Baxter, actress

He's a gentleman. And so far he's the only one I've met in this business of self-promoting sons of bitches. —Michael Curtiz, director

God! The man's an ignoramus. —Margaret Sullavan, actress and costar in *So Red the Rose* ('35)

Randy Scott was a gentleman and nothing like most Western stars. —Sam Peckinpah, director

✦ First Sexual Experience
Unknown.

✦ Wives
Marion (Mariana) DuPont Somerville, heiress
Marie Patricia Stillman, heiress

✦ Did You Know?
During the period in the early 1930s when Scott and Cary Grant were living together as a "couple," they both went through unusual marriages. First, Cary married Virginia Cherrill, then he went "back" to Scott, who in the meantime had also married. So, Grant moved into a house right next door to the newlywed Randolph Scotts. A year later, Scott divorced his wife and moved back into a house with Cary. Scott and Grant ended up living together for almost ten years.

Lovers, Flings, or Just Friends?

Wendy Barrie, actress
Virginia Cherrill, actress
Gary Cooper, actor
Vivienne Gay, actress
Cary Grant, actor
Howard Hughes, aviation and cinema mogul
Dorothy Lamour, actress
Mister Blackwell, fashion designer and critic
Margaret Sullavan, actress (costar in *So Red the Rose*, '35)
Lupe Velez, actress

Tom Selleck 1945–

✦ He Said

It isn't antigay to say you are heterosexual.

I was an awkward kid. I discovered that I liked girls, but I was too shy to let them know it.

✦ They Said

He genuinely seems to like women. For an actor, that's rare. —Bess Armstrong, actress

He's the biggest Boy Scout in America. —John Hillerman, actor and costar in his first television series

At thirty-six, he's got the body of an NFL linebacker and the head of a Viking sea lord. . . . His dimples could hold a split of champagne apiece. —*People* magazine

✦ First Sexual Experience

Unknown for certain, but Selleck has said, "I was a virgin past the time I should have been."

✦ Wives

Jacqueline Ray, divorcée
Jillie Mack, actress

✦ Did You Know?

How did Selleck get his part as a "hunk" in *Myra Breckenridge* ('70)? Well, for one thing, he—along with the other handsome possibilities for the role—auditioned in Mae West's dressing room at 8:00 P.M. one evening. To make the whole matter more interesting, neither Selleck nor the other actors have ever revealed what the audition consisted of.

What was Selleck's reaction when a national tabloid said he was gay? He sued and within a very quick time made them apologize for the falseness of their statements on the subject.

Lovers, Flings, or Just Friends?

Phyllis Elizabeth Davis, actress (costar in *Terminal Island*, '73)

Phyllis Forberg, student

De-Ahna Ray, exotic dancer

Mimi Rogers, actress

Francine York, actress

Lovers, Flings, or Just Friends?

Mia Farrow, actress

Francesa Hilton, daughter of Zsa Zsa Gabor

Alice Joyce, stewardess

Sophia Loren, actress (costar in *The Millionairess*, '61)

Liza Minnelli, singer-actress

Princess Margaret, British royalty

Nanette Newman, British actress

Tracy Redd, actress (costar in *Dr. Strangelove*, '64)

Janette Scott, British actress

Christina Wachmeister, Swedish socialite

Peter Sellers 1925–1980

✦ He Said

I was looking for a mother replacement with a sexual life as well.
—On why he married

When a marriage or love affair is over, I just have to get rid of everything associated with it.

I'm not a funny man offstage. I'm a serious person. I don't crack jokes. Don't call me a comedian.

Having no genuine personality of my own gives me such a complex, you know.

✦ They Said

He was an emotional and physical bully, especially to ladies.
—Blake Edwards, director

I can't say that Peter was in love with his mother, but it was a classic love-hate relationship. —Anne Howe, spouse

I would squirm with embarrassment at the demeaning lengths he would stoop to in order to ingratiate himself with the Royal family. It was contemptible. —Britt Ekland, actress and spouse

I would defy anyone to tell me what was nice about him. —Blake Edwards, director

He was totally absorbed by the present. I don't think he ever had a dream about himself which he wanted to realize. He was an "instant man." —Anonymous friend

✦ First Sexual Experience
Unknown.

✦ Wives
Anne Howe (Hayes), Australian actress
Britt Ekland, actress (costar in *After the Fox*, '66)
Miranda Quarry, socialite
Lynn Frederick, actress (costar in *The Prisoner of Zenda*, '79)

✦ Did You Know?
Sellers was another star who loved erotic photos—actually, photos of him and some of his ladies cavorting naked, which he took himself.

Sellers, a man who had already had heart attacks and heart surgery, continued to use amyl nitrate as a sexual stimulant almost until his final heart attack.

David O. Selznick 1901–1965

✦ He Said

If you hold out, you might get loaned out. —Threatening Shirley Temple, who was under contract to him, in an effort to woo her

✦ They Said

David was crazy about women. As a sex object he could not have seemed delectable. But how do you know when everyone wants careers? —Dorothy Paley, family friend

He was very sexually oriented. He had very strong needs. —Marcella Bannett, his secretary

You know, he'd try and rip your clothes off. —Joan Fontaine, actress

He was like a wonderful, brand-new, beautifully designed, and very expensive show—he wasn't creative, but he was a piece of work. —Katharine Hepburn, actress

✦ First Sexual Experience

Lost his virginity at age seventeen to the daughter of a movie executive, at whose Long Island beach house he was staying while recuperating from influenza.

✦ Wives

Irene Mayer, daughter of studio chief Louis B. Mayer
Jennifer Jones, actress

✦ Did You Know?

David O. had a well-deserved reputation as a physical klutz. Once while standing preening nude before a mirror, he managed to slam a drawer shut on his genitals.

Until he was married, Selznick's father undressed him for bed each evening, then tucked him under the covers.

Selznick was a drug freak, quite partial to Benzedrine and barbiturates, who often crushed Benzedrine tablets into his hand, then licked the pieces up.

Lovers, Flings, or Just Friends?

Jean Arthur, actress
Constance Bennett, actress
Ingrid Bergman, actress
Joan Crawford, actress
Joan Fontaine, actress
Shirley Harden, secretary
Ann Harding, actress
Laura Harding, American Express heiress
Nancy Kelly, actress
Carole Lombard, actress
Marina, Countess Cicogna, Italian nobility
and lots of starlets and bit players he lured onto the "casting couch," who nicknamed him C.O.D (for cash on delivery)

Lovers, Flings, or Just Friends?

Anouk Aimée, French actress (costar in *The Appointment*, '69)

April Ashley, British transsexual

Ingrid Bergman, actress (costar in *The Yellow Rolls-Royce*, '64)

Dyan Cannon, actress

Julie Christie, actress (costar in *Doctor Zhivago*, '65)

Anjanette Comer, actress

Catherine Deneuve, actress (costar in *Mayerling*, '68)

Ava Gardner, actress (costar in *Mayerling*, '68)

Yane Le Maullaur, French one-time fiancée

Sophia Loren, actress (costar in *More Than a Miracle*, '67)

Barbara Parkins, actress

Barbra Streisand, actress-singer (costar in *Funny Girl*, '68)

Annette Stroyberg, French actress

Marilu Toto, Italian actress

Viviane Ventura, actress-author

Omar Sharif 1932–

✦ He Said

I love sex, wine, and food—after a hard's day work, they are my rewards.

The fact that I entertain many girls is only because I am searching always for the right one.

A woman mustn't contradict me openly. I can contradict a woman because I'm a man and because arrogance is the nature of man.

I couldn't love a woman who couldn't or wouldn't blush.

Aggressive feminists scare me.

✦ They Said

In spite of the passionate lover he played on the screen, he was rarely romantic. —Roger Vadim, French director, who calls Sharif an "excellent friend"

For him, kissing a woman is to embrace part of the universe. —Astrologer who prepared a chart on Sharif

✦ First Sexual Experience

Lost his virginity when he was about seventeen to a prostitute in a parked car in Heliopolis, a suburb of Cairo.

✦ Wives

Faten Hamama, Egyptian actress (costar in *The Blazing Sun*, '53)
Sohair Ramzi, actress

✦ Did You Know?

Sharif was once accosted in a Dallas hotel room by a woman armed with a gun. She forced him to strip, then demanded that he make love to her. Motioning to his flaccid penis, he insisted that "it's not possible at the moment."

Sharif was originally scheduled to make his American film debut in *Joseph and His Brethren* (never filmed) with Rita Hayworth. The actress became involved with singer Dick Haymes and traipsed off to Mexico with him, causing the film's cancellation.

When a photo was released from *Funny Girl* ('68) showing Sharif and Streisand kissing, it caused a furor in his homeland of Egypt. Since the actress was Jewish and had raised money for Israel, Egyptian papers branded Sharif a traitor and demanded that he be stripped of his citizenship. The threat was never carried through.

Benjamin "Bugsy" Siegel 1906–1947

✦ He Said

I'm gonna kill 'im! He's using that name I hate! —Frequently said, and expressing his distaste for his nickname

Out here, the politicians don't run for office. We run them. —Describing California, and in particular Hollywood and Los Angeles, in the 1940s

✦ They Said

He thought he was God's gift to women. —Abe Zwillman, mobster

If anyone or anything was his mistress, it was that Las Vegas hotel. —Virginia Hill, his moll, whose nickname was the Flamingo and for whom Siegel's infamous hotel was named

He used to go to bed at night with a chin strap to keep his profile good, and he wore those shades over his eyes. —George Raft, actor and close friend

Crooks, as well as shady ladies, like to mingle with celebrities. Bugsy loved to socialize. He'd turn up dressed to the nines, to have a drink or play poker as the guest of all kinds of people. —Hedda Hopper, gossip columnist

✦ First Sexual Experience
Unknown.

✦ Wives
Esta Krakower, childhood sweetheart
Virginia Hill, mobster moll

✦ Did You Know?
Siegel owned five of Jean Harlow's pubic hairs, each mounted in a small gold locket. Obtained without Harlow's permission by another mobster lover when she underwent an emergency operation, they originally sold for $500 each.

Siegel, possessed of a notoriously violent temper, planned on killing Loretta Young, until his attorney, Jerry Giesler, dissuaded him from doing it. Young had sought to purchase Siegel's home, on which he had already drastically reduced the price, when termite damage was discovered. She wanted Siegel to pay for the damage, plus the inspection report. He refused, and so she backed out of the deal. Infuriated, Siegel sought retaliation until Giesler intervened.

Lovers, Flings, or Just Friends?

Wendy Barrie, actress

Ketti Gallian, French starlet

Jean Harlow, actress

Marie "The Body" McDonald, actress

Marilyn Monroe, actress

Dorothy Dentice Taylor, Countess di Frasso, socialite

Sophie Tucker, singer and last of the Red-Hot Mamas

Mae West, actress

Lovers, Flings, or Just Friends?

Lauren Bacall, actress

Jacqueline Bisset, actress (costar in *The Detective*, '68)

Joan Blackman, actress

Jill Corey, singer

Angie Dickinson, actress

Marlene Dietrich, singer-actress

Patty Duke, actress

Anita Ekberg, actress

Eva Gabor, actress

Zsa Zsa Gabor, actress

Judy Garland, singer-actress

Grace Kelly, actress

Hope Lange, actress

Shirley MacLaine, actress

Marisa Mell, actress

Sylvia Miles, actress

Marilyn Monroe, actress

Kim Novak, actress

Juliet Prowse, dancer-actress

Lee Radziwill, socialite

Nancy Davis Reagan, actress-political wife

Lee Remick, actress

Jill St. John, actress

Elizabeth Taylor, actress

Lana Turner, actress

Gloria Vanderbilt, socialite

Natalie Wood, actress

plus many prostitutes, because with them he doesn't have to be *Frank Sinatra*, and other assorted starlets, singers, waitresses, and women of all occupations

Frank Sinatra 1915–1998

✦ He Said

If I had as many love affairs as you've given me credit for, I'd now be speaking to you from a jar in the Harvard Medical School.

Every time I sing a song I make love to them. I'm a boudoir singer.

If I hadn't made it in show business, I'd have been a mobster myself.

✦ They Said

When Sinatra dies, they're giving his zipper to the Smithsonian. —Dean Martin, singer-actor

Mais oui . . . the Mercedes-Benz of men! —Marlene Dietrich, who should have known, since she was a hard driver once she got into the seat

The problems were never in bed. We were always great in bed. —Ava Gardner, quipping on the good parts of their marriage after it had soured

He was no DiMaggio. —Marilyn Monroe, assessing the Sinatra bed manner

A complete shit. —Lauren Bacall, after being dumped rather abruptly by Ole Blue Eyes

He's the most fascinating man in the world, but don't stick your hand in the cage. —Tommy Dorsey, who gave Frank his early start and then had a contract dispute with him

When he gets to heaven, Frank's gonna give God a hard time for making him bald. —Marlon Brando

I was not impressed with the creeps and Mafia types he kept around him. —Prince Charles

✦ First Sexual Experience
Unknown.

✦ Wives
Nancy Barbato
Ava Gardner, actress
Mia Farrow, actress
Barbara Marx, ex-wife of Zeppo Marx

✦ Did You Know?
What's the word on skinny Frank's physical endowment? Maybe spouse Ava Gardner tipped everyone off when she said, "Well, there's only 10 pounds of Frank, but there's 110 pounds of cock."

Red Skelton 1913–1997

✦ He Said

All men make mistakes, but those who are married find out about them sooner.

I'm nuts and I know it.

I dood it. —Skelton's most famous line in films, radio, and television

✦ They Said

In my opinion, if he had his choice of getting laid or getting a laugh, I think he'd opt for the latter. —A former comedy writer who worked for Skelton

I think I learned every four-letter word I've ever heard from Red. He used the filthiest language on the set imaginable. He'd shock me so I'd go back to my dressing room and cry. —Esther Williams, who costarred with Skelton in several films

Basically a very sad clown. —Lucille Ball

✦ First Sexual Experience
Unknown.

✦ Wives

Edna Marie Stillwell, theater usherette
Georgia Maureen Davis, actress
Lothian Toland, daughter of cinematographer Gregg Toland

✦ Did You Know?

While waiting for a complicated scene setup on *A Southern Yankee* ('48), Skelton took an MGM contract actress, stunning as a doll, into his dressing room. As she was on her knees in front of Skelton performing oral sex on him, an accidental explosion rocked the set. Pictures fell off the wall, the dressing room rocked, the windows rattled, and Skelton climaxed almost simultaneously. He patted her on the head and said, "Good girl!"

Skelton once told a friend that as a child he'd been employed as the towel boy in an Indiana whorehouse. The friend said he had no way of knowing whether Skelton was telling the truth or not.

Skelton played a particularly grim joke on dancer-actress Ann Miller and her mother. When she told him that the duo was soon to take their first plane ride, Skelton gave them a wrapped package a few days later, cautioning them not to open it until after their plane was aloft. When they opened the present, they found a beautiful leather scrapbook—full of photos and articles about plane crashes.

Lovers, Flings, or Just Friends?

Muriel Morris Chase, starlet

Arlene Dahl, actress

Ann Sothern, actress (costar in *Maisie Gets Her Man*, '42)

Lupe Velez, actress

Lovers, Flings, or Just Friends?

Diana Barrymore, actress
Yvonne De Carlo, actress
Judy Garland, actress
Betty Grable, actress
Lana Turner, actress
Irene Wrightsman, heiress
plus lots of other stars, starlets, and assorted other young females when he was a "swinging" bachelor

Robert Stack 1919–

✦ He Said
Seldom does Hollywood shake off its self-satisfied superiority and remember its beginning as a nondescript village of nickelodeon salesmen.

The surest road to disaster in Hollywood is to know, or be brash enough to remember, the humblest origins of any of our great leaders.

✦ They Said
You kiss better than Farley Granger. —Lee Radziwill, who costarred with him in her one disastrous attempt at an acting career

I could make this kid a star, but he doesn't need me. He's not hungry enough. —Jack Warner, head of Warner Bros. Studios

✦ First Sexual Experience
Lost his virginity at sixteen to a petite redhead with a "big smile and boobs to match" who took tap-dancing lessons, as did Stack, from the Ernest Belcher School of Dance.

✦ Wives
Rosemarie Bowe, starlet

✦ Did You Know?
One of the treasured possessions found among the items residing in Anne Frank's hiding place was a photograph of Robert Stack.

Stack's father was the advertising executive who created the slogan, "The Beer That Made Milwaukee Famous," and his mother was a member of Rudolph Valentino's wedding party.

Who was Stack's roommate during the summer of 1940 in his Hollywood Hills bachelor apartment? None other than one John Fitzgerald Kennedy. Stack characterized his libidinous buddy by saying, "I've known many of the great Hollywood stars and only a very few of them seemed to hold the attention for women that JFK did."

Sylvester Stallone 1946–

✦ He Said

I would go to school chiefly to flirt.

I'm not handsome in the classical sense. The eyes droop, the mouth is crooked, the teeth aren't straight, the voice sounds like a Mafioso pallbearer, but somehow it all works.

Love makes you do stupid things! It makes you dumb!

They wanted to know if I'd take off my clothes. "Why not?" I said, "I take them off for free at home every night." —Answering why he accepted $100 to appear in a soft-porn film (*Party at Kitty and Stud's*) when he was broke

I am the manifestation of my own fantasy.

✦ They Said

Sylvester Stallone . . . I bet he has pimples on his ass. —John Waters, director

Sly is a great kisser. —Dolly Parton, costar in *Rhinestone* ('84)

His biggest asset: a face that would look well upon a three-toed sloth. —Russell Davies, critic

In life he handles himself well, except in the realm of women. There he acts like the rest of us. —Burgess Meredith, actor

Sly loves women and he loves women loving him. —Linda Gray, actress

✦ First Sexual Experience

Two tales have surfaced about Stallone's loss of his virginity. One says that he lost it to the girlfriend of a fellow student at Manor High School. The girl's boyfriend followed them and caught them in the act, provoking a fight with the naked Stallone. The other says he lost it to a girl named Ingrid, who a day later was sharing her charms with lots of the other guys he knew.

✦ Wives

Sasha Czack, movie usher
Brigitte Nielsen, model-actress

✦ Did You Know?

Stallone sued a Canadian tabloid after they printed that his body was so ravaged by steroids and diseases that he was impotent and had had a penis pump implant.

Stallone once considered going off to Australia to become a sheepherder before he succeeded in films.

Lovers, Flings, or Just Friends?

Susan Anton, actress
Naomi Campbell, model
Maryam D'Abo, actress
Devin de Vasquez, *Playboy* centerfold (June 1985)
Janice Dickinson, model
Angie Everhart, model
Jennifer Flavin, model
Cornelia Guest, socialite
Mary Hart, television personality
Joyce Ingalls, actress (costar in *Paradise Alley*, '78)
Farrah Fawcett, actress
Joanna Pacula, actress
Delia Sheppard, model-actress (costar in *Rocky V*, '90)
Alana Collins Hamilton Stewart, divorcée
Janine Turner, actress (costar in *Cliffhanger*, '92)
Vanna White, television personality

Jimmy Stewart 1908–1997

✦ He Said

My bachelor years, let me tell you, were wonderful . . . just wonderful. Boy, did I have some good times.

Oh, you just look and look and look and you get older and older and older. However, one never gets too old to stop looking.
—Remarking on why he was taking so long to get married; he finally married at age forty-one

I don't pick a story, I pick a director.

✦ They Said

She took one look at Jimmy Stewart and began to rub her hands.
—Joe Pasternak, producer of *Destry Rides Again* ('39), remembering how Marlene Dietrich reacted to her costar in the film

James Stewart is the most nearly normal of all Hollywood stars.
—Louella Parsons, gossip columnist

He has an alert, kiddish, eagle-beaked appearance, and everybody likes him. —*Colliers* magazine

✦ First Sexual Experience

Unknown for certain, but could have lost his virginity to actress Margaret Sullavan, whom he met during his junior year in college when she was already a sexual predator.

✦ Wives

Gloria McLean, divorcée

✦ Did You Know?

Marlene Dietrich told novelist and sometime lover Erich Marie Remarque that she and Stewart started having sex when they met for wardrobe fittings on *Destry Rides Again* ('39). She also claimed that she became pregnant from their first sexual encounter and had had an abortion.

Shortly after he entered the air corps in World War II, one Hollywood columnist estimated that in his time in Hollywood the lanky, homespun Stewart had "dated" 263 different "glamour" girls of the films.

Stewart was one of the few actors—another was Errol Flynn—to suffer a personal loss in the Vietnam War. His son, Ronald, a marine, was killed in fighting at Quang Tri, south of the demilitarized zone.

Lovers, Flings, or Just Friends?

June Allyson, actress (costar in *The Glenn Miller Story*, '53)

Wendy Barrie, actress (costar in *Speed*, '36)

Diana Barrymore, actress

Olivia de Havilland, actress

Marlene Dietrich, singer-actress (costar in *Destry Rides Again*, '39)

Mitzi Gaynor, actress-singer

Jean Harlow, actress (costar in *Wife vs. Secretary*, '36)

Rita Hayworth, actress

Katharine Hepburn, actress (costar in *The Philadelphia Story*, '40)

Grace Kelly, actress (costar in *Rear Window*, '54)

Jeanette MacDonald, singer-actress

Ginger Rogers, actress (costar in *Vivacious Lady*, '38)

Rosalind Russell, actress

Norma Shearer, actress

Simone Simon, actress (costar in *Seventh Heaven*, '37)

Margaret Sullavan, actress (costar in *The Shop Around the Corner*, '40)

Lana Turner, actress

Loretta Young, actress

Robert Taylor 1911–1969

✦ He Said

Well, I am a red-blooded man and I resent people calling me "pretty"—and for your information, I've got hair on my chest!
—Snapping at the press, who had always made fun of his "pretty boy" image

I was a punk kid from Nebraska who's had an awful lot of the world's good things dumped in his lap.

✦ They Said

So beautiful—and so dumb. —Greta Garbo, actress and costar in *Camille* ('36)

I had an awful crush on Bob Taylor. You might say I had my eye on him. We had quite a laugh when I told him about it thirty years later. —Pat Nixon, who, as Thelma "Pat" Ryan, worked as an extra on Taylor's film *Small Town Girl* ('36)

✦ First Sexual Experience
Unknown.

✦ Wives

Barbara Stanwyck, actress (costar in *This Is My Affair*, '37)
Ursula Thiess, German actress-model

✦ Did You Know?

While making *The Conspirator* ('50) with Elizabeth Taylor, Robert Taylor kept getting an erection in his scenes with her. He finally discussed his problem with the cameraman, who helpfully tried to focus as many shots as possible above Robert Taylor's waist.

Taylor brooded about his "pretty boy" image and often feared that he might actually be a homosexual. In fact, he consulted with a psychologist over his fears.

Taylor's famous widow's peak hairline wasn't real. His hair actually squared off straight across his forehead, but his studio (MGM) had his hairs plucked, one by one, to create the widow's peak.

When Taylor was signed to make *The Gorgeous Hussy* ('36) with costar Joan Crawford, Hollywood wags asked, "To which one of them does the title refer?"

Lovers, Flings, or Just Friends?

Marina Besti, Italian actress

Gilmor Brown, theatrical teacher and director

Virginia Bruce, actress (costar in *Times Square Lady*, '35)

Yvonne De Carlo, actress

Lia Dileo, Italian actress

Greta Garbo, actress (costar in *Camille*, '36)

Ava Gardner, actress (costar in *The Bribe*, '49)

Janet Gaynor, actress (costar in *Small Town Girl*, '36)

John Gilbert, actor

Sheilah Graham, gossip columnist

Virginia Grey, actress

Irene Hervey, actress

Sybil Merritt, starlet

Eleanor Parker, actress (costar in *Above and Beyond*, '52)

Tyrone Power, actor

Lane Trumbel, starlet

Lana Turner, actress (costar in *Johnny Eager*, '42)

plus many other women, particularly prostitutes from the brothel maintained by his studio

Michael "Mike" Todd 1907–1957

✦ He Said

I'll never marry an actress. To live with an actress, you gotta be able to worry about her hair, and when her bosoms start to drop, she gets panicky and runs to the nearest headshrinker.

If there are any more geniuses like me around, I'd be self-conscious.

I've been broke many times, but never poor. Poor is a state of mind.

✦ They Said

I don't think he needed her more than she needed him, but they fell in love, and he taught her everything he knew about sex, good and bad. —Hedda Hopper, gossip columnist, on Todd and his wife Elizabeth Taylor

Mike Todd definitely belongs on a runaway horse. —Joe E. Lewis, comedian, commenting on Todd's predilection for living life at a superhectic pace

✦ First Sexual Experience
Unknown.

✦ Wives
Bertha Freshman, student
Joan Blondell, actress
Elizabeth Taylor, actress

✦ Did You Know?
Did Todd kill his first wife? They had an argument and, somehow, a knife was introduced into the fray. Her hand got slashed, which meant she had to be rushed to the hospital. She died suddenly during surgery, supposedly from a reaction to the anesthetic. Was Todd "more involved" with his wife's death than we know? After all, he did once break the arm of his second wife, actress Joan Blondell, during an argument.

Urbane man about New York City, Todd was directly responsible for the Ma and Pa Kettle series of films during the fifties. He was involved with Universal Studios and attended a special showing of *The Egg and I* ('47), in which the homespun couple made their first appearance. He made a casual comment that the Ma and Pa Kettle characters should be featured in a series of films, which he thought would be quite successful. Todd was correct: The series made lots of money for Universal.

Lovers, Flings, or Just Friends?

Nancy Berg, model
Marlene Dietrich, singer-actress
Evelyn Keyes, actress
Gypsy Rose Lee, stripper
Anita Loos, author
Lorraine Manville, heiress
Marilyn Monroe, actress
Muriel Page, dancer
Jean Simmons, actress

Mel Tormé 1925–1999

✦ He Said

Say what you will about the naive, narrow films of the thirties and forties, it is difficult to recall any of them that exhibited the questionable taste on display in certain more recent films.

Then shut your mouth, dear! —Snapping at Hollywood columnist Virginia Graham, who had admitted that she hadn't read his book *The Other Side of the Rainbow*, about Judy Garland, even though she was berating him about it

✦ They Said

There's me and Tony Bennett and Mel Tormé. —Frank Sinatra, on the few real saloon singers left

Sinatra's successor. —Mike Levin, reviewing in *Down Beat* magazine

An untalented amateur in a Little Lord Fauntleroy suit. —George Frazier, in a scathing review

✦ First Sexual Experience

Lost his virginity, when he was age seventeen, to a "dark-haired, pretty woman in her early thirties" named Dorothy. She had been "recruited" for the assignment by some members of the band he was traveling with.

✦ Wives

Florence Ann Gertrude "Candy" Toxton, starlet
Arlene Mills
Janette Scott, British actress
Ali Severson, tax attorney

✦ Did You Know?

Tommy Dorsey, exceptionally proud of his wife, an MGM starlet named Pat Dane, had her remove her clothing and show her breasts to Tormé, saying, "How about those, huh, kid?"

Tormé said he believed *fart* to be the most detestable word in the English language.

Lovers, Flings, or Just Friends?

Cathy Down, actress
Ava Gardner, actress
Lorry Hamilton, whose father was a John Dillinger henchman
Raven (Evelyn) McBride, starlet
Marilyn Maxwell, actress
Marilyn Monroe, actress
Lana Turner, actress

Spencer Tracy 1900–1967

✦ He Said

Write anything you want about me. Make up something. Hell, I don't care.

All an actor owes the public is a good performance.

I just show up and try not to bump into the furniture. —Defining his technique for acting

✦ They Said

Spence was a very disturbed man. He was a mean drunk and a bastard. —Joan Crawford, actress

He made women feel warm and wanted, but there was no flattery about him. —Loretta Young, actress

A tiny thing about Spencer: He made the best cup of coffee in the world. —Katharine Hepburn, actress

✦ First Sexual Experience

Unknown.

✦ Wives

Louise Treadwell, actress

✦ Did You Know?

Tracy wasn't the "normal" type of alcoholic—he'd have remarkably long periods of sobriety. He was a "binge" alcoholic, given to intense, short periods of drinking. It wasn't unusual for him to disappear completely during these drinking spells. He'd check into a hotel with a suitcase loaded with liquor bottles. Then he'd strip, settle himself into the bathtub, and drink himself into a stupor for days or weeks at a time. Once his binge was over, Tracy would return to his acting almost completely sober.

John Travolta 1954–

✦ He Said

It was only after I got into show business that girls liked me.

A confirmed bachelor is a guy who believes in wine, women, and "so long." I'm a confirmed bachelor.

I'm not an old-fashioned romantic. I believe in love and marriage, but not necessarily with the same person.

Your traditional well-built woman, meaning large breasts, small waist, good hips, good butt, good legs. That's my sexual ideal.

The gay rumor about male stars is such a classic that it didn't surprise me to hear it about me, because I'd heard it about the others.

✦ They Said

He has this strange androgynous quality. —Lorne Michaels, producer

He is the street Tyrone Power. —Allen Carr, producer

The sensitivity and sensuality are very strong. It's as if he has every dichotomy—masculinity, femininity, refinement, crudity. You see him, you fall in love a little bit. —Lily Tomlin, costar in *Moment by Moment* ('79)

✦ First Sexual Experience

Probably lost his virginity to a girl who attended the same school he did in New Jersey. He's said that he was thirteen years old when it happened, but won't name the girl, having said only that she wasn't African American.

✦ Wives

Kelly Preston, actress (costar in *The Experts*, '89)

✦ Did You Know?

Paul Barresi, a star of porn films, claimed in articles in the *New York Post* and the *National Enquirer* to have had an affair with Travolta. According to Barresi, he and Travolta had sex "dozens of times" during the period when John was also seeing Debra Winger and Olivia Newton-John. Barresi later apologized for "going public" about his affair with Travolta, claiming he was hard-pressed for money to support his children. Shortly after the revelation, Travolta married actress Kelly Preston rather abruptly and fathered a child. Barresi had predicted Travolta's response to his revelations would probably be a quick marriage.

Lovers, Flings, or Just Friends?

Nancy Allen, actress (costar in *Carrie*, '76)

Paul Barresi, porn star

Marisa Berenson, actress

Karen Lynn Gorney, actress (costar in *Saturday Night Fever*, '77)

Marilu Henner, actress

Diana Hyland, actress (costar in *The Boy in the Plastic Bubble*, '77)

Olivia Newton-John, singer-actress (costar in *Grease*, '78)

Joan Prather, actress (costar in *The Devil's Rain*, '75)

Marcia Strassman, actress

Lily Tomlin, actress (costar in *Moment by Moment*, '79)

Debra Winger, actress

Roger Vadim 1928–2000

✦ He Said

The problem is to make the woman know that she wants you.

Lies or half-truths are harder for me to live with than the certainty of infidelity.

✦ They Said

If only Vadim had been jealous, things might have worked out.
—Brigitte Bardot, on how her infidelities failed to rouse Vadim's emotions

✦ First Sexual Experience

Lost his virginity on June 6, 1944 (D-Day), in a hayloft in Normandy, to Françoise, a fellow theater student.

✦ Wives

Brigitte Bardot, actress (directed her in *And God Created Woman*, '56)

Annette Stroyberg, actress (directed her in *Les Liaisons Dangereuses*, '59)

Jane Fonda, actress (directed her in *Barbarella*, '68)

Catherine Schneider, socialite heiress

Marie-Christine Barrault, actress

✦ Did You Know?

Bardot's family were such devout Catholics and moralists that they forced Vadim to spend his wedding night with their daughter on the family's living room sofa. He and Brigitte had only held the civil ceremony, with the religious ceremony scheduled for the next day. In her family's eyes, the couple wasn't "properly" married yet.

What did Vadim think of Bardot, his first wife? Well, he said, "One night with her was worth a lifetime."

Rudolph Valentino 1895–1926

✦ He Said

A love affair with a stupid woman is like a cup of cold coffee.

To generalize on women is dangerous. To specialize on them is infinitely worse.

A man should control his life. Mine is controlling me. I don't like it.

✦ They Said

I don't think the girls will like him, because he's too foreign looking. —D. W. Griffith, director

A weak man, and a bit on the stupid side as well. —Colleen Moore, silent screen actress

He was one who was catnip to women. —H. L. Mencken, author

When it came to making love, Rudolph Valentino preferred a plate of spaghetti. —Anonymous silent film actress

With Rudolph Valentino the motion picture camera for the first time really showed what it could do in the way of creating a personality. —Adela Rogers St. Johns, writer

His acting is largely confined to protruding his large, almost occult eyes until the vast areas of white are visible; drawing back the lips of his wide, sensuous mouth to bare his gleaming teeth; and flaring his nostrils. —Adolph Zukor, head of Paramount Studios

✦ First Sexual Experience

Undoubtedly lost his virginity as a young man in Castellaneta, Italy. He was caught making love with young ladies on at least two occasions by their fathers, who severely thrashed him.

✦ Wives

Jean Acker, actress (their marriage was never consummated; she locked him out of the bedroom minutes after the ceremony ended)
Natacha Rambova, dancer

✦ Did You Know?

When Valentino died, his body wasn't placed in the funeral home. A wax dummy was used instead, because it was feared that the crowds might defile the corpse. The public who viewed the "exhibit" never suspected the difference.

Lovers, Flings, or Just Friends?

Agnes Ayres, actress (costar in *The Sheik*, '21)

Vilma Banky, actress (costar in *The Eagle*, '25)

Ray "Rae" Bourbon, female impersonator

Marion Davies, actress

Elinor Glyn, novelist

Sessue Hayakawa, silent screen actor

Norman Kerry, silent screen actor

Beatrice "Bea" Lillie, actress

June Mathis, actress-screenwriter

Mae Murray, actress (costar in *The Little Big Person*, '19)

Nita Naldi, actress

Alla Nazimova, actress (costar in *Camille*, '21)

Pola Negri, actress

Ramon Novarro, actor

Alice Terry, actress

and lots of lonely, wealthy women—mostly married—when he was working as a dancer-gigolo

Rudy Vallee 1901–1986

✦ He Said

I never felt that physically and facially I was anything of a ladykiller, but I had a great reputation for being a cocksman. I wasn't, really, because fucking wasn't the most important thing to me.

People called me the guy with the cock in his voice. Maybe that's why in eighty-four years of life I've been with over 145 women and girls.

✦ They Said

Always taken with young girls. —Joan Fontaine, actress

In fact, Rudy's whole life has been one of a pursuit of romance for romance itself. —Eleanor Norris, fourth wife

✦ First Sexual Experience

Valle has said he lost his virginity when he was six years old, when he and several other boys accompanied a little girl behind a local lakeside icehouse.

✦ Wives

Leona Cauchois, whose father invented the tea ball

Fay Webb, starlet

Bettejane Greer, singer

Eleanor Norris, student

✦ Did You Know?

Vallee had a fetish for long painted fingernails, black satin dresses, and high-heeled shoes. He particularly liked it when he could encourage one of his, as he put it, "usual dark-haired females" to dress up this way for him.

Luchino Visconti 1906–1976

✦ He Said

When I was young, homosexuality was a forbidden fruit, something special, a fruit to be gathered with care, not what it is today—hundreds of homosexuals showing off, dancing together in a gay bar.

What are actors, after all? They are thoroughbreds. Nervous and sensitive. They have to be fondled or rebuked according to the occasion.

Always they want to lower the picture, to make it pleasing to the most uneducated man in the smallest town in the most faraway state. —Complaining about Hollywood's mentality

✦ They Said

Now here's a man who loves little boys, it's as simple as that. He's a throwback to the old Roman emperors. —Burt Lancaster, actor

He didn't fall in love often and was not promiscuous and never forgot you. —Anonymous lover

Luchino was extremely sensitive to beauty, in men and women. I must say with dismay that he became almost blind when confronted with beauty. Even imbeciles were judged well if they were beautiful. —Adriana Asti, confidante

He is a tyrant. —Maria Callas, opera diva

✦ First Sexual Experience

Probably involved a boy in the stables on his father's estate. His first kiss from a female was from Wanda Toscanini, daughter of the famed conductor, who later married Vladimir Horowitz.

✦ Wives

Luchino never married, although he was engaged once.

✦ Did You Know?

Visconti established a "trend" for society everywhere when he was a young man. He became enamored of a French luggage maker because all his pieces were decorated with his initials—the same as Visconti's: *LV*. Thus, he popularized the works of Louis Vuitton.

Exactly one year after Visconti's death, Helmut Berger tried to commit suicide in Rome.

Visconti's father was the Duke of Modrone, a title conferred on the Italian family by Napoleon.

Lovers, Flings, or Just Friends?

Helmut Berger, actor (directed him in *The Damned*, '69)

Clara Calamai, Italian actress

Maria Callas, opera diva

Gabrielle "Coco" Chanel, couturier

Alain Delon, actor (directed him in *Rocco and His Brothers*, '60)

Maria Denis, Italian actress

Marlene Dietrich, singer-actress

Massimo Girotti, Italian actor (directed him in *Ossessione*, '42)

Farley Granger, actor (directed him in *Senso*, '53)

Horst, German photographer

Anna Magnani, actress (directed her in *Bellissima*, '51)

Elsa Morante, wife of writer Alberto Moravia

Princess of Gerace, Italian nobility

Irma Windisch-Graetz, Austrian aristocrat

Franco Zeffirelli, director

Lovers, Flings, or Just Friends?

Linda Christian, actress

Joan Collins, actress (costar in *Stopover Tokyo*, '57)

Mona Freeman, actress

Terry Moore, actress (costar in *Beneath the Twelve Mile Reef*, '53)

Lori Nelson, actress

Jean Peters, actress (costar in *Broken Lance*, '54)

Stephanie Powers, actress

Debbie Reynolds, actress

Tina Sinatra, actress

Barbara Stanwyck, actress (costar in *Titanic*, '53)

Lana Turner, actress

Henry Willson, agent

Susan Zanuck, daughter of studio head

Robert Wagner 1930–

✦ He Said
I'm no longer the pretty boy with a beach ball in one hand and a tennis racquet in the other.

✦ They Said
Our life together never really ended. It was just interrupted. We had each other in our youth, and now we have each other in our prime. —Natalie Wood, commenting on their second marriage

✦ First Sexual Experience
Unknown.

✦ Wives
Natalie Wood, actress (costar in *All the Fine Young Cannibals*, '59)
Marion Marshall, actress-model
Natalie Wood, actress
Jill St. John, actress

✦ Did You Know?
Wagner was "discovered" by Henry Willson, the same agent who "discovered" Rock Hudson, Tab Hunter, Guy Madison, and Tony Curtis, among others. Willson, a notorious homosexual, was famed for finding handsome, well-built young men and fashioning careers for them.

During the making of *The Pink Panther* ('64), Wagner was required to appear in a bathtub scene with Capucine. In order to make the soap suds appear fluffier, a powerful chemical was added to the water, but the two stars weren't warned about it. Wagner got the chemical in his eyes and damaged his corneas. For a few days, until his treatment succeeded, it appeared that he would either lose his eyesight completely or suffer irreversible harm.

Robert Walker 1914–1951

✦ He Said

Everyone has problems, but I couldn't live with mine. I wasn't an alcoholic, but I was on the way to being one. Liquor was an outlet—an escape.

I basically felt inadequate, unwanted, and unloved ever since I was born. I was always trying to make an escape from life.

My personal life has been completely wrecked by David Selznick's obsession for my wife [Jennifer Jones]. What can you do to fight such a powerful man?

✦ They Said

He was a talented, sensitive, fey guy who combined the comic abilities of Jack Lemmon with a heart-grabbing little-boy-lost appeal. —Tay Garrett, Walker's first director

✦ First Sexual Experience

Unknown, but possibly lost his virginity in Central America or Mexico, since he made four voyages there while working on a banana boat while in his early twenties.

✦ Wives

Jennifer Jones, actress (costar in *Since You Went Away*, '44)
Barbara Ford, daughter of director John Ford

✦ Did You Know?

Walker died unexpectedly—almost instantaneously—after being given an injection of sodium amytal by his psychiatrist and an associate doctor while having a hysterical fit. A close friend of Walker's was present when the injection was given, having held him down for it. He's said that for years afterward he felt guilty; he felt it was almost as if he'd helped kill his friend.

Lovers, Flings, or Just Friends?

Nancy Davis (Reagan), actress

Elizabeth Firestone, socialite

Judy Garland, singer-actress

Ava Gardner, actress (costar in *One Touch of Venus*, '48)

Ida Lupino, actress

Peter Lawford, actor

Diana Lynn, actress

Lee Russell Marshall, divorcée

Kay Scott Nearay, starlet

Phyllis Thaxter, actress

Marie Windsor, actress

Lovers, Flings, or Just Friends?

Anita Ekberg, actress

Marilyn Miller, actress

Patsy Ruth Miller, actress

Jacqueline Park, starlet

Irene Rich, silent screen actress

plus lots of starlets and prostitutes through the years

Jack L. Warner 1892–1978

✦ He Said

Give an actor a break and he'll fuck you.

Most of the time, fortunately, I don't really care what people think of Jack Warner.

I have created enough stars, if I may use the word create *modestly, to fill the Hollywood skies.*

We took you up from oblivion and brought you to where you are now. —Railing at the ingratitude of his actors

I have a theory of relatives, too. Don't hire them. —Telling scientist Albert Einstein, famed for his Theory of Relativity, about his own philosophical musings

✦ They Said

Working for Warner Brothers is like trying to fuck a porcupine. It's one prick against a hundred. —Wilson Mizner, screenwriter

In some ways, Jack was a moral man. He never engaged in any of the dressing room nonsense. —Bette Davis, actress, who held a longtime contract at Warner Bros. studio

He was unreasonable; he was tyrannical. —Olivia de Havilland, actress, who finally sued to break her contract with Warner Bros.

Among the moguls I have known in Hollywood, he was by far the most dangerous. Tricky as hell. —Gottfried Reinhardt, producer-writer

✦ First Sexual Experience
Unknown.

✦ Wives
Irma Solomons, heiress
Ann Paige, starlet

✦ Did You Know?
Wonder why the men in Warner Bros. films don't show any chest hair? Jack Warner had a phobia about it being shown on the screen. He also wouldn't permit the female employees at the studio to wear pants to work.

Warner, of humble Jewish origins, always appreciated the richer, more famous social circle of friends he'd been able to join. One of his fondest memories—which he felt confirmed his acceptance by these people—was of the time that he and the Duke of Windsor urinated together on a rosebush while they were both vacationing in the south of France.

Denzel Washington 1954–

✦ He Said

Temptation is all around, it's all around, you know, and I haven't been perfect.

I was reading where they said—what is it?—95 percent of men have hired a prostitute at one time or another. I am saying, Well, I'm in that 5.

Female singers touch me more than anyone else.

When we had that first child, acting became making a living. The child was life.

God, family, work. Football. —Naming the important things in his life

My parents' divorce made me want to make my marriage work.

✦ They Said

Like me some Denzel. —Spike Lee, director, mouthing the phrase supposedly uttered by Washington's African-American female admirers

As good-looking as he is, he doesn't seem egotistic. —Halle Berry, actress

You remind me exactly of Robert Redford. You have that look of the romantic but masculine gentleman. —Alan Pakula, director

He's a very witty guy. —Tom Hanks, actor

He has intellectual weight, spiritual gravity, and a powerful sexual and romantic presence. —Kenneth Branagh, actor-director

Denzel qualifies as a respectable lover—and in the way that Hollywood deals with love. —Ossie Davis, actor

✦ First Sexual Experience
Unknown.

✦ Wives
Pauletta Pearson, actress

✦ Did You Know?
The rumor mill was abuzz in 1993 over a remark that Washington was alleged to have made to a fellow male African-American actor. It was said that young Will Smith, scheduled to star in *Six Degrees of Separation* as a young scam artist, had solicited the older actor's advice about a brief homosexual kissing scene in the film. Did Washington tell the younger actor, "Don't you go kissing no man in a film," as was reported? A later statement from him clarified his words to Smith, but didn't really seem to deny that he'd made the comment.

Lovers, Flings, or Just Friends?

In 1994, Washington was named as one of Hollywood's least-faithful husbands by *People*. Despite their assertion, none of the names of his purported partners have yet surfaced.

Lovers, Flings, or Just Friends?

Clara Bow, actress

Joan Crawford, actress

Marlene Dietrich, singer-actress (costar in *Pittsburgh*, '42)

Paulette Goddard, actress (costar in *Reap the Wild Wind*, '42)

Sigrid Gurie, actress (costar in *Three Faces West*, '40)

Osa Massen, actress

Carmen Miranda, actress-singer

Gail Russell, actress (costar in *Angel and the Badman*, '47)

Martha Scott, actress (costar in *In Old Oklahoma*, '43)

Pat Stacy, personal secretary

Claire Trevor, actress (costar in *Stagecoach*, '39)

John Wayne 1907–1979

✦ He Said
Women scare the hell out of me. . . . I've always been afraid of them.

I couldn't be a philanderer. I tried it—but it made me feel cheap and dirty.

✦ They Said
He walks like a fairy. He's the only man in the world who can do that. —William Wellman, director

He was attractive to women and he was attracted by women, but he was uneasy around them because he occasionally liked to use . . . I guess you'd call them "vulgarities." —Michael Wayne, his son

Get him out of the saddle—you got nothing. —Joan Crawford, actress

A face alive with humor, and a sharp wit. Dangerous when aroused. —Katharine Hepburn, costar in *Rooster Cogburn* ('75)

✦ First Sexual Experience
Probably lost his virginity to some young lady while a student at Glendale High School in Glendale, California. Wayne has said that he often spent time "picking up a certain type of girl on Saturday nights."

✦ Wives
Josephine Alicia Saenz, socialite
Esperanza Baur Dias Ceballos, Mexican actress-prostitute
Pilar Palette Weldy, Peruvian starlet

✦ Did You Know?
Who was the one man who tried to make his sexual dreams about Wayne come true? None other than Laurence Harvey, his costar in *The Alamo* ('60). The British bisexual tried the blunt approach, telling Wayne, "Please, Duke. Tonight. Just one time. I'll be the queen, if you'll be the king." The Duke passed on his chance to be a king with a queen.

Who was the best lay Wayne ever had? According to him it was Marlene Dietrich, because he said, "Best lay I've ever had."

Representatives of Governor George Wallace contacted Wayne in 1968 about his being on Wallace's American Independent Party ticket as the vice presidential candidate. Wayne declined, stating he had no interest in political office.

Johnny Weissmuller 1904–1984

✦ He Said

I wish I could have stayed a middle of the roader between my early apprehension toward girls and later infatuation. It might have saved a few fireworks.

I went to the back lot at MGM, they gave me a G-string and said, "Can you climb a tree?" —Remembering his training as an actor

✦ They Said

Hiyah, Johnny! I didn't recognize you with your clothes on. —Normal greeting during his Tarzan days

Dahling! You are the kind of man a woman like me must shanghai and keep under lock and key until both of us are entirely spent. Prepare a leave for ten days! —Tallulah Bankhead, being outrageous, as usual, in pursuit of a man

If I saw Weissmuller scratching his groin, I knew either his loincloth was too tight or he was pulling at his foreskin. —Richard Thorpe, director

He's a sissy! —Elmo Lincoln, the first screen Tarzan

✦ First Sexual Experience
Unknown.

✦ Wives
Camilla Louier
Bobbie Arnst, singer
Lupe Velez, actress
Beryel Scott, socialite
Allene Gates, golfer
Gertrudis Maria Theresa Elizabeth Bauman, divorcée

✦ Did You Know?

MGM paid a substantial, for those days, amount of money to convince Weissmuller's second wife to divorce him; the studio thought he would be a hotter property single.

During World War II at a bond rally, Weissmuller auctioned off a Tarzan "yell" by himself for $50,000. It went to a rich Texan.

Lovers, Flings, or Just Friends?

Tallulah Bankhead, actress
Linda Christian, actress
Joan Crawford, actress
Eleanor Holm, Olympic swimming medalist
plus lots and lots of chorus girls and starlets

Orson Welles 1915–1986

✦ He Said

I was in Hollywood during the war, when there was no competition. There was nobody I missed. —Talking about his sexual conquests in the early forties

I am like Casanova. Not a sexual acrobat—because I'm not. But because I am willing to wait under the window until four-thirty in the morning. I'm that kind of romantic fellow.

From my earliest years I was the Lillie Langtry of the older homosexual set. Everyone wanted me.

You see, the Italians believe that any young boy is meat for a quick seduction, and it will have no effect on him or on the masculinity of the grown man.

I always seduce actors. I make them fall in love with me.

Seventy-five percent of what I say in interviews is false.

✦ They Said

Orson Welles. You should cross yourself when you say his name. —Marlene Dietrich, holding His Largeness in high esteem

It's like meeting God without dying. —Dorothy Parker, writer and noted wit

There, but for the grace of God, goes God. —Herman J. Manckiewicz, coscreenwriter of *Citizen Kane* ('41)

Orson spent all his money on women. That's why he didn't have the money to make films. —Eartha Kitt, singer-actress

✦ First Sexual Experience

Lost his virginity when he was nine years old to a group of female cousins, on his mother's side, in Woodstock, Illinois. He had gone to stay with them after his mother's death. He said, "They had their way with me to whatever extent that may be."

✦ Wives

Virginia Nicolson, socialite
Rita Hayworth, actress
Paolo Mori, Countess di Girfalco, Italian socialite

✦ Did You Know?

Welles was accused of being a "queer" in a confrontation at Hollywood's Brown Derby restaurant by actor Guinn "Big Boy" Williams. To emphasize his disgust at Welles, Williams cut off Orson's tie with a knife during their argument.

Lovers, Flings, or Just Friends?

Lucille Ball, actress

Marc Blitzstein, composer

Corinne Calvet, actress

Francis Carpenter, actor

Jack Carter, actor

Dorothy Comingore, actress (costar in *Citizen Kane*, '40)

Dolores Del Rio, actress

Marlene Dietrich, singer-actress (costar in *Touch of Evil*, '58)

Hilton Edwards, actor

Geraldine Fitzgerald, actress

Judy Garland, singer-actress

Lena Horne, singer-actress

John Houseman, actor-producer

Eartha Kitt, singer-actress

Barbara Laage, French actress

Marilyn Monroe, actress

Maria Montez, actress

Tamara Toumanova, ballerina

Gloria Vanderbilt, socialite

Vera Zorina, ballerina

and a gypsy in Rome who taught him how to walk with a live chicken between his legs; several girls in the Presbyterian choir of a church in Woodstock, Illinois; several ballerinas; lots of Brazilian women; a concubine of the Moroccan Pasha of Marrakesh, Thami el-Glaoui; *and* women in brothels in Singapore and Shanghai

Michael Wilding 1912–1979

✦ He Said

I do not believe in love at first sight, simply because I have never experienced it.

My first and most lasting impression of Hollywood was that of living in a cell and working in a factory.

How could such a goddess find the ideal companion in me? —On his fling with Marlene Dietrich

✦ They Said

He says he cannot live without me, and then he goes and fucks Taylor. . . . It must be those huge breasts of hers—he likes them to dangle in his face. —Marlene Dietrich, outraged when Wilding, with whom she was having a torrid affair, rather suddenly became the second Mr. Elizabeth Taylor

I could never get over the looks of any of Michael's ladies. He's been surrounded by dazzlingly beautiful, talented women all his life. —Peter Graves, actor

You eat my food, you drink my wine, you fuck my women, yet you won't do press-ups with me? —Stewart Granger, close friend, decrying Wilding's refusal to work out with him

✦ First Sexual Experience

Probably lost his virginity in Belgium when he was a young student there.

✦ Wives

Kay Young, actress
Elizabeth Taylor, actress
Susan Nell, socialite
Margaret Leighton, actress

✦ Did You Know?

Did Wilding have a gay side? Rumors flew, and when he became engaged to Taylor, they came to a head. Gossip Hedda Hopper tried to dissuade Taylor from marrying Wilding by citing stories of his involvement with men. She even documented the charges in one of her books, which prompted a lawsuit from the actor. The offending passage about him was removed, but the wondering continued to dog him all his life.

Lovers, Flings, or Just Friends?

Ingrid Bergman, actress (costar in *Under Capricorn*, '49)

Noël Coward, playwright-entertainer

Marlene Dietrich, actress-singer

Paulette Goddard, actress

Stewart Granger, actor and close friend

Sally Gray, actress (costar in *Carnival*, '46)

Rita Hayworth, actress

Barbara Hutton, ultra-wealthy socialite

Glynis Johns, actress

Marie McDonald, actress

Karen von Unge, Swedish actress

Diana Wynyard, actress

Lovers, Flings, or Just Friends?

Molly Madden, model

Robin Williams 1952–

✦ He Said

Cocaine is God's way of saying you're making too much money.

The prospect of sex was scary back then, just because it was the first time. Now it can be lethal. —Contrasting the difference between becoming sexually aware when he did and doing so at the present time

I'd not exactly been the ideal husband. I'd been running around doing all kinds of things—drugs, affairs—but my wife had too. —Remembering why his first marriage collapsed

I can't remember a lot, thankfully. —Commenting on the wild phase in his life

✦ They Said

Robin's purity of spirit is so unmistakeable, so winning. —Pam Dawber, actress

It was never any one woman, it was lots of women. —Valerie Velardi, spouse, on what she disliked about their marriage

He has that glaze in his eye, you know he's in another place. —Billy Crystal, comedian

Throughout his life, he's always felt alone with his imagination. —Christopher Reeve, actor and close friend during Williams's early years in New York City

There is no filter between his brain and his mouth. —Larry Brezner, show business manager

✦ First Sexual Experience

Unknown.

✦ Wives

Valerie Velardi, graduate student
Marsha Garces, nanny

✦ Did You Know?

Robin's wild druggie days did lead him into some now-sad situations. For instance, he was one of the last people to see John Belushi alive. He spent some time with his fellow comedian in his hotel room shortly before Belushi overdosed and died. Did Robin indulge with Belushi that night? He's said no, while others have alleged he did.

While film stars often appear on the cover of magazines, Williams certainly has a dubious honor in that aspect. During the run of his television show *Mork and Mindy,* he was the cover subject on an issue of *Hairdo Ideas.*

Thomas Lanier "Tennessee" Williams 1911–1983

✦ He Said

All homosexuals have to live with a deep wound that never heals.

It is most disturbing to think that the head beside you on the pillow might be thinking too. —Explaining why he liked basically ignorant rough trade for sex

I cannot write any sort of story unless there is at least one character in it for whom I have physical desire.

To know me is not to love me. At best, it is to tolerate me.

In fact, I would guess that chance acquaintances or strangers have usually been kinder to me than friends—which does not speak too well for me.

✦ They Said

Miss Nancy —His father's derogatory nickname for him as a child

Eyes very beautiful, teeth very ugly. He is surrounded by admirers, accepts their compliments gracefully, but longs to be off by himself where he can behave badly. —Cecil Beaton, photographer

A pudgy, taciturn, mustached little man without any obvious distinction. —Harold Acton, historian-socialite

✦ First Sexual Experience

Lost his virginity to Bette Reitz, a fellow student at the University of Iowa, when he was twenty-six. He had previously ejaculated with males, but claimed that he hadn't had sex with any of them. He also claimed that he never masturbated until he was twenty-five years old.

✦ Wives

Williams remained a bachelor, though he did form several male relationships of some length.

✦ Did You Know?

When playwright Thornton Wilder criticized to his face Williams's portrayal of southern womanhood by the travails of Blanche DuBois in *A Streetcar Named Desire*, Williams retorted, "This man has never had a good lay in his life."

After his first meeting with John F. Kennedy, Williams told Gore Vidal he found Kennedy's ass attractive. When Gore passed the remark on to the complimentee, Kennedy replied, "That's very exciting."

Lovers, Flings, or Just Friends?

Danny Aikman, adagio dancer

Diana Barrymore, actress

Warren Beatty, actor

Elvi Bordelon, boardinghouse owner

Marlon Brando, actor

Bill Cannastra, law student

Robert Carroll, writer

William Inge, playwright

John F. Kennedy, president

Kip Kiernan, model-dancer

Frank Merlo, sailor

Frederick Nicklaus, writer

Bette Reitz, student

Pancho Rodriguez y Gonzalez, hotel worker

Ned Rorem, composer

Lovers, Flings, or Just Friends?

Skye Aubrey, actress

Sherry Britton, stripper

Bette Davis, actress (costar in *Old Acquaintance*, '43)

Harriet Vine Douglas, actress-dancer

Sophia Loren, actress (costar in *Five Miles to Midnight*, '62)

Elaine Stritch, actress

Gig Young 1913–1978

✦ He Said

When I discovered liquor I thought I'd found the magic potion.
—Remarking on why he liked to drink so heavily

✦ They Said

He was not just a guy who wanted to get laid, frankly. It was the chase he enjoyed. —Peter Brook, casting executive and carousing friend

Not a sweeter man would you ever want to meet. Blew his fucking wife's brains out and his brains out. —George C. Scott, commenting on the tragedy that ended Young's life

✦ First Sexual Experience

Lost his virginity at sixteen to a "slim-waisted, full-breasted" twenty-eight-year-old blonde, who followed him home from basketball practice one evening.

✦ Wives

Sheila Stapler, actress
Sophie Rothstein, drama coach
Elizabeth Montgomery, actress
Elaine Whitman, real-estate agent
Ruth Hannalore "Kim" Schmidt, Australian script supervisor

✦ Did You Know?

Young was one of the few Hollywood men to elude the clutches of Joan Crawford. She frequently invited him to drinks in her dressing room and called him darling, but bungled her big chance with him. Joan put the make on him too abruptly, and Young was "put off" when she did so; the invitations for drinks and affectionate name-calling quickly ceased on Crawford's part after the rejection.

Darryl F. Zanuck 1902–1979

✦ He Said

You've had nothing until you've had me. I am the biggest and the best. I can go all night and all day.

Any of my indiscretions were with people, not actresses.

✦ They Said

The only thing bigger than his cigar is his cock, which he's not too shy to show or put into use. —Ava Gardner, actress

He had two categories of women—broads and librarians. —Anne Baxter, actress

Darryl, undersized, with prominent buckteeth, always seemed to be overcompensating to prove his potency. —Myrna Loy, actress

Zanuck bore a striking resemblance to Bugs Bunny. When he entered a room, his front teeth preceded him by about three seconds. —Marlon Brando, actor

✦ First Sexual Experience

Lost his virginity at thirteen in a field outside Oakdale, Nebraska, to a local minister's daughter.

✦ Wives

Virginia Fox, actress and ex–Mack Sennett Bathing Beauty

✦ Did You Know?

Every afternoon at 4:00 P.M. was Zanuck's sex break. At that time, a girl, selected by Zanuck himself, from the Twentieth Century–Fox studio lot, would come to his office. Once she entered, the door was locked from the inside. Thereafter no calls or interruptions were permitted and all work in the offices adjacent to Zanuck's ceased. When he was finished, the girl left by a side door, and Zanuck unlocked his office for work to resume. Rarely did the same girl come twice, but there were exceptions.

Zanuck liked to expose himself and masturbate in front of the starlets he was pursuing, as he said, "to get those broads' juices running." He also liked to open his pants in his office and pull out his erect penis in front of various female stars. Corinne Calvet was among those who was treated—or mistreated—to the exhibition.

According to France's renowned Madame Claude (real name Fernande Grudet), who ran an exclusive, international call-girl service, Zanuck liked to see two women making love to each other. After he became excited watching them, he'd choose one of them as his sex partner.

Lovers, Flings, or Just Friends?

Wendy Barrie, actress

Dolores Costello, actress

Linda Darnell, actress

Bella Darvi, actress

Irina Demick, actress

Edna Freund, stenographer and later operator of a Hollywood call-girl service

Genevieve Gilles, actress

Juliette Greco, actress-singer

Ann Harding, actress

Xaviera Hollander, author-prostitute

Carole Landis, actress

Marilyn Monroe, actress

Maria Montez, actress

Alla Nazimova, actress

Merle Oberon, actress

Simone Simon, actress

Gene Tierney, actress

plus probably thousands of women, mainly starlets, whom he summoned to his office each afternoon for his notorious "fuck" break

Bibliography

....

Autobiographies, Biographies, Memoirs, Reminiscences, and Anecdotes

Aadland, Florence, as told to Tedd Thomey. *The Big Love*. Lancer Books, 1961.

Adams, Cindy, and Susan Crimp. *Iron Rose*. Dove Books, 1995.

Adams, Edie, and Robert Windeler. *Sing a Pretty Song. . . .* William Morrow, 1990.

Agan, Patrick. *Hoffman vs. Hoffman*. Robert Hale, 1986.

Aherne, Brian. *A Proper Job*. Houghton Mifflin, 1969.

Alam, Asadollah. *The Shah and I*. St. Martin's, 1991.

Alexander, Paul. *Boulevard of Broken Dreams: The Life, Times, and Legend of James Dean*. Viking, 1994.

Allyson, June, and Frances Spatz Leighton. *June Allyson*. G. P. Putnam's Sons, 1982.

Alpert, Hollis. *The Barrymores*. Dial Press, 1964.

Altman, Diana. *Hollywood East*. Hawthorn Books, 1992.

Andersen, Christopher. *Citizen Jane: The Turbulent Life of Jane Fonda*. Henry Holt, 1990.

———. *Jagger Unauthorized*. Delacorte Press, 1993.

———. *Madonna Unauthorized*. Simon and Schuster, 1991.

———. *Michael Jackson: Unauthorized*. Simon and Schuster, 1994.

Anderson, Loni, and Larkin Warren. *My Life in High Heels*. William Morrow, 1995.

Anger, Kenneth. *Hollywood Babylon*. Associated Press Professional Services, 1965.

———. *Hollywood Babylon: II*. E. P. Dutton, 1984.

Ankerich, Michael C. *Broken Silence: Conversations With Twenty-Five Silent Film Stars*. McFarland, 1993.

Ann-Margret. *Ann-Margret: My Story*. G. P. Putnam's Sons, 1994.

Anthony, Jolene M. *Tom Cruise*. St. Martin's, 1988.

Arce, Hector. *Gary Cooper: An Intimate Biography*. William Morrow, 1979.

———. *The Secret Life of Tyrone Power*. William Morrow, 1979.

Arden, Eve. *Three Phrases of Eve*. St. Martin's, 1985.

Arnaz, Desi. *A Book*. William Morrow, 1976.

Arnold, William. *Shadowland*. McGraw-Hill, 1978.

Ashley, Elizabeth. *Actress: Postcards From the Road*. M. Evans, 1978.

Astor, Mary. *A Life on Film*. Delacorte Press, 1971.

———. *Mary Astor: My Story*. Doubleday, 1959.

Aumont, Jean-Pierre. *Sun and Shadow*. W. W. Norton, 1977.

Bacall, Lauren. *Lauren Bacall by Myself*. Alfred A. Knopf, 1978.

———. *Now*. Alfred A. Knopf, 1994.

Bach, Steven. *Marlene Dietrich: Life and Legend*. William Morrow, 1992.

Bacon, James. *Hollywood Is a Four-Letter Word*. Henry Regnery, 1976.

———. *Made in Hollywood*. Contemporary Books, 1977.

Baker, Carroll. *Baby Doll*. Arbor Books, 1983.

Baker, Jean-Claude, and Chris Chase. *Josephine: The Hungry Heart*. Random House, 1993.

Ball, Lucille, with Betty Hannah Hoffman. *Love Lucy*. G. P. Putnam's Sons, 1996.

Barker, Malcolm J., with T. C. Sobey. *Living With the Queen*. Barricade Books, 1991.

Barlett, Donald L., and James B. Steele. *Empire: The Life, Legend, and Madness of Howard Hughes*. W. W. Norton, 1979.

Barrymore, Diana. *Too Much, Too Soon*. Henry Holt, 1957.

Basquette, Lina. *Lina: De Mille's Godless Girl*. Derlinger's Publishers, 1990.

Baxter, Anne. *Intermission*. G. P. Putnam's Sons, 1976.

Baxter, John. *Fellini*. St. Martin's, 1993.

Beck, Marilyn. *Marilyn Beck's Hollywood*. 1973.

Bego, Mark. *The Best of Modern Screen*. St. Martin's, 1986.

———. *Rock Hudson*. Signet, 1986

Behlmer, Rudy. *Memo From Darryl F. Zanuck: The Golden Years at Twentieth Century–Fox*. Grove Press, 1993.

———. *Inside Warner*. Viking, 1985.

Behr, Edward. *The Good Frenchman: The True Story of the Life and Times of Maurice Chevalier*. Villard Books, 1993.

Behrman, S. N. *People in a Diary: A Memoir*. Little, Brown, 1972.

Bell, Simon, with Richard Curtis and Helen Fielding. *Who's Had Who*. Warner Books, 1990.

Bender, Marylin. *The Beautiful People*. Coward-McCann, 1967.

Bennett, Joan, and Lois Kibbee. *The Bennett Playbill*. Holt, Rinehart and Winston, 1970.

Benson, Ross. *Charles: The Untold Story*. St. Martin's, 1993.

Berg, A. Scott. *Goldwyn*. Alfred A. Knopf, 1989.

Bergen, Candice. *Knock Wood*. G. K. Hall, 1984.

Bergman, Ingmar. *The Magic Lantern*. Viking, 1988.

Bergman, Ingrid, and Alan Burgess. *Ingrid Bergman: My Story*. Delacorte Press, 1980.

Berle, Milton. *B. S. I Love You*. McGraw-Hill, 1988.

Berle, Milton, with Haskel Frankal. *Milton Berle: An Autobiography*. Delacorte Press, 1974.

Bernard, Matt. *Mario Lanza*. Macfadden-Bartell, 1971.

Bibb, Porter. *It Ain't as Easy as it Looks*. Crown, 1993.

Black, Jonathan. *Streisand*. Leisure Books/Norden, 1980.

Blair, Clay Jr., and Joan Blair. *The Search for JFK*. Berkley, 1976.

Blake, Michael F. *Lon Chaney: The Man Behind the Thousand Faces*. Vestal Press, 1990.

Bloom, Claire. *Leaving a Doll's House*. Little, Brown, 1996.

———. *Limelight and After*. Harper and Row, 1982.

Bly, Nellie. *Barbra Streisand: The Untold Story*. Pinnacle Books, 1994.

———. *Marlon Brando: Larger Than Life*. Pinnacle Books, 1994.

———. *The Kennedy Men*. Kensington Books, 1996.

———. *Oprah! Up Close and Down Home*. Zebra Books, 1993.

Bogart, Stephen Humphrey. *In Search of My Father*. E. P. Dutton, 1995.

Bona, Damien. *Opening Shots*. Workman, 1994.

Bonderoff, Jason. *Tom Selleck: An Unauthorized Biography*. Signet/NAL, 1983.

Bosworth, Patricia. *Montgomery Clift*. Harcourt Brace Jovanovich, 1978.

Botham, Noel, and Peter Donnelly. *Valentino: The Love God*. Ace Books, 1976.

Bova, Joyce. *Don't Ask Forever*. Kensington Books, 1994.

Bowie, Angela. *Backstage Passes*. G. P. Putnam's Sons, 1993.

Bradshaw, Jon. *Dreams Money Can Buy*. William Morrow, 1985.

Brady, Frank. *Citizen Welles*. Charles Scribner's Sons, 1989.

———. *Onassis: An Extravagant Life*. Prentice-Hall, 1977.

Brady, Kathleen. *Lucille*. Hyperion, 1994.

Bragg, Melvyn. *Richard Burton: A Life*. Little, Brown, 1988.

Brando, Anna Kashfi, and E. P. Stein. *Brando for Breakfast*. Crown, 1979.

Brando, Marlon. *Songs My Mother Taught Me*. Random House, 1994.

Braun, Eric. *Deborah Kerr*. W. H. Allen, 1977.

Brenman-Gibson, Margaret. *Clifford Odets: American Playwright—The Years from 1906 to 1940*. Atheneum, 1981.

Brian, Denis. *Tallulah Darling: A Biography of Tallulah Bankhead*. Pyramid, 1972.

Brooks, Louise. *Lulu in Hollywood*. Alfred A. Knopf, 1982.

Brown, David. *Star Billing*. Weidenfeld and Nicolson, 1985.

Brown, Peter H. *Marilyn: The Last Take*. E. P. Dutton, 1992.

Brown, Peter Harry. *Kim Novak: The Reluctant Goddess*. St. Martin's, 1986.

———. *Such Devoted Sisters: Those Fabulous Gabors*. St. Martin's, 1985.

Brown, Peter Harry, and Pamela Ann Brown. *The MGM Girls: Behind the Velvet Curtain*. St. Martin's, 1983.

Brown, Peter Harry, and Pat H. Broeske. *Howard Hughes: The Untold Story*. E. P. Dutton, 1996.

Brownlow, Kevin. *The Parade's Gone By. . . .* University of California Press, 1968.

Brunette, Peter. *Roberto Rossellini*. Oxford University Press, 1987.

Bruno, Michael. *Venus in Hollywood*. Lyle Stuart, 1970.

Brynner, Rock. *Yul: The Man Who Would Be King*. Simon and Schuster, 1989.

Burton, Humphrey. *Leonard Bernstein*. Doubleday, 1994.

Burton, William Westbrook. *Conversations About Bernstein*. Oxford University Press, 1995.

Cafarakis, Christian. *The Fabulous Onassis: His Life and Loves*. William Morrow, 1972.

Callow, Simon. *Charles Laughton: A Difficult Actor*. Grove Press, 1987.

————. *Orson Welles: The Road to Xanadu*. Viking, 1995.

Calvet, Corinne. *Has Corinne Been a Good Girl?* St. Martin's, 1983.

Callan, Michael Feeney. *Julie Christie*. St. Martin's, 1984.

————. *Richard Harris*. Sidgwick & Jackson, 1990.

Canales, Luis. *Imperial Gina*. Branden, 1990.

Capote, Truman. *Answered Prayers: The Unfinished Novel*. Random House, 1987.

————. *Music for Chameleons*. Random House, 1980.

Carey, Gary. *All the Stars in Heaven: Louis B. Mayer's MGM*. E. P. Dutton, 1981.

————. *Anita Loos*. Alfred A. Knopf, 1988.

————. *Judy Holliday: An Intimate Life Story*. Seaview Books, 1982.

Cary, Diana Serra. *Hollywood's Children*. Houghton Mifflin, 1979.

Carne, Judy. *Laughing on the Outside, Crying on the Inside*. Rawson Associates, 1985.

Caserta, Peggy. *Going Down With Janis*. Dell, 1974.

Cassini, Igor, with Jeanne Molli. *I'd Do It All Over Again*. G. P. Putnam's Sons, 1977.

Cassini, Oleg. *In My Own Fashion*. Simon and Schuster, 1987.

Castle, William. *Step Right Up: I'm Going to Scare the Pants Off America*. G. P. Putnam's Sons, 1976.

Catalano, Grace. *Brad Pitt: Hot and Sexy*. Bantam Books, 1995.

Celebrity Research Group. *Bedside Book of Celebrity Gossip*. Crown, 1984.

Celebrity Service International. *Earl Blackwell's Entertainment Celebrity Register*. Visible Ink, 1991.

Chandler, Charlotte. *I, Fellini*. Random House, 1995.

————. *The Ultimate Seduction*. Doubleday, 1984.

Chaplin, Charles. *My Autobiography*. Simon and Schuster, 1964.

Chaplin, Saul. *The Golden Age of Movie Musicals and Me*. University of Oklahoma Press, 1994.

Christian, Linda. *Linda: My Own Story*. Crown, 1962.

Citron, Stephen. *Noël and Cole: The Sophisticates*. Oxford University Press, 1993.

Clarke, Donald. *Wishing on the Moon: The Life and Times of Billie Holliday*. Viking, 1994.

Clarke, Gerald. *Capote: A Biography*. Simon and Schuster, 1988.

Clayson, Alan. *Ringo Starr*. Paragon House, 1991.

Clinch, Minty. *Burt Lancaster*. Stein and Day, 1985.

————. *Robert Redford*. New English Library, 1989.

Coe, Jonathan. *Humphrey Bogart: Take It and Like It*. Grove Weidenfeld, 1991.

Cole, Gerald, and Wes Farrell. *The Fondas*. W. H. Allen, 1984.

Collier, James Lincoln. *Duke Ellington*. Oxford University Press, 1987.

Collins, Joan. *Joan Collins: Past Imperfect*. W. H. Allen, 1978.

Collins, Nancy. *Hard to Get*. Random House, 1990.

Colman, Juliet Benita. *Ronald Colman: A Very Private Man*. William Morrow, 1975.

Colombo, John Robert, ed. *Popcorn in Paradise*. Holt, Rinehart and Winston, 1979.

Conner, Floyd. *Lupe Velez and Her Lovers*. Barricade Books, 1993.

———. *Pretty Poison: The Tuesday Weld Story*. Barricade Books, 1995.

Conover, David. *Finding Marilyn: A Romance*. Grosset and Dunlap, 1981.

Conrad, Earl. *Billy Rose: Manhattan Primitive*. World, 1968.

Considine, Shaun. *Barbra Streisand*. Delacorte Press, 1985.

———. *Bette and Joan: The Divine Feud*. E. P. Dutton, 1989.

———. *Mad as Hell: The Life and Work of Paddy Chayefsky*. Random House, 1994.

Cooper, Jackie, and Dick Kleiner. *Please Don't Shoot My Dog*. William Morrow, 1981.

Crane, Cheryl. *Detour: A Hollywood Story*. William Morrow, 1988.

Crawford, Joan, with Jane Kerner Ardmore. *A Portrait of Joan*. Doubleday, 1962.

Crawley, Tony. *Bébé: The Films of Brigitte Bardot*. Citadel Press, 1977.

Crivello, Kirk. *Fallen Angels*. Citadel Press, 1988.

Crowther, Bosley. *Hollywood Rajah*. Holt, Rinehart and Winston, 1960.

Curcio, Vincent. *Suicide Blonde: The Life of Gloria Grahame*. William Morrow, 1989.

Curtis, James. *Between Flops*. Harcourt Brace Jovanovich, 1982.

Curtis, Tony, and Barry Paris. *Tony Curtis: The Autobiography*. William Morrow, 1993.

Curtiss, Thomas Quinn. *Erich von Stroheim*. Farrar, Straus and Giroux, 1971.

Daly, Marsha. *Steve Martin: An Unauthorized Biography*. Signet/NAL, 1980.

———. *Sylvester Stallone: An Illustrated Life*. St. Martin's, 1995.

Dandridge, Dorothy, and Earl Conrad. *Everything and Nothing: The Dorothy Dandridge Tragedy*. Abelard-Schuman, 1970.

Dardis, Tom. *Keaton: The Man Who Wouldn't Lie Down*. Charles Scribner's Sons, 1979.

———. *Some Time in the Sun*. Charles Scribner's Sons, 1976.

Darin, Dodd. *Dream Lovers*. Warner Books, 1994.

David, Catherine. *Simone Signoret*. Overlook Press, 1993.

David, Lester. *Jacqueline Kennedy Onassis: A Portrait of Her Private Years*. Birch Lane Press, 1994.

David, Lester, and Jhan Robbins. *Richard and Elizabeth*. Funk and Wagnalls, 1977.

Davidson, Bill. *The Real and Unreal*. Harper and Brothers, 1961.

———. *Spencer Tracy: Tragic Idol*. E. P. Dutton, 1987.

Davis, Bette. *The Lonely Life*. G. P. Putnam's Sons, 1962.

———. *This 'n' That*. G. P. Putnam's Sons, 1987.

Davis, John H. *The Kennedys: Dynasty and Disaster 1848–1984*. McGraw-Hill, 1984.

Davis, Judith. *Richard Gere: An Unauthorized Biography*. Signet/NAL, 1983.

Davis, Sammy Jr., and Burt Boyar with Jane Boyar. *Why Me: The Sammy Davis Jr. Story*. Farrar, Straus and Giroux, 1989.

Davis, Sammy Jr., *Hollywood in a Suitcase*. William Morrow, 1980.

Davis, Ronald L. *Hollywood Beauty: Linda Darnell and the American Dream*. University of Oklahoma Press, 1991.

———. *The Glamour Factory*. Southern Methodist University Press, 1993.

———. *John Ford: Hollywood's Old Master*. University of Oklahoma Press, 1995.

De Carlo, Yvonne, and Doug Warren. *Yvonne: An Autobiography*. St. Martin's, 1987.

De Cordova, Fred. *Johnny Came Lately*. Simon and Schuster, 1988.

de Havilland, Olivia. *Every Frenchman Has One*. Random House, 1961.

Dent, Alan. *Mrs. Patrick Campbell*. Museum Press, 1961.

deRosso, Diana. *James Mason*. Lennard Publishing, 1989.

Des Barres, Pamela. *I'm With the Band: Confessions of a Groupie*. Beech Tree Books, 1987.

———. *Take Another Little Piece of My Heart*. William Morrow, 1992.

Deutsch, Armand. *Bogie and Me*. G. P. Putnam's Sons, 1991.

Dewey, Donald. *Marcello Mastroianni*. Birch Lane Press, 1993.

Diane, Jacobs. *Christmas in July: The Life and Art of Preston Sturges*. University of California Press, 1992.

Dick, Bernard. *The Merchant Prince of Poverty Row*. University of Kentucky Press, 1993.

Dick, Bernard F. *Hellman in Hollywood*. Fairleigh-Dickinson University Press, 1982.

Dickens, Norman. *Jack Nicholson: The Search for a Superstar*. New American Library, 1975.

DiOrio, Al. *Barbara Stanwyck*. Coward-McCann, 1983.

———. *Borrowed Time*. Running Press, 1981.

———. *Little Girl Lost: The Life and Hard Times of Judy Garland*. Arlington House, 1973.

Dougan, Andy. *Untouchable*. Thunder's Mouth Press, 1996.

Douglas, Kirk. *The Ragman's Son*. Simon and Schuster, 1988.

Downing, David. *Jack Nicholson*. Stein and Day, 1984.

Duberman, Martin Bauml. *Paul Robeson*. Alfred A. Knopf, 1988.

Du Bois, Diana. *In Her Sister's Shadow*. Little, Brown, 1995.

Duke, Patty, and Kenneth Turan. *Call Me Anna: The Autobiography of Patty Duke*. Bantam Books, 1987.

Duke, Pony, with Jason Thomas. *Too Rich: The Family Secrets of Doris Duke*. HarperCollins, 1996.

Dunaway, David King. *Huxley in Hollywood*. Harper and Row, 1989.

Dunaway, Faye. *Looking for Gatsby*. Simon and Schuster, 1995.

Dundy, Elaine. *Finch, Bloody Finch: A Life of Peter Finch*. Holt, Rinehart and Winston, 1980.

Durgnat, Raymond, and Scott Simmon. *King Vidor: American*. University of California Press, 1988.

Edmonds, Andy. *Bugsy's Baby*. Birch Lane Press, 1993.

———. *Hot Toddy*. William Morrow, 1989.

Edwards, Anne. *Early Reagan*. William Morrow, 1987.

———. *Judy Garland: A Biography*. Simon and Schuster, 1974.

————. *Shirley Temple: American Princess*. William Morrow, 1988.

————. *Throne of Gold: The Lives of the Aga Khans*. William Morrow, 1995.

————. *Vivien Leigh*. Simon and Schuster, 1977.

Edwards, Larry. *Buster: A Legend in Laughter*. McGwinn & McGuire, 1995.

Edwards, Michael. *In the Shadow of the King: Priscilla, Elvis, and Me*. St. Martin's, 1988.

Eells, George. *Final Gig*. Harcourt Brace Jovanovich, 1991.

————. *Hedda and Louella*. G. P. Putnam's Sons, 1972.

————. *Ginger, Loretta, and Irene Who?* G. P. Putnam's Sons, 1976.

————. *Robert Mitchum: A Biography*. Franklin Watts, 1984.

————. *The Life That Late He Led*. G. P. Putnam's Sons, 1967.

Eells, George, and Stanley Musgrove. *Mae West*. William Morrow, 1982.

Eisenschitz, Bernard. *Nicholas Ray*. Faber and Faber, 1993.

Ekland, Britt. *True Britt*. Prentice-Hall, 1980.

Eliot, Marc. *Burt!: The Unauthorized Biography*. Dell, 1982.

————. *Walt Disney: Hollywood's Dark Prince*. Birch Lane Press, 1993.

Epstein, Edward Z. *Portrait of Jennifer*. Simon and Schuster, 1995.

Esposito, Joe, and Elena Cumans. *Good Rockin' Tonight*. Simon and Schuster, 1994.

Evans, Peter. *Ari: The Life and Times of Aristotle Socrates Onassis*. Summit Books, 1986.

————. *Bardot: Eternal Sex Goddess*. Leslie Frewin, 1972.

————. *Peter Sellers: The Mask Behind the Mask*. New English Library, 1980.

————. *The Kid Stays in the Picture*. Hyperion, 1994.

Eyeles, Allen. *James Stewart*. Stein and Day, 1984.

Eyman, Scott. *Ernst Lubitsch: Laughter in Paradise*. Simon and Schuster, 1993.

————. *Mary Pickford: America's Sweetheart*. Donald I. Fine, 1990.

Fairbanks, Douglas Jr. *A Hell of a War*. St. Martin's, 1993.

————. *The Salad Days*. Doubleday, 1988.

Fairey, Wendy W. *One of the Family*. W. W. Norton, 1992.

Farber, Stephen, and Marc Green. *Hollywood Dynasties*. Delilah Communications, 1984.

————. *Hollywood on the Couch*. William Morrow, 1993.

Faulkner, Trader. *Peter Finch*. Taplinger Publishing, 1979.

Feibleman, Peter. *Lilly*. William Morrow, 1988.

Feinman, Jeffrey. *Hollywood Confidential*. Playboy Press, 1976.

Ferris, Paul. *Richard Burton*. Coward, McCann and Geoghegan, 1981.

Fine, Marshall. *Bloody Sam*. Donald I. Fine, 1991.

Fisher, Clive. *Noël Coward*. St. Martin's, 1992.

Fisher, Eddie. *Eddie: My Life and Loves*. Harper and Row, 1981.

Fishgall, Gary. *Against Type: The Biography of Burt Lancaster*. Scribner, 1995.

Fitz-Simon, Christopher. *The Boys*. Nick Hern Books, 1994.

Flamini, Roland. *Ava*. Coward, McCann and Geoghegan, 1983.

————. *Scarlett, Rhett, and a Cast of Thousands*. Macmillan, 1975.

————. *Thalberg*. Crown, 1994.

Fleming, Karl, and Ann Taylor Fleming. *The First Time*. Simon and Schuster, 1975.

Fonda, Henry. *Fonda: My Life*. New American Library, 1981.

Fontaine, Joan. *No Bed of Roses: An Autobiography*. William Morrow, 1978.

Ford, Glenn, and Margaret Redfield. *Glenn Ford: RFD Beverly Hills*. Hewitt House, 1970.

Fountain, Leatrice Gilbert. *Dark Star*. St. Martin's, 1985.

Francisco, Charles. *Gentleman: The William Powell Story*. St. Martin's, 1985.

Frank, Gerold. *Judy*. Harper and Row, 1975.

Frankel, Jennie Louise, Terrie Maxine Frankel, and Joanne Parrent. *You'll Never Make Love in This Town Again*. Dove Books, 1995.

Freedland, Michael. *Cagney*. Stein and Day, 1975.

————. *Gregory Peck*. William Morrow, 1980.

————. *Jolson*. Stein and Day, 1972.

————. *Maurice Chevalier*. William Morrow, 1981.

————. *Peter O'Toole*. St. Martin's, 1982.

————. *The Secret Life of Danny Kaye*. St. Martin's, 1985.

————. *Sophie: The Sophie Tucker Story*. Woburn Press, 1978.

————. *The Two Lives of Errol Flynn*. William Morrow, 1978.

Frewin, Leslie. *The Late Mrs. Dorothy Parker*. Macmillan, 1986.

Frischauer, Willi. *Bardot: An Intimate Biography*. Michael Joseph, 1978.

————. *Behind the Scenes of Otto Preminger*. William Morrow, 1974.

Fussell, Betty Harper. *Mabel*. Tichnor and Fields, 1982.

Gabler, Neal. *Winchell: Gossip, Power, and the Culture of Celebrity*. Alfred A. Knopf, 1995.

Gabor, Eva. *Orchids and Salami*. Doubleday, 1954.

Gabor, Zsa Zsa. *Zsa Zsa Gabor: My Story*. World, 1960.

Gabor, Zsa Zsa, and Wendy Leigh. *One Lifetime Is Not Enough*. Delacorte Press, 1991.

Gaines, Steven, and Sharon Churcher. *Obsession: The Life and Times of Calvin Klein*. Birch Lane Press, 1994.

Galante, Pierre. *Mademoiselle Chanel*. Henry Regnery, 1973.

Gardner, Ava. *Ava: My Story*. Bantam Books, 1990.

Gausberg, Alan L. *Edward G. Robinson: Little Caesar*. New England Library, 1983.

Geist, Kenneth L. *Pictures Will Talk*. Charles Scribner's Sons, 1978.

George, Don. *Sweet Man: The Real Duke Ellington*. G. P. Putnam's Sons, 1981.

Gibson, Barbara. *The Kennedys: The Third Generation*. Thunder's Mouth Press, 1993.

Gilbert, Julie. *Opposite Attraction*. Pantheon Books, 1995.

Glatt, John. *Lost in Hollywood: The Fast Times and Short Life of River Phoenix*. Donald I. Fine, 1995.

Gil-Montero, Martha. *Brazilian Bombshell*. Donald I. Fine, 1989.

Godfrey, Lionel. *The Life and Crimes of Errol Flynn*. St. Martin's, 1977.

Goldberg, Robert, and Gerald Jay Goldberg. *Citizen Turner*. Harcourt Brace, 1995.

Goldman, Albert. *Elvis*. McGraw-Hill, 1981.

———. *Ladies and Gentlemen—Lenny Bruce!!* Random House, 1974.

———. *The Lives of John Lennon*. William Morrow, 1988.

Goldman, Herbert G. *Fanny Brice: The Original Funny Girl*. Oxford University Press, 1992.

———. *Jolson: The Legend Comes to Life*. Oxford University Press, 1988.

Goldsmith, Barbara. *Little Gloria . . . Happy at Last*. Alfred A. Knopf, 1980.

Goldstein, Toby. *Sally Field*. PaperJacks, 1988.

———. *William Hurt: The Man, the Actor*. St. Martin's, 1987.

Goodman, Ezra. *Fifty-Year Decline and Fall of Hollywood*. Simon and Schuster, 1961.

Gottfried, Martin. *All His Jazz: The Life and Death of Bob Fosse*. Bantam Books, 1990.

———. *Jed Harris: The Curse of Genius*. Little, Brown, 1984.

———. *Nobody's Fool: The Lives of Danny Kaye*. Simon and Schuster, 1994.

Gottlieb, Polly Rose. *The Nine Lives of Billy Rose*. Crown, 1968.

Govoni, Albert. *Cary Grant: An Unauthorized Biography*. Henry Regnery, 1971.

Graham, Don. *No Name on the Bullet*. Viking Penguin, 1989.

Graham, Sheilah. *Confessions of a Hollywood Columnist*. William Morrow, 1969.

———. *Garden of Allah*. Crown, 1970.

———. *Hollywood Revisited*. St. Martin's, 1985.

———. *How to Marry Super Rich*. Grosset and Dunlap, 1974.

Granger, Stewart. *Sparks Fly Upward*. Granada, 1981.

Gray, Marianne. *La Moreau*. Donald I. Fine, 1994.

Greenwood, Earl. *The Boy Who Would Be King*. E. P. Dutton, 1990.

Gregory, Adela, and Milo Speriglio. *Crypt 33: The Saga of Marilyn Monroe—The Final Word*. Birch Lane Press, 1993.

Grobel, Lawrence. *Conversations with Capote*. New American Library, 1985.

———. *The Hustons*. Charles Scribner's Sons, 1989.

Gronowicz, Antoni. *Garbo: Her Story*. Simon and Schuster, 1990.

Grosland, Margaret. *Piaf*. G. P. Putnam's Sons, 1985.

Grossman, Barbara W. *Funny Woman*. Indiana University Press, 1991.

Gross, Michael. *Model*. William Morrow, 1995.

Groteke, Kristi, and Marjorie Rosen. *Mia and Woody: Love and Betrayal*. Carroll and Graf, 1994.

Gubernick, Lisa Rebecca. *Squandered Fortune: The Life and Times of Huntington Hartford*. G. P. Putnam's Sons, 1991.

Guiles, Fred Lawrence. *Joan Crawford: The Last Word*. Birch Lane Press, 1995.

———. *Marion Davies*. McGraw-Hill, 1972.

———. *Norma Jean: The Life of Marilyn Monroe*. McGraw-Hill, 1979.

———. *Stan: The Life of Stan Laurel*. Stein and Day, 1980.

Gussow, Mel. *Don't Say Yes Until I Finish Talking: A Biography of Darryl Zanuck*. Doubleday, 1971.

Guthrie, Lee. *The Lives and Loves of Cary Grant*. Drake, 1977.

Hadleigh, Boze. *Bette Davis Speaks*. Barricade Books, 1996.

———. *Conversations With My Elders*. St. Martin's, 1976.

———. *Hollywood Babble On*. Birch Lane Press, 1994.

———. *Hollywood Gays*. Barricade Books, 1996.

———. *Hollywood Lesbians*. Barricade Books, 1994.

———. *The Vinyl Closet*. Los Hombres Press, 1992.

Hall, Elaine Blake. *Burt and Me: My Days and Nights With Burt Reynolds*. Pinnacle Books, 1994.

Hall, William. *Raising Caine*. Prentice-Hall, 1981.

Hamblett, Charles. *Who Killed Marilyn Monroe?* Leslie Frewin, 1966.

Hamilton, Nigel. *JFK: Reckless Youth*. Random House, 1992.

Haney, Lynn. *Naked at the Feast*. Dodd, Mead, 1981.

Hanna, David. *Come Up and See Me Sometime: A Confidential Biography of Mae West*. Tower, 1976.

Hanna, Robert. *Robert Redford*. Nordon Publications, 1978.

Hanut, Eryk. *I Wish You Love: Conversations With Marlene Dietrich*. Frog, 1996.

Harmetz, Aljean. *Rolling Thunder and Other Movie Business*. Alfred A. Knopf, 1983.

———. *Round Up the Usual Suspects*. Hyperion, 1992.

Harris, Marlys J. *The Zanucks of Hollywood*. Crown, 1989.

Harris, Radie. *Radie's World*. G. P. Putnam's Sons, 1975.

Harris, Warren G. *Audrey Hepburn*. Simon and Schuster, 1994.

———. *Lucy and Desi*. Simon and Schuster, 1991.

———. *Natalie and R. J.: Hollywood's Star-Crossed Lovers*. Doubleday, 1988.

———. *The Other Marilyn*. Arbor House, 1985.

Harrison, Elizabeth. *Love, Honor, and Dismay*. Doubleday, 1977.

Harrison, Rex. *Rex: An Autobiography*. William Morrow, 1975.

Hart, Kitty Carlisle. *Kitty*. Doubleday, 1988.

Haskins, James, and Kathleen Benson. *Lena*. Stein and Day, 1984.

Hayman, Ronald. *Tennessee Williams: Everyone Else Is an Audience*. Yale University Press, 1993.

Hayward, Brooke. *Haywire*. Alfred A. Knopf, 1977.

Head, Edith, and Paddy Calistro. *Edith Head's Hollywood*. E. P. Dutton, 1983.

Helms, Alan. *Young Man From the Provinces*. Faber and Faber, 1995.

Henner, Marilu, with Jim Jerome. *By All Means Keep on Moving*. Pocket Books, 1994.

Henreid, Paul, and Julius Fast. *Ladies' Man*. St. Martin's, 1984.

Henry, William A. III. *The Great One: The Life and Legend of Jackie Gleason*. Doubleday, 1992.

Herman, Jan. *A Talent for Trouble*. G. P. Putnam's Sons, 1995.

Herndon, Venable. *James Dean: A Short Life*. Doubleday, 1974.

Heymann, C. David. *Liz*. Birch Lane Press, 1995.

———. *Poor Little Rich Girl*. Lyle Stuart, 1983.

———. *A Woman Named Jackie*. Lyle Stuart, 1989.

Hickey, Des, and Gus Smith. *The Prince: The Public and Private Life of Laurence Harvey*. Leslie Frewin, 1975.

Higham, Charles. *Audrey: The Life of Audrey Hepburn*. Macmillan, 1984.

———. *Ava: A Life Story*. Delacorte Press, 1974.

———. *Bette*. Macmillan, 1981.

———. *Brando*. New American Library, 1987.

———. *Charles Laughton*. Doubleday, 1976.

———. *Errol Flynn: The Untold Story*. Doubleday, 1980.

———. *Howard Hughes: The Secret Life*. G. P. Putnam's Sons, 1993.

———. *Kate: The Life of Katharine Hepburn*. W. W. Norton, 1975.

———. *The Life of Marlene Dietrich*. W. W. Norton, 1988.

———. *Lucy: The Real Life of Lucille Ball*. St. Martin's, 1986.

———. *Merchant of Dreams: L. B. Mayer, MGM, and the Secret Hollywood*. Donald I. Fine, 1993.

———. *Orson Welles: The Rise and Fall of an American Genius*. St. Martin's, 1985.

———. *Rose*. Pocket Books, 1995.

———. *Sisters*. Coward-McCann, 1984.

———. *Ziegfeld*. Henry Regnery, 1972.

Higham, Charles, and Roy Moseley. *Cary Grant: The Lonely Heart*. Harcourt Brace Jovanovich, 1989.

———. *Princess Merle: The Romantic Life of Merle Oberon*. Coward-McCann, 1983.

Hirschhorn, Clive. *Gene Kelly*. St. Martin's, 1984.

Hoare, Philip. *Noël Coward*. Simon and Schuster, 1995.

Holley, Val. *James Dean*. St. Martin's, 1995.

Holtzman, Will. *Judy Holliday*. G. P. Putnam's Sons, 1982.

Hopper, Hedda. *From Under My Hat*. Doubleday, 1952.

———. *The Whole Truth and Nothing But*. Doubleday, 1963.

Hoskyns, Barney. *Montgomery Clift: Beautiful Loser*. Bloomsbury, 1991.

Hotchner, A. E. *Doris Day: Her Own Story*. William Morrow, 1976.

———. *Sophia Living and Loving: Her Own Story*. William Morrow, 1979.

Houseman, Victoria. *Made in Heaven*. Bonus Books, 1991.

Howard, Ronald. *In Search of My Father*. St. Martin's, 1980.

Hudson, Rock, and Sara Davidson. *Rock Hudson: His Story*. Avon Books, 1986.

Hunter, Allan. *Faye Dunaway*. St. Martin's, 1986.

———. *Tony Curtis: The Man and His Movies*. St. Martin's, 1985.

Huston, John. *An Open Book: An Autobiography*. Alfred A. Knopf, 1980.

Hyams, Joe. *Bogie*. Signet/NAL, 1966.

———. *Mislaid in Hollywood*. Peter H. Wyden, 1973.

Hyams, Joe, and Jay Hyams. *James Dean: Little Boy Lost*. Warner Books, 1992.

Infield, Glenn. *Leni Riefenstahl*. Thomas Y. Crowell, 1976.

Israel, Lee. *Miss Tallulah Bankhead*. G. P. Putnam's Sons, 1972.

Jablonski, Edward. *Gershwin*. Doubleday, 1987.

Jackson, Carlton. *Hattie*. Madison Books, 1990.

Jeffries, J. T. *Jessica Lange*. St. Martin's, 1986.

Jenkins, Garry. *Daniel Day-Lewis: The Fire Within*. St. Martin's, 1995.

Jennings, Dean. *We Only Kill Each Other*. Prentice-Hall, 1967.

Jerome, Stuart. *Those Crazy Wonderful Years When We Ran Warner Brothers*. Lyle Stuart, 1983.

Jordan, Rene. *The Greatest Star: The Barbra Streisand Story*. G. P. Putnam's Sons, 1975.

Joyce, Aileen. *Julia: The Untold Story of America's Pretty Woman*. Pinnacle Books, 1993.

Kahn, E. J. *Jock: The Life and Times of John Hay Whitney*. Doubleday, 1981.

Kanin, Garson. *Hollywood*. Viking, 1974.

———. *Tracy and Hepburn: An Intimate Memoir*. Bantam Books, 1972.

Kashner, Sam, and Nancy Schoenberger. *A Talent for Genius: The Life and Times of Oscar Levant*. Villard Books, 1994.

Katz, Ephraim. *The Film Encyclopedia*. Second edition, HarperCollins, 1994.

Kazan, Elia. *A Life*. Alfred A. Knopf, 1988.

Keith, Slim, with Annette Tapert. *Slim: Memories of a Rich and Imperfect Life*. Simon and Schuster, 1990.

Kelley, Kitty. *Elizabeth Taylor: The Last Star*. Simon and Schuster, 1981.

———. *His Way: The Unauthorized Biography of Frank Sinatra*. Bantam Books, 1986.

———. *Jackie Oh!* Ballantine, 1979.

———. *Nancy Reagan: The Unauthorized Biography*. Simon and Schuster, 1991.

Kendall, Alan. *George Gershwin*. Universe Books, 1987.

Kessler, Judy. *Inside People*. Villard Books, 1994.

Kessler, Ronald. *The Sins of the Father*. Warner Books, 1996.

Kesting, Jürgen, translated by John Hunt. *Maria Callas*. Northeastern University Press, 1993.

Keyes, Evelyn. *I'll Think About That Tomorrow*. E. P. Dutton, 1991.

———. *Scarlett O'Hara's Younger Sister, or My Lively Life in or out of Hollywood*. Lyle Stuart, 1977.

Kidd, Charles. *Debrett Goes to Hollywood*. Weidenfeld and Nicolson, 1986.

Kiernan, Thomas. *Jane: An Intimate Biography of Jane Fonda*. G. P. Putnam's Sons, 1973.

———. *The Life and Times of Roman Polanski*. Grove, 1982.

———. *The Roman Polanski Story*. Grove, 1980.

———. *Repulsion*. New English Library, 1980.

———. *Sir Larry: The Life of Laurence Olivier*. Times Books, 1981.

Kirkpatrick, Sidney D. *A Cast of Killers*. E. P. Dutton, 1986.

Kissel, Howard. *David Merrick: The Abominable Showman*. Applause, 1993.

Kitt, Eartha. *Alone With Me*. Henry Regnery, 1976.

———. *Confessions of a Sex Kitten*. Barricade, 1991.

———. *Thursday's Child*. Duell, Sloan & Pearce, 1956.

Klurfield, Herman. *Winchell: His Life and Times*. Praeger, 1976.

Kobal, John. *People Will Talk*. Alfred A. Knopf, 1985.

———. *Rita Hayworth: The Time, the Place, and the Woman*. W. W. Norton, 1978.

Koch, Stephen. *Double Lives: Spies and Writers in the Secret Soviet War of Ideas Against the West*. Free Press, 1994.

Koffler, Kevin J. *The New Breed: Actors Coming of Age*. Henry Holt, 1988.

Konolige, Kit. *The Richest Women in the World*. Macmillan, 1985.

Korda, Michael. *Charmed Lives*. Random House, 1979.

Koski, John, and Mitchell Symons. *Movielists*. Chapmans, 1992.

Koszarski, Richard. *The Man You Loved to Hate*. Oxford University Press, 1983.

Kotsilibas-Davis, James. *The Barrymores: The Royal Family in Hollywood*. Crown, 1981.

Kotsilibas-Davis, James, and Myrna Loy. *Being and Becoming*. Alfred A. Knopf, 1987.

Kramer, Freda. *Jackie: A Truly Intimate Biography*. Grosset and Dunlap, 1979.

Kulik, Karol. *Alexander Korda: The Man Who Could Work Miracles*. Arlington, 1975.

Lacey, Robert. *Grace*. G. P. Putnam's Sons, 1994.

Laffey, Bruce. *Beatrice Lillie*. Wynwood Press, 1989.

LaGuardia, Robert. *Monty: A Biography of Montgomery Clift*. Arbor House, 1977.

LaGuardia, Robert, and Gene Arceri. *Red: The Tempestuous Life of Susan Hayward*. Macmillan, 1985.

Lake, Veronica, with Donald Bain. *Veronica*. Citadel Press, 1971.

Lamarr, Hedy. *Ecstasy and Me: My Life as a Woman*. Bartholomew, 1966.

Lambert, Gavin. *Norma Shearer*. Alfred A. Knopf, 1990.

Lamour, Dorothy. *My Side of the Road*. Prentice-Hall, 1980.

Lamparski, Richard. *Lamparski's Hidden Hollywood*. Simon and Schuster, 1981.

———. *Whatever Became of. . . ?* (Second series). Crown, 1968.

Landau, Deborah. *Janis Joplin: Her Life and Times*. Paperback Library, 1971.

Latham, Aaron. *Crazy Sundays: F. Scott Fitzgerald in Hollywood*. Viking, 1971.

Lawford, Patricia S. *The Peter Lawford Story*. Carroll and Graf, 1988.

Lawrence, Jerome. *Actor: The Life and Times of Paul Muni*. G. P. Putnam's Sons, 1974.

Lax, Eric. *Woody Allen*. Alfred A. Knopf, 1991.

Leamer, Laurence. *The Kennedy Women*. Villard Books, 1994.

———. *The King of the Night*. William Morrow, 1989.

Leaming, Barbara. *Bette Davis: A Biography*. Summit Books, 1992.

———. *If This Was Happiness*. Viking, 1989.

———. *Katharine Hepburn*. Crown, 1995.

———. *Orson Welles*. Viking, 1985.

———. *Polanski, the Filmmaker as Voyeur*. Simon and Schuster, 1982.

Lee, Jennifer. *Tarnished Angel*. Thunder's Mouth Press, 1991.

Leigh, Janet. *There Really Was a Hollywood*. Doubleday, 1984.

Leigh, Janet, with Christopher Nickens. *Psycho*. Harmony Books, 1995.

Leigh, Wendy. *Arnold*. Congdon and Weed, 1990.

———. *Liza: Born a Star*. E. P. Dutton, 1993.

———. *Prince Charming: The John F. Kennedy Jr. Story*. E. P. Dutton, 1993.

Lenburg, Jeff. *Dustin Hoffman: Hollywood's Antihero*. St. Martin's, 1983.

———. *Peekaboo: The Story of Veronica Lake*. St. Martin's, 1983.

Lenburg, Jeff, Greg Lenburg, and Randy Skretvedt. *Steve Martin: The Unauthorized Biography*. St. Martin's, 1980.

Lenzner, Robert. *The Great Getty*. Crown, 1985.

Leonard, Maurice. *Mae West: Empress of Sex*. Birch Lane Press, 1992.

LeRoy, Mervyn. *Mervyn LeRoy: Take One*. Hawthorne Books, 1984.

Leverich, Lyle. *Tom: The Unknown Tennessee Williams*. Crown, 1995.

Levy, Emanuel. *George Cukor: Master of Elegance*. William Morrow, 1994.

Levy, Shawn. *King of Comedy: The Life and Art of Jerry Lewis*. St. Martin's, 1996.

Lewis, Arthur H. *It Was Fun While It Lasted*. Trident Press, 1973.

Lewis, Judy. *Uncommon Knowledge*. Simon and Schuster, 1994.

Lewis, Roger. *The Life and Death of Peter Sellers*. Century, 1994.

Linet, Beverly. *Ladd*. Arbor House, 1979.

———. *Star-Crossed: The Story of Jennifer Jones and Robert Walker*. G. P. Putnam's Sons, 1986.

———. *Susan Hayward: Portrait of a Survivor*. Atheneum, 1980.

Loos, Anita. *A Girl Like I*. Viking, 1966.

———. *The Talmadge Girls*. Viking, 1978.

Lovelace, Linda, and Mike McGrady. *Ordeal*. Berkley, 1980.

MacGraw, Ali. *Moving Pictures*. Bantam Books, 1991.

Machlin, Milt. *Libby*. Tower, 1980.

MacLaine, Shirley. *My Lucky Stars*. Bantam Books, 1995.

Madden, Nelson C. *The Real Howard Hughes Story*. Manor, 1976.

Madsen, Axel. *Chanel: A Woman of Her Own*. Henry Holt, 1990.

———. *Gloria and Joe*. Arbor House, 1988.

———. *John Huston: A Biography*. Doubleday, 1978.

———. *The Sewing Circle*. Birch Lane Press, 1995.

———. *Stanwyck*. HarperCollins, 1994.

Madsen, Axel, and William Wyler. *William Wyler*. Thomas Y. Crowell, 1973.

Mailer, Norman. *Marilyn: A Biography*. Grosset and Dunlap, 1973.

Mair, George. *Oprah Winfrey: The Real Story*. Birch Lane Press, 1994.

Maltin, Leonard, ed. *Leonard Maltin's TV Movies and Video Guide*. NAL Penguin, 1996.

Mannering, Derek. *Mario Lanza*. Robert Hale, 1991.

Mansfield, Stephanie. *The Richest Girl in the World*. G. P. Putnam's Sons, 1992.

Manso, Peter. *Brando: The Biography*. Hyperion, 1994.

Marsh, Dave, and James Bernard. *The New Book of Rock Lists*. Fireside, 1994.

Martin, Mary. *My Heart Belongs*. Quill, 1984.

Martin, Pete. *Hollywood Without Makeup*. J. B. Lippincott, 1948.

Martin, Ralph S. *Seeds of Destruction: Joe Kennedy and His Sons*. G. P. Putnam's Sons, 1995.

Marx, Arthur. *Everybody Loves Somebody Sometime (Especially Himself)*. Hawthorne Books, 1974.

———. *Goldwyn*. W. W. Norton, 1976.

———. *The Nine Lives of Mickey Rooney*. Stein and Day, 1986.

———. *Red Skelton*. E. P. Dutton, 1979.

———. *The Secret Life of Bob Hope*. Barricade Books, 1993.

Marx, Kenneth S. *Star Stats: Who's Whose in Hollywood*. Price/Stern/Sloan, 1979.

Marx, Samuel. *A Gaudy Spree: Literary Hollywood When the West Was Fun*. Franklin Watts, 1987.

———. *Mayer and Thalberg: The Make-Believe Saints*. Random House, 1975.

Mason, James. *Before I Forget*. Hamish Hamilton, 1981.

Maychick, Diana. *Audrey Hepburn: An Intimate Portrait*. Birch Lane Press, 1993.

———. *Meryl Streep*. St. Martin's, 1984.

Maychick, Diana, and L. Avon Borgo. *Heart to Heart With Robert Wagner*. St. Martin's, 1986.

McAdams, William. *Ben Hecht*. Charles Scribner's Sons, 1990.

McBride, Mary Margaret. *The Life Story of Constance Bennett*. Star Library Publications, 1932.

McCabe, John. *Babe: The Life of Oliver Hardy*. Citadel Press, 1989.

McClelland, Doug. *Hollywood on Hollywood: Tinseltown Talks*. Faber and Faber, 1975.

———. *Star Speak: Hollywood on Everything*. Faber and Faber, 1987.

McGee, Tom. *The Girl With the Million Dollar Legs*. Vestal Press, 1995.

McGilligan, Patrick. *A Double Life: George Cukor*. St. Martin's, 1991.

———. *Jack's Life: A Biography of Jack Nicholson*. W. W. Norton, 1994.

McGovern, Dennis, and Deborah Grace Winer. *Sing Out, Louise!* Schirmer/Macmillan, 1993.

McKay, Keith. *Robert De Niro: The Hero Behind the Masks*. St. Martin's, 1986.

McKelway, Claire. *Gossip: The Life and Times of Walter Winchell*. Viking, 1940.

Meade, Marion. *Buster Keaton: Cut to the Chase*. HarperCollins, 1995.

———. *Dorothy Parker: What Fresh Hell Is This?* Villard Books, 1988.

Meredith, Burgess. *So Far, So Good*. Little, Brown, 1994.

Merrill, Gary, and John Cole. *Bette, Rita, and the Rest of My Life*. Lance Tapley, 1988.

Merryman, Richard. *Mank*. William Morrow, 1978.

Messick, Hank. *The Beauties and the Beasts*. David McKay, 1973.

Meyers, Jeffrey. *Scott Fitzgerald*. HarperCollins, 1994.

Miles, Sarah. *Serves Me Right*. Macmillan, 1994.

Milland, Ray. *Wide-Eyed in Babylon*. William Morrow, 1974.

Millar, Ingrid. *Liam Neeson*. St. Martin's, 1995.

Miller, Ann, with Norma Lee Browning. *Miller's High Life*. Doubleday, 1972.

Milton, Joyce. *Tramp: The Life of Charlie Chaplin*. HarperCollins, 1996.

Minnelli, Vincente, with Hector Arce. *I Remember It Well*. Doubleday, 1974.

Mix, Olive Stokes. *The Fabulous Tom Mix*. Prentice-Hall, 1975.

Mix, Paul E. *The Life and Legend of Tom Mix*. A. S. Barnes, 1972.

Moats, Alice-Leone. *The Million Dollar Studs*. Delacorte, 1977.

Monaco, James. *American Film Now*. New American Library, 1984.

Montgomery, Paul L. *Eva, Evita*. Pocket Books, 1979.

Moore, Terry. *The Beauty and the Billionaire*. Pocket Books, 1984.

Mordden, Ethan. *Movie Star: A Look at the Women Who Made Hollywood*. St. Martin's, 1983.

Morella, Joe. *Paul and Joanne: A Biography of Paul Newman and Joanne Woodward*. Delacorte Press, 1988.

Morella, Joe, and Edward Z. Epstein. *Brando: The Unauthorized Biography*. Crown, 1973.

———. *The "It" Girl: The Incredible Story of Clara Bow*. Delacorte Press, 1976.

———. *Jane Wyman*. Delacorte Press, 1985.

———. *Lana: The Public and Private Lives of Miss Turner*. Citadel Press, 1971.

———. *Loretta Young: An Extraodinary Life*. Delacorte Press, 1986.

———. *Mia: The Life of Mia Farrow*. Delacorte Press, 1991.

———. *Paulette: The Adventurous Life of Paulette Goddard*. St. Martin's, 1985.

Morella, Joseph, and George Mazzei. *Genius and Lust: The Creative and Sexual Lives of Cole Porter and Noël Coward*. Carroll and Graf, 1995.

Morgan, Henry. *Here's Morgan*. Barricade Books, 1995.

Morley, Sheridan. *Gertrude Lawrence*. McGraw-Hill, 1981.

———. *James Mason: Odd Man Out*. Harper and Row, 1989.

———. *The Other Side of the Moon*. Harper and Row, 1983.

Morris, George. *John Garfield*. Jove Publications, 1977.

Moseley, Leonard. *Zanuck*. Little, Brown, 1984.

Moseley, Roy. *Rex Harrison*. St. Martin's, 1987.

Blackwell, Mr., with Vernon Patterson. *From Rags to Bitches*. General Publishing Group, 1995.

Mungo, Ray. *Palm Springs Babylon*. St. Martin's, 1993.

Munn, Michael. *Charlton Heston*. St. Martin's, 1986.

———. *The Hollywood Murder Casebook*. St. Martin's, 1987.

———. *Hollywood Rogues*. St. Martin's, 1991.

———. *The Kid From the Bronx: A Biography of Tony Curtis*. W. H. Allen, 1984.

———. *Kirk Douglas.* St. Martin's, 1985.

Munshower, Suzanne. *The Diane Keaton Scrapbook.* Grosset and Dunlap, 1979.

———. *Don Johnson: An Unauthorized Biography.* Signet/NAL, 1986.

———. *John Travolta.* Grosset and Dunlap, 1976.

Naremore, James. *The Films of Vincente Minnelli.* Cambridge University Press, 1993.

Nash, Alana, with Billy Smith, Marty Lacker, and Lamar Fike. *Elvis Aaron Presley.* HarperCollins, 1995.

Neal, Patricia. *As I Am.* Simon and Schuster, 1988.

Negri, Pola. *Memoirs of a Star.* Doubleday, 1970.

Negulesco, Jean. *Things I Did and Things I Think I Did.* Simon and Schuster, 1984.

Newman, Phyllis. *Just in Time: Notes From My Life.* Simon and Schuster, 1988.

Nicholas, Margaret. *The World's Greatest Lovers.* Octopus Books, 1985.

Niven, David. *Bring on the Empty Horses.* G. P. Putnam's Sons, 1975.

———. *The Moon's a Balloon.* Coronet, 1971.

Norman, Barry. *The Film Greats.* Hodder and Staughton, 1985.

Odets, Clifford. *The Time Is Ripe: The 1940 Journal of Clifford Odets.* Grove Press, 1988.

Offen, Ron. *Cagney.* Henry Regnery, 1972.

Ogden, Christopher. *Life of the Party.* Little, Brown, 1994.

Onyx, Narda. *Water, World, and Weissmuller.* Vion, 1964.

Oppenheimer, Jerry, and Jack Vitek. *Idol: Rock Hudson.* Villard Books, 1986.

Oremano, Elena. *Paul Newman.* St. Martin's, 1989.

Outerbridge, James. *Without Makeup, Liv Ullman: A Photobiography.* William Morrow, 1979.

Palmer, Laura Kay. *Osgood and Anthony Perkins.* McFarland, 1991.

Papich, Stephen. *Remembering Josephine.* Bobbs-Merrill, 1976.

Paris, Barry. *Garbo.* Alfred A. Knopf, 1995.

———. *Louise Brooks.* Alfred A. Knopf, 1989.

Parish, James Robert. *The Fox Girls.* Arlington House, 1971.

———. *The Glamour Girls.* Rainbow Books, 1977.

———. *Great Western Stars.* Ace Books, 1976.

———. *The Hollywood Beauties.* Arlington House, 1978.

———. *The Hollywood Reliables.* Arlington House, 1980.

———. *The Jeanette MacDonald Story.* Mason/Charter, 1976.

———. *The Paramount Pretties.* Castle Books, 1972.

———. *The RKO Gals.* Rainbow Books, 1977.

———. *The Swashbucklers.* Arlington House, 1976.

———. *The Tough Guys.* Arlington House, 1976.

Parish, James Robert, and Ronald L. Bowers. *The MGM Stock Company: The Golden Years.* Arlington House, 1973.

Parish, James Robert, and Lennard DeCarl. *Hollywood Players: The Forties.* Arlington House, 1976.

Parish, James Robert, and William T. Leonard. *The Funsters.* Arlington House, 1979.

Parish, James Robert, and Michael R. Pitts. *Hollywood Songsters*. Garland, 1991.

Parish, James Robert, and Don E. Stanke. *The Debonairs*. Arlington House, 1975.

———. *The Forties Gals*. Arlington House, 1980.

———. *Hollywood Baby Boomers*. Arlington House, 1993.

———. *The Leading Ladies*. Arlington House, 1977.

Parish, James Robert, and Steven Whitney. *Vincent Price Unmasked*. Drake, 1974.

Parker, John. *Polanski*. Victor Gollancz, 1993.

———. *Sean Connery*. Contemporary Books, 1993.

———. *The Joker Is Wild: The Biography of Jack Nicholson*. Anaya, 1991.

———. *Warren Beatty: The Last Great Lover of Hollywood*. Carroll and Graf, 1993.

Parton, Dolly. *Dolly: My Life and Other Unfinished Business*. HarperCollins, 1994.

Passingham, Kenneth. *Sean Connery*. St. Martin's, 1983.

Pastos, Spero. *Pin-Up: The Story of Betty Grable*. G. P. Putnam's Sons, 1986.

Payn, Graham. *My Life With Noël Coward*. Applause Books, 1994.

Pearson, John. *Painfully Rich*. St. Martin's, 1995.

Peary, Danny. *Closeups*. Workman, 1978.

Pepitone, Lena, and William Stadiem. *Marilyn Monroe Confidential*. Simon and Schuster, 1979.

Peters, Margot. *The Barrymores*. Alfred A. Knopf, 1990.

Peyser, Joan. *Bernstein*. Birch Tree Books, 1987.

———. *The Memory of All That*. Simon and Schuster, 1993.

Pickard, Roy. *Jimmy Stewart: A Life in Film*. St. Martin's, 1992.

Pierce, Patrica Jobe. *The Ultimate Elvis: Day by Day*. Simon and Schuster, 1994.

Poitier, Sidney. *This Life*. Alfred A. Knopf, 1980.

Polanski, Roman. *Roman*. William Morrow, 1984.

Powell, Jane. *The Girl Next Door*. William Morrow, 1988.

Preminger, Otto. *Preminger: An Autobiography*. Doubleday, 1977.

Pryor, Richard. *Pryor Convictions*. Pantheon Books, 1995.

Queenan, Joe. *If You're Talking to Me, Your Career Must Be in Trouble*. Hyperion, 1994.

Quinn, Anthony. *One Man Tango*. HarperCollins, 1995.

———. *The Original Sin*. Little, Brown, 1972.

Quirk, Lawrence J. *Claudette Colbert*. Crown, 1985.

———. *Fasten Your Seat Belts: The Passionate Life of Bette Davis*. William Morrow, 1990.

———. *The Films of Fredric March*. Citadel Press, 1971.

———. *Jane Wyman: The Actress and the Woman*. Dembner Books, 1986.

———. *The Kennedys in Hollywood*. Taylor, 1996.

———. *Margaret Sullavan: Child of Fate*. St. Martin's, 1986.

————. *Norma*. St. Martin's, 1988.

————. *Totally Uninhibited: The Life and Wild Times of Cher*. William Morrow, 1991.

Ramer, Jean. *Duke: The Real Story of John Wayne*. Universal Award House, 1973.

Rasponi, Lanfranco. *International Nomads*. G. P. Putnam's Sons, 1966.

Rathbone, Basil. *In and Out of Character*. Doubleday, 1962.

Reagan, Ronald, and Richard G. Hubler. *Where's the Rest of Me?* Karz, 1981.

Redgrave, Deidre, with Danaë Brook. *To Be a Redgrave: Surviving Amidst the Glamour*. Linden Press/Simon and Schuster, 1982.

Reed, Donald A. *Robert Redford*. Sherbourne Press, 1976.

Reed, Oliver. *Reed About Me*. W. H. Allen, 1979.

Reed, Rex. *Big Screen, Little Screen*. Macmillan, 1971.

————. *Conversations in the Raw*. World, 1969.

————. *Do You Sleep in the Nude?* New American Library, 1968.

————. *People Are Crazy Here*. Delacorte Press, 1974.

————. *Travolta to Keaton*. William Morrow, 1979.

————. *Valentines and Vitriol*. Delacorte Press, 1977.

Reeves, Michael. *Travolta! A Photo Biography*. Jove Publications, 1978.

Reeves, Richard. *President Kennedy: Profile of Power*. Simon and Schuster, 1993.

Renay, Liz. *My First 2,000 Men*. Barricade Books, 1992.

Resnick, Sylvia S. *Burt Reynolds: An Unauthorized Biography*. St. Martin's, 1983.

Reynolds, Burt. *My Life*. Little, Brown, 1994.

Reynolds, Debbie, and David Patrick Columbia. *Debbie: My Life*. William Morrow, 1988.

Reynolds, Simon, and Joy Press. *The Sex Revolt*. Harvard University Press, 1995.

Rich, Sharon. *Sweethearts*. Donald I. Fine, 1994.

Richards, David. *Played Out: The Jean Seberg Story*. Random House, 1981.

Richman, Harry. *A Hell of a Life*. Duell, Sloan and Pearce, 1966.

Riefenstahl, Leni. *A Memoir*. St. Martin's, 1992.

Riese, Randall. *Her Name Is Barbra*. Birch Lane Press, 1993.

————. *The Unabridged James Dean*. Contemporary Books, 1991.

————. *The Unabridged Marilyn: Her Life From A to Z*. Congdon and Weed, 1987.

Riley, Lee. *Teen Dreams: Tom Cruise*. Pinnacle Books, 1985.

Riley, Lee, and David Shumacher. *The Sheens: Martin, Charlie, and Emilio*. St. Martin's, 1989.

Riva, Maria. *Marlene Dietrich*. Alfred A. Knopf, 1993.

Rivera, Geraldo, with Daniel Paisner. *Exposing Myself*. Bantam Books, 1991.

Rivkin, Allen, and Laura Kerr. *Hello, Hollywood*. Doubleday, 1962.

Robb, Brian J. *Johnny Depp: A Modern Rebel*. Plexus, 1996.

————. *River Phoenix: A Short Life*. HarperCollins, 1995.

Robbins, Jhan. *Yul Brynner: The Inscrutable King.* Dodd, Mead, 1987.

Roberts, Randy, and James S. Olson. *John Wayne: American.* Simon and Schuster, 1995.

Robertson, James C. *The Casablanca Man: The Cinema of Michael Curtiz.* Routledge, 1993.

Robinson, Edward G., with Leonard Spigelgass. *All My Yesterdays.* Hawthorn Books, 1973.

Robinson, Jeffrey. *Bardot: An Intimate Portrait.* Donald I. Fine, 1994.

Rodriguez, Elena. *Dennis Hopper: A Madness to His Method.* St. Martin's, 1988.

Rogers, Ginger. *Ginger: My Story.* HarperCollins, 1991.

Rollyson, Carl. *Lillian Hellman: Her Legend and Her Legacy.* St. Martin's, 1985.

Rooney, Mickey. *Life Is Too Short.* Villard Books, 1991.

Rose, Frank. *The Agency.* HarperCollins, 1995.

Rosen, Majorie. *Popcorn Venus.* Coward, McCann and Geoghegan, 1973.

Rossellini, Roberto. *My Method: Writings and Interviews.* Marsilio, 1992.

Rovin, Jeff. *Stallone! A Hero's Story.* Pocket Books, 1985.

———. *TV Babylon.* Signet, 1987.

Rubin, Sam, and Richard Taylor. *Mia Farrow: Flower Child, Madonna, Muse.* St. Martin's, 1989.

Russell, Jane. *Jane Russell: My Path and Detours.* Franklin Watts, 1985.

Russell, Ken. *Altered States.* Bantam Books, 1982.

———. *A British Picture: An Autobiography.* William Heinemann, 1989.

Rutledge, Leigh W. *The Gay Book of Lists.* Alyson Publications, 1987.

Sanders, Coyne Steven. *Rainbow's End: The Judy Garland Show.* Zebra Books, 1992.

Sandford, Christopher. *Mick Jagger: Primitive Cool.* St. Martin's, 1993.

Sanello, Frank. *Cruise: The Unauthorized Biography.* Taylor, 1995.

Saroyan, Aram. *Trio.* Linden Press/Simon and Schuster, 1985.

Satchell, Tim. *Astaire.* Hutchison, 1987.

Saxton, Martha. *Jayne Mansfield and the American Fifties.* Houghton Mifflin, 1975.

Scagnetti, Jack. *The Life and Loves of Gable.* Jonathan Davis, 1976.

Schanke, Robert A. *Shattered Applause: The Lives of Eva Le Gallienne.* Southern Illinois University Press, 1992.

Schatz, Thomas. *The Genius of the System: Hollywood Filmmaking in the Studio Era.* Pantheon Books, 1988.

Schickel, Richard. *Clint Eastwood.* Alfred A. Knopf, 1996.

Schoell, William. *The Films of Al Pacino.* Citadel Press, 1995.

Scott, Michael. *Maria Meneghini Callas.* Northeastern University Press, 1991.

Seagrave, Kerry. *Politicians' Passions.* S. P. I. Books, 1992.

Seagrave, Kerry, and Linda Martin. *The Continental Actress.* McFarland, 1990.

Sealy, Shirley. *The Celebrity Sex Register.* Simon and Schuster, 1982.

Seay, Davin. *Mick Jagger: The Story Behind the Rolling Stone.* Birch Lane Press, 1993.

Segaloff, Nat. *Hurricane Billy.* William Morrow, 1990.

Segrest, Meryle. *Leonard Bernstein: A Life.* Alfred A. Knopf, 1994.

Sellers, Michael, with Sarah and Victoria Sellers. *P. S. I Love You.* Collins, 1981.

Selznick, Irene Mayer. *A Private View.* Alfred A. Knopf, 1983.

Servadio, Gaia. *Luchino Viscounti: A Biography.* Weidenfeld and Nicolson, 1982.

Seward, Ingrid. *Royal Children.* St. Martin's, 1993.

Sharif, Omar, and Marie-Thérèse Guinchard. *The Eternal Male: My Own Story.* Doubleday, 1977.

Shaw, Artie. *The Trouble With Cinderella.* Farrar Straus and Young, 1952.

Shevey, Sandra. *The Marilyn Scandal.* William Morrow, 1988.

Shepherd, Donald. *Duke: The Life and Times of John Wayne.* Doubleday, 1985.

Shepherd, Donald, and Robert F. Slatzer. *Bing Crosby: The Hollow Man.* St. Martin's, 1981.

Shepherd, Jack. *Jack Nicholson.* St. Martin's, 1991.

Shipman, David. *Judy Garland: The Secret Life of an American Legend.* Hyperion, 1993.

———. *The Great Movie Stars: The Golden Years.* Bonanza Books, 1970.

———. *The Great Movie Stars: The Independent Years.* Little, Brown, 1991.

———. *The Great Movie Stars: The International Years.* St. Martin's, 1972.

———. *Movie Talk.* St. Martin's, 1988.

Shulman, Irving. *Harlow: An Intimate Biography.* Random House, 1964.

———. *Valentino.* Trident Press, 1967.

Siciliano, Enzo. *Pasolini.* Random House, 1982.

Simpson, Harold B. *Audie Murphy: American Soldier.* Hill Junior College Press, 1975.

Sinclair, Andrew. *Spiegel: The Man Behind the Movies.* Little, Brown, 1987.

Singer, Kurt. *The Charles Laughton Story.* Winston, 1976.

Sklar, Robert. *City Boys.* Princeton University Press, 1992.

Skolsky, Sidney. *Don't Get Me Wrong, I Love Hollywood.* G. P. Putnam's Sons, 1975.

Slater, Leonard. *Aly.* Random House, 1965.

Slide, Anthony. *Great Pretenders.* Wallace-Homestead, 1986.

Smith, Bruce. *Costly Performance—Tennessee Williams: The Last Stage.* Paragon House, 1990.

Smith, Gus. *Richard Harris.* Robert Hale, 1990.

Smith, R. Dixon. *Ronald Colman, Gentleman of the Cinema.* McFarland, 1991.

Smith, Ronald L. *Johnny Carson.* St. Martin's, 1987.

———. *Sweethearts of Sixties TV*. St. Martin's, 1989.

Smith, Sally Bedell. *In All His Glory: The Life of William S. Paley*. Simon and Schuster, 1990.

Souhami, Diana. *Greta and Cecil*. HarperCollins, 1994.

Spada, James. *Grace: The Secret Lives of a Princess*. Doubleday, 1987.

———. *More Than a Woman*. Bantam Books, 1993.

———. *Peter Lawford: The Man Who Kept the Secrets*. Bantam Books, 1991.

———. *Streisand: Her Life*. Crown, 1995.

———. *Streisand: The Woman and the Legend*. Doubleday, 1981.

Speck, Gregory. *Hollywood Royalty*. Birch Lane Press, 1996.

Speigel, Penina. *McQueen: Untold Story of a Bad Boy in Hollywood*. Doubleday, 1986.

Sperling, Cass Warner, and Cork Millner with Jack Warner Jr. *Hollywood Be Thy Name*. Prima, 1994.

Spoto, Donald. *Blue Angel: The Life of Marlene Dietrich*. Doubleday, 1992.

———. *The Kindness of Strangers: The Life of Tennessee Williams*. Little, Brown, 1985.

———. *Laurence Olivier: A Biography*. HarperCollins, 1992.

———. *Madcap: The Life of Preston Sturges*. Little, Brown, 1990.

———. *Marilyn Monroe: A Biography*. HarperCollins, 1993.

———. *A Passion for Life*. HarperCollins, 1995.

———. *Rebel: The Life and Legend of James Dean*. HarperCollins, 1996.

Stack, Robert, with Mark Evans. *Strait Shooting*. Macmillan, 1980.

Stadiem, William. *Too Rich: The High Life and Tragic Death of King Farouk*. Carroll and Graf, 1991.

Stallings, Penny. *Flesh and Fantasy*. St. Martin's, 1978.

———. *Rock 'n' Rock Confidential*. Little, Brown, 1984.

Stassinopoulos, Arianna. *Maria Callas: The Woman Behind the Legend*. Simon and Schuster, 1981.

Steel, Dawn. *They Can Kill You, But They Can't Eat You*. Pocket Books, 1993.

Stenn, David. *Bombshell: The Life and Death of Jean Harlow*. Doubleday, 1993.

———. *Clara Bow: Runnin' Wild*. Doubleday, 1988.

Stine, Whitney. *Stars and Star Handlers*. Roundtable, 1985.

Stirling, Monica. *A Screen of Time: A Study of Luchino Visconti*. Harcourt Brace Jovanovich, 1979.

St. Johns, Adela Rogers. *Love, Laughter, and Tears: My Hollywood Story*. Doubleday, 1978.

Straight, Raymond. *Mrs. Howard Hughes*. Galloway House, 1970.

———. *The Tragic Secret Life of Jayne Mansfield*. Henry Regnery, 1974.

Strait, Raymond, and Leif Henie. *Queen of Ice, Queen of Shadows: The Unsuspected Life of Sonja Henie*. Stein and Day, 1985.

Strait, Raymond, and Terry Robinson. *Lanza: His Tragic Life*. Prentice-Hall, 1980.

Strasberg, Susan. *Bittersweet*. G. P. Putnam's Sons, 1980.

———. *Marilyn and Me*. Warner Books, 1992.

Stuart, Otis. *Perpetual Motion: The Public and Private Lives of Rudolph Nureyev*. Simon and Schuster, 1995.

Swanson, Gloria. *Swanson on Swanson*. Random House, 1980.

Swindell, Larry. *Body and Soul: The Story of John Garfield*. William Morrow, 1975.

———. *Charles Boyer: The Reluctant Lover*. Doubleday, 1983.

———. *Screwball: The Life of Carole Lombard*. William Morrow, 1975.

Taheri, Amin. *The Unknown Life of the Shah*. Hutchison, 1991.

Taraborrelli, Randy. *Call Her Miss Ross*. Carol Publishing Group, 1989.

———. *Michael Jackson: The Magic and the Madness*. Ballantine, 1991.

Taylor, Robert Lewis. *W. C. Fields: His Follies and Fortunes*. Doubleday, 1967.

Terrill, Marshall. *Steve McQueen*. Donald I. Fine, 1993.

Theodoracopulos, Taki. *Princes, Playboys, and High-Class Tarts*. Karz-Cohl Publishing, 1984.

Theodoracopulos, Taki, and Jeffrey Bernard. *High Life—Low Life*. Jay Landesman, 1981.

Thomas, Bob. *Clown Prince of Hollywood*. McGraw-Hill, 1990.

———. *Golden Boy: The Untold Story of William Holden*. St. Martin's, 1983.

———. *I Got Rhythm: The Ethel Merman Story*. G. P. Putnam's Sons, 1985.

———. *Joan Crawford: A Biography*. Simon and Schuster, 1978.

———. *King Cohn*. G. P. Putnam's Sons, 1967.

———. *Liberace*. St. Martin's, 1987.

———. *Marlon, Portrait of the Rebel as an Artist*. Random House, 1966.

———. *Thalberg: Life and Legend*. Doubleday, 1969.

———. *Winchell*. Doubleday, 1971.

Thomas, Tony. *The Dick Powell Story*. Riverwood Press, 1993.

———. *Cads and Cavaliers*. A. S. Barnes, 1973.

Thompson, Dave. *Travolta*. Taylor, 1996.

Thompson, Douglas. *Clint Eastwood: Riding High*. Smith Gryphon, 1992.

Thompson, Verita, with Donald Shepherd. *Bogie and Me*. St. Martin's, 1982.

Thomson, David. *Showman*. Alfred A. Knopf, 1992.

———. *Warren Beatty and Desert Eyes: A Life and a Story*. Doubleday, 1987.

Thorson, Scott, with Alex Thorleifson. *Behind the Candelabra: My Life with Liberace*. E. P. Dutton, 1988.

Tierney, Gene. *Gene Tierney: Self-Portrait*. Wyden Books, 1979.

Todd, Ann. *The Eighth Veil*. G. P. Putnam's Sons, 1981.

Todd, Michael Jr. *A Valuable Property*. Arbor House, 1983.

Toffel, Neile McQueen. *My Husband, My Friend*. Atheneum, 1986.

Tonetti, Claretta. *Luchino Viscounti*. Twayne Publishers, 1983.

Tormé, Mel. *It Wasn't All Velvet*. Viking Penguin, 1988.

Tornabene, Lyn. *Long Live the King: A Biography of Clark Gable*. G. P. Putnam's Sons, 1975.

Toshes, Nick. *Dino: Living High in the Dirty Business*. Doubleday, 1992.

Turner, Lana. *Lana: The Lady, the Legend, the Truth*. E. P. Dutton, 1982.

Tyler, Gregg. *The Joy of Hustling*. Manor Books, 1976.

Tynan, Kathleen. *Tynan*. William Morrow, 1987.

Ullman, Liv. *Changing*. Alfred A. Knopf, 1977.

———. *Choices*. Alfred A. Knopf, 1985.

Vadim, Roger. *Bardot, Deneuve, Fonda*. Simon and Schuster, 1986.

———. *Memoirs of the Devil*. Harcourt Brace Jovanovich, 1975.

Valentine, Tom, and Patrick Mahn. *Daddy's Duchess*. Lyle Stuart, 1987.

Vallee, Rudy. *Let the Chips Fall. . . .* Stackpole Books, 1975.

Vallee, Rudy, and Gil McKean. *My Time Is Your Time*. Ivan Obolensky, 1962.

Van Doren, Mamie. *Playing the Field: My Story*. G. P. Putnam's Sons, 1987.

van Gelder, Peter. *That's Hollywood*. HarperCollins, 1990.

Van Rensselear, Philip. *Million Dollar Baby: An Intimate Portrait of Barbara Hutton*. G. P. Putnam's Sons, 1979.

VanDerBeet, Richard. *George Sanders: An Exhausted Life*. Madison Books, 1990.

Vanderbilt, Gloria. *Black Knight, White Knight*. Alfred A. Knopf, 1987.

Vermilye, Jerry. *Ida Lupino*. Pyramid, 1977.

Vickers, Hugo. *Cecil Beaton*. Little, Brown, 1985.

———. *Loving Garbo*. Random House, 1994.

Vidal, Gore. *Palimpsest*. Random House, 1995.

Vidor, King. *King Vidor on Film Making*. David McKay, 1972.

———. *A Tree Is a Tree*. Harcourt Brace, 1953.

Wagner, Walter. *You Must Remember This*. G. P. Putnam's Sons, 1975.

Walker, Alexander. *Fatal Charm*. St. Martin's, 1992.

———. *Garbo: A Portrait*. Macmillan, 1980.

———. *It's Only a Movie, Ingrid: Encounters on and off Screen*. Headline Book Publishing, 1988.

———. *Peter Sellers*. Macmillan, 1981.

———. *Rudolph Valentino*. Stein and Day, 1976.

Walker, Alexander, ed. *No Bells on Sunday: The Rachel Roberts Journals*. Harper and Row, 1984.

Wallace, Irving, et al. *Intimate Sex Lives of Famous People*. Delacorte Press, 1981.

Wallis, Hal, and Charles Higham. *Starmaker*. Macmillan, 1980.

Walsh, Raoul. *Every Man in His Time*. Farrar, Straus and Giroux, 1974.

Wansell, Geoffrey. *Haunted Idol: The Story of the Real Cary Grant*. William Morrow, 1983.

Wapshott, Nicholas. *Peter O'Toole*. Beaufort Books, 1983.

Warhol, Andy. *The Andy Warhol Diaries*. Warner Books, 1989.

Warner, Jack L., with Dean Jennings. *My First One Hundred Years in Hollywood*. Random House, 1965.

Warren, Doug. *Betty Grable: The Reluctant Movie Queen*. St. Martin's, 1981.

Waters, John. *Shock Value*. Dell, 1981.

Waterbury, Ruth. *Richard Burton: His Intimate Story*. Pyramid, 1965.

Wayne, Jane Ellen. *Ava's Men*. Prentice-Hall, New York, 1990.

———. *Clark Gable: Portrait of a Misfit*. St. Martin's, 1993.

———. *Cooper's Women*. Prentice-Hall, 1988.

———. *Crawford's Men*. Prentice-Hall, 1988.

———. *Gable's Women*. Prentice-Hall, 1987.

———. *Grace Kelly's Men*. St. Martin's, 1991.

———. *Lana: The Life and Loves of Lana Turner*. St. Martin's, 1995.

———. *Marilyn's Men*. St. Martin's, 1992.

———. *Robert Taylor: The Man With the Perfect Face*. St. Martin's, 1973, 1987.

———. *Stanwyck*. Arbor House, 1985.

Weddle, David. *If They Move . . . Kill 'Em!: The Life and Times of Sam Peckinpah*. Grove Press, 1994.

Weiss, Murray, and Bill Hoffman. *Palm Beach Babylon*. Birch Lane Press, 1992.

West, Mae. *Goodness Had Nothing to Do With It*. Bernard McFadden, 1970.

Westbrook, Robert. *Intimate Lies*. HarperCollins, 1995.

Westmore, Frank, and Muriel Davidson. *The Westmores of Hollywood*. J. B. Lippincott, 1976.

Wheeler, David, and Mike Wrenn. *Bitch . . . Bitch . . . Bitch*. Dell, 1990.

White, Carol, with Clifford Harlow. *Carol Comes Home*. New English Library, 1982.

Wilding, Michael, and Pamela Wilcox. *The Wilding Way*. St. Martin's, 1982.

Wilk, Max, ed. *The Wit and Wisdom of Hollywood*. Atheneum, 1971.

Wilkerson, Tichi, and Marcia Borie. *Hollywood Legends: The Golden Years of the Hollywood Reporter*. Tale Weaver, 1988.

Wilkie, Jane. *Confessions of an Ex–Fan Magazine Writer*. Doubleday, 1981.

Williams, John A., and Dennis A. Williams. *If I Stop I'll Die: The Comedy and Tragedy of Richard Pryor*. Thunder's Mouth Press, 1991.

Wilson, Earl. *I Am Gazing Into My Eight-Ball*. Doubleday, Doran, 1945.

———. *Let 'Em Eat Cheesecake*. Doubleday, 1949.

———. *Show Business Laid Bare*. G. P. Putnam's Sons, 1974.

———. *Sinatra: An Unauthorized Biography*. Macmillan, 1976.

Winchell, Walter. *Winchell Exclusive*. Prentice-Hall, 1975.

Windeler, Robert. *Julie Andrews*. St. Martin's, 1983.

———. *Burt Lancaster*. St. Martin's, 1984.

Winecoff, Charles. *Split Image: The Life of Anthony Perkins*. E. P. Dutton, 1996.

Winters, Shelley. *Shelley . . . Also Known as Shirley*. William Morrow, 1980.

———. *Shelley II: The Middle of My Century*. Simon and Schuster, 1989.

Wolfe, Jane. *Blood Rich: When Oil Billions, High Fashions, and Royal Intimacies Are Not Enough*. Little, Brown, 1993.

Worrell, Denice. *Icons*. Atlantic Monthly Press, 1989.

Wray, Fay. *On the Other Hand*. St. Martin's, 1989.

Wright, William. *All the Pain That Money Can Buy*. Simon and Schuster, 1991.

———. *Heiress*. New Republic Books, 1978.

————. *Lillian Hellman: The Image, The Woman.* Simon and Schuster, 1986.

Yablonsky, Lewis. *George Raft.* McGraw-Hill, 1974.

Yule, Andrew. *Life on the Wire.* Donald I. Fine, 1991.

————. *Picture Shows.* Limelight Editions, 1992.

————. *Sean Connery.* Donald I. Fine, 1992.

Zaslow, Jeffrey. *Take It From Us: Advice From 262 Celebrities on Everything That Matters to Them and to You.* Bonus Books, 1995.

Zec, Donald. *Marvin: The Story of Lee Marvin.* St. Martin's, 1980.

————. *Some Enchanted Egos.* Allison and Busby, 1972.

Zeltner, Irwin F. *What the Stars Told Me.* Exposition Press, 1971.

Zetterling, Mai. *All Those Tomorrows.* Grove Press, 1986.

Ziegfeld, Patricia. *The Ziegfelds' Girl: Confessions of an Abnormally Happy Childhood.* Little, Brown, 1964.

Zierold, Norman. *The Moguls: Hollywood's Merchants of Myth.* Silman-James Press, 1991.

————. *Sex Goddesses of the Silent Screen.* Henry Regnery, 1973.

Zolotow, Maurice. *Shooting Star: A Biography of John Wayne.* Simon and Schuster, 1974.

Zorina, Vera. *Zorina.* Farrar, Straus and Giroux, 1986.

Newspapers, Periodicals

Celebrity Sleuth
Los Angeles Times
Movieline
Newsweek
People
Playboy
Playgirl
Premiere
San Francisco Chronicle
San Francisco Examiner
Time
US
Vanity Fair

Television Programs

Barbara Walters Interviews (ABC)
Hard Copy (syndicated)
Hollywood Babylon (VH-1)
Jonathan Ross Presents . . . (VH-1)